Contents

Romanticism
&
Melody

Volume II

by

George Colerick

Published by
JUVENTUS
LONDON

JUVENTUS publications include:
Musical Humour, Parody and Burlesque
New Chekhovs
Filmed Musicals

First published in 2009 by JUVENTUS,
16 Kensington Hall Gardens,
London W14 9LS

Copyright© 2009 by George Colerick

British Library Cataloguing-in-Publication Data

A catalogue record for this book
is available from the British Library

Typeset by YHT Ltd, London
Printed and bound by Biddles Ltd, King's Lynn

Preface

In childhood a beautiful love song should offer promise of future happiness. From the age of nine I have retained very strong feelings for the wondrously tender *Parlez-moi d'amour*. I cannot believe that it will join the infinite ranks of the forgotten songs; the French are surely keeping it alive.

The more conformist of us boys often spent our money on at least one Hollywood film weekly, discussing certain features of the female stars, but rarely their voices. Hollywood did introduce some 'foreign', mainly exotic music, 'Latin', 'gipsy', Russian. We did not realise the effect was mainly to take the juice out of the original. One exception was individual and wholesome: Carmen Miranda, vital, childlike and delightfully what we would now call *over the top* as she performed in her *Souss American Vay*. She was for many briefly the tip of Brazil's musical iceberg. There would have been other singers from distant parts equally to be enjoyed, but we were scarcely given the chance to hear them.

Until the expansion of recorded music sales during the 1950s, there had not been much prestige in showing enthusiasm for music. Yet we assumed we were being offered the best and latest in 'rhythm', what was called 'dance music'. This was in obligingly 'strict' tempo, to the advantage of those who wanted to master the intricacies of ballroom dancing. That skill seemed rather effeminate to one 14-year old until a school Xmas party when evident shyness with girls from another school forced a rethink. I still have good reason to be glad about my conversion. Yet as a dance-club regular, I have heard more bad music in my life than is good for me.

Alongside the jazz influence, American music owed an enormous amount to composers among Jewish immigrants, though Gershwin and Kern were deceased by 1945. Jazz and swing had great vitality, a late Romantic development, producing many classics loved today. There must have been at least two dozen popular songs I most liked then which are still often heard. This facility would have encouraged me several decades later to write my first related book, though as a child, I had few casual lifelines to 'great' music. We of the Catholic minority benefited from medieval music, not thought of as 'classical' or highbrow; the *Dies Irae* and *Tantum Ergo* became part of our weekly routine.

Most families had had very modest record collections and my father's reflected his Irish ancestry, as well as a few popular classics. Most importantly, as a child I was intrigued by what the BBC played often, without any hype, what they called 'overtures'. I had no idea of their interesting link to operas, but they all had beautiful melodies and built up to exciting climaxes with rapidly changing rhythms. In contrast music at school seemed nothing but collective singing lessons, quite boring.

At the age of 15–16, only the most fortunate were promoted to the VI Form, where our elders made it brutally clear that we were to set aside childish things, particularly weak jokes. They told us that during lunch breaks, on alternate days in the common room 'traditional' music would be played, jazz and 'classical'. I knew almost nothing about these terms, but we soon realised that *Tuxedo Junction, Bach goes to Town* and Tchaikovsky's Fifth could be equally enjoyable. Their melodies and harmonies had a common origin, and syncopation was not a 20th century invention. By the age of 17, some groups among us had decided that music, poetry or classic novels were more important than a career or 'romance', matters to be deferred for years. This puzzled our relatives and there were big clashes about priorities and behaviour. Yet it was a very civilised 'teenage rebellion. We had no money either for alcohol or luxuries, and materialism hardly troubled us; though some of us might be drifting into intellectual arrogance. There were no music recordings to borrow from libraries so we sneaked free hearings at the local record shop which had a compliant manager.

Certain school friends wondered why I appeared to prefer Brahms to Beethoven or Wagner; I was fascinated by his melodies with dreamy flow, and cross-rhythms. Some relatives expressed concern at my state of mind because I was hearing sounds they could not detect in music which left them cold. The opening of the Second Symphony suggested to me gliding through a beautiful garden, but it was the start of his Third Symphony which reflected some deep human drama more real for me than Wagner's. A bar or two is often enough to identify Brahms, and what no-one else could have written, such as the song, *The Melody draws me*. As for the suggestions that he was too academic or cautious, what of the suspenseful openings of his four concertos?

I had a strong feeling for rhythm but no desire to play drums, though for a time, I learnt clarinet, thinking I might enjoy the freedom of playing jazz; but lacked the patience. Today most music regarded here as 'popular' lacks the stimulating effects of acceleration, slowing down, unexpected developments and brief silences. Not too much is generally demanded in quality of melody which is often subordinate to the lyrics. This may explain why soccer fans world-wide nearly always choose songs over 100 years old.

I assimilated large areas of the 'classical' orchestral repertoire in rapid time, being much helped by acquiring a tape-recorder. This was the original type, reel-to-reel, technically excellent. These were eventually replaced on commercial grounds by an appalling design, the cassette, with its fragile, absurdly narrow tape. It was a quasi-monopolistic trick on the consumers, cheap production for profit. The BBC radio output became the basis of my music knowledge, and I disdained the spending of 'good money' on recordings. As a result, I went for a very broad range of musical experience, rather than comparing interpretations. My writing now concentrates on the compositions, not the performers.

Many British and American schoolchildren already in the 1960s could hardly think of more than one living composer, Bert Bacharach; at least, he had just established a distinct musical personality. Are all great composers, like poets, dead? Most of the 'serious' ones alive have been partly to blame because they cannot or will not compose for the broad public; and 'popular' record labels had started to omit composers' names, if any had been employed. Because commercial music is largely based on the cliché, arranging is much simpler and cheaper than composing. Mass production, with marketing the main cost, brings very high profits: standardisation on a global scale reduces genuine variety. As a result, people are being cut off from their own national cultures as never before; this is causing great concern to governments throughout the world. It was the monumental achievement of the BBC in the radio age that under Lord Reith's guidance it worked towards an integrated society. It offered the whole of Britain for the first and only time not only clear, attractive English: but the best informed, the finest entertainment, the highest standards of taste. Now opposing trends dominate in the media and we are deeply divided culturally with communication between social groups ever more difficult.

Many of us relate important turns in our musical perspectives to single events. During National Service in Germany my preference for that country's music increased. At a party, when a girl burst out unannounced with a beautifully trained voice into operetta, I wished I had a voice to join her and became permanently attracted to the Viennese style. For years, Richard Strauss' works obscured my valuation of other nations' opera, but the passion and realism of Verdi's *Masked Ball* and *Don Carlos* heard at Covent Garden converted me to the Italian masterpieces. Visiting several countries by car in 1965 was a much valued chance to experience Central European music live. Yes, in Budapest men were still offering women roses in the restaurants, the violinist was at hand, and the public dances could be uninhibited as far away as Siofok by Lake Balaton. Who cared about politics?

As a lecturer I organised college opera visits and was specially curious about their expressed musical reactions which included valuable cognitive experiences. Seated at the rear of the theatre, some students were astonished that the singers could throw their voices so far without microphones. Probably it was for many a first perception of the potential of fully trained voices.

Though there is broad enthusiasm for music, most English are inarticulate about it, the other peoples in our islands perhaps less so. Despite the richness of our language, conversation is often laced with dull clichés and misused adjectives. Blame the media! Unlike in some other countries I visited for some time, such as Hungary, Sweden and Finland, most of some 300 overcrowded English radio stations are seriously under-funded and do not attempt to offer a fair range of musical experience. When eight undergraduates were once competing in *University Challenge*, none of them knew what a concerto was, and the chairman expressed his disgust. That incident led me to write one of the following chapters.

1 *The Onset of Romanticism: Beethoven*

At the first rehearsal of Beethoven's Fifth Symphony, the performers were more amused than shocked at the sound and intensity of its opening. A few years earlier, reactions would been more hostile but by 1805, social attitudes were becoming more enlightened following the impact of the French Revolution. Beethoven was the man to exploit this new freedom, and with his originality and vision, he would become the greatest influence on Romantic and 19th century music.

Beethoven grew up during the great Classical period of the late 18th century, with its sophisticated musical forms. He left Bonn for Vienna in the early 1790s where he was taught briefly by Joseph Haydn. His early compositions showed a special admiration for Mozart's works. In particular, sonata form as then established was to be the model for the first movement of all symphonies, and so remained well into the 20th century. Its logic was its strength. Song has always tended to be more interesting for having two contrasting melodies. In the symphony, so-called sonata form strengthened this with two subjects or groups of themes. The first was to be developed, leading to a climax then a resolution. It was optional whether the finale followed that pattern.

Variety was assured at first by a sequence of tempi in the four movement symphony: slow introduction, then a brisk first movement (*allegro*): next slower (*andante*) or slow (*lento*): then minuet and trio¹ finale (*allegro*) or very fast (*presto*). The last three movements had freer use of two themes (ABA, ABAB or ABABA), contrasting in shape, mood, pace and key. It was the most perfectly satisfying form for a work lasting some half an hour. Chamber music conformed to sonata form but tended to omit the third movement, the dance. This, the stately minuet, was unsuited to Beethoven who decided to replace that 3/4 rhythm with a very energetic one, a *scherzo*, Italian for joke.

Genius is privileged to break rules; Haydn would have recognised he had one on his hands though he found him a difficult pupil. Beethoven had started his composing life, choosing the piano sonata as the main form for developing his creative skills. This early phase of composing lasted roughly until 1803, the date of his *Eroica Symphony*. Conceived on a larger scale, more powerful than anything beforehand, it had been dedicated to Napoleon, but when he made himself Emperor of the French in 1804, Beethoven furiously tore out the title page. Freedom meant that much to him, both politically and for his creative self.

At first sympathetic to the Revolution, with the French advancing and briefly occupying Vienna, he was in full political disillusion, and he gradually turned to religion. Those were the years when his impending deafness ended his career as a pianist, and threatened his composing facility. There were also disappointments in love, so that Beethoven was facing one of several critical phases in his emotional life.

Yet this had a positive effect on his creativity, and his middle period is now considered as having lasted until about 1815. It passed the bounds of traditional harmony, form and emotional restraint during the first of these years. The Fifth Symphony's power was startling, the orchestra was at times used percussively. Other creative high points included the *Appassionata* Sonata, his opera, *Fidelio*, and the Triple Concerto.

Later came the Seventh Symphony, a sequence of dances, and two very commanding works, the Fifth Piano Concerto and probably the greatest of all piano trios, the opus 97, named after his friend, the musician Archduke Rudolph. He had shown ways to break the Classical mould, influencing the early Romantics who came to prominence a few years after his death in 1827.

Beethoven could not live comfortably with other humans, a state of depression around 1815 curtailing his composing for some two years. He then came back helped by a much stronger model, a 6-octave Broadwood grand piano, and his *Hammerklavier* Sonata exploited this power to the full, so marking the start of his final period. Yet three more sonatas completed his purposes for the instrument. For the short period remaining to his life, he turned his attention to the string quartet, and he composed no other chamber music afterwards. There were to be five quartets, uniquely complex in style and development, not understood by many at the time, but related to intense spiritual experiences. They included a movement in which

Beethoven gave thanksgiving to God for recovery from an illness.

He was experimenting with melody and harmonies. The *Grosse Fugue* which was to be the finale of the opus 130 quartet was so dominant that Beethoven was advised to separate it from the other movements, so that it became his final publication. One century later, Stravinsky praised it as a masterpiece of his own speciality, rhythm.

Beethoven cared for the fate of humanity, eventually finding inspiration for grand statements by 1823 in his *Missa Solemnis* and Ninth Symphony, the *Choral*. This was larger and more complex than any previous symphony. Though the first three movements are very imposing, they are then subjected to an unprecedented ritual. In a sequence of orchestral recitative, their themes are in turn rejected, then a soloist in a moment of great drama introduces the dominant melody to the words of Schiller's *Ode to Joy*, the *Choral* finale. This movement eclipsed his *Choral Fantasy* written years earlier, a most original single movement, vigorous and extrovert, later regarded as an apparent run-in.

The Ninth Symphony and the *Missa Solemnis* with the last sonatas and quartets are works that the music world is still learning from two centuries later.

2 Schubert: 1823

Schubert was a Viennese boy, the first great composer to be without a patron, in that sense an amateur, a poor music teacher. A bachelor, even his emotional life was impoverished though exaggerated through legend, and his health was always poor. 1823 was to be a critical year in his tragically short career. Aged 26, behind him was his youth when he had shown such precocious talent for song-writing. If that had come easy to him, symphonic writing is for all a challenge involving a kind of apprenticeship, of which many composers later destroy the evidence. Spontaneous and unpretentious, such a thought would not have occurred to Schubert, and his first six symphonies exist as his 'juvenilia' but as such, a considerable achievement. They had been written much under the influence of Joseph Haydn who had died in 1809.

By 1823, Schubert's early maturity had been advanced by a degree of suffering, and the new awareness that he had few years left. Not concerned with material things, he was disordered and much of his work was lost or mislaid. That year, he spent some time in hospital under treatment for an incurable venereal disease. Though the chronology can never be certain, he completed by that year two movements of what one day would be world famous as his *Unfinished Symphony*. In the structure most suited to important public statements, he had suddenly shown maturity and musical individuality. It makes interesting contrast with his Fifth Symphony, quite Classical, written seven years earlier but with Schubert's personality.

The missing two movements of the *Unfinished Symphony* have been one of the largest puzzles in musical history. Did he stop work on it around the time of his hospital stay? This cannot explain why he did not finish several other works. Perhaps he realised it could stand best as it was; even Brahms who was strict about symphonic form thought so. More likely, he felt the urgency to express more rapidly the many ideas within him. He had just one more such work and most ambitious in scope, the Ninth.[2] As for the *Unfinished*, part of a third movement exists

4

and allegedly the fourth appeared some months later as the first entr'acte in incidental music to the play, *Rosamunde*. It was sometimes played as a substitute with the symphony though some have argued that it lacks the nature of a finale. Its status remains in question.

With the briefest of introductions, the apprehensive first subject builds up to an impassioned climax, the relief coming in the form of a flowing melody which has become one of the best loved in all symphonies. Listeners might relate the restrained sense of menace to Schubert's condition in 1823. Thinking partly of his emotive use of the cello section, Julius Harrison writes of skill in imposing the 'hushed effect':

> *Not only were his melodies scattered about the instruments with deep feeling for their characteristic tone colours, but the actual range of dynamics was enlarged.*

The following movement maintains a similar pace, more serene but having an affinity in a work noted for its darker harmonies. This *Unfinished Symphony* is the first great orchestral work in today's repertoire by a young composer breaking away from the Classical style. The *Rosamunde* music also from 1823 was its accomplice, deservedly sharing its popularity. It was composed for an inferior play *Rosamunde* which disappeared after a few performances. In the event that was hardly a loss.

Its now famous overture was written for an opera, then switched. It broke away from the fashionable Rossini style of dramatic contrasts in tone and pace, and has subtle changes in key and harmony.[3] That also applies to the ten other movements he wrote, an exceptionally tuneful score not specially tied to the story but broadly suiting a domestic comedy. Neither a descriptive nor dramatic approach was necessary and the *Rosamunde* music stands now well on its own as a concert suite. Apart from the two concluding movements, the first a light chorus, there is often a wistful note touched by the clarinets in their middle range, and in a song, unusually for contralto voice. Benign influences are felt in two choruses representing the outer world and nature. The carefree finale has a rare trotting rhythm and was known as the 'Russian air'. That and a plaintive slow movement, have become specially familiar Schubert, and he used them both for other works. Several 'musicals' were once made about his life and work, often as a pastiche, with the *Rosamunde* music prominent.

To German Romantics around 1820, the term 'wanderer' was associated with personal freedom, escaping conventional responsibilities, communing with nature like Byron and Shelley. In an 1816 song with this title, Schubert interpreted it more in the sense of an outsider, an unfortunate one, as he saw himself despite his enviable band of musical companions. The song was in 1823 placed with a set of variations in the slow movement of the *Wandererfantasie*. This work was shaped like a sonata but thematically linked over three movements. The significance of this was taken up years later and developed by Franz Liszt.

Song and operatic aria were quite distinct by the time of Schubert. He perfected the German song, the *Lied*, a great lyrical form essentially intimate, whereas though he wrote many arias, he failed in opera, which is essentially dramatic. Even so, he had a facility for interpreting texts by the greatest writers such as Goethe or average ones, his muse fired more by ideas than the words. In 1823, his choice was *Die schöne Müllerin* (The fair Maid of the Mill), and to a modest text he wrote a great song cycle on the ancient theme of unrequited love. It was entirely a plaint by the youth, the girl seemingly uninvolved at any time. Her indifference is indicated in the eighth of the twenty songs; her later interest in a young hunter, dressed in fashionable green, causes jealousy. The growing despondency of the young man is reflected in music near in feeling to its sequel *Winterreise* (Winter Journey), which sinks towards despair with the same character considering suicide.

Die schöne Müllerin is a lover's narration, drawing in literary clichés of that early Romantic era; he addresses and is consoled by the brook which powers the mill. The music enhances a simple story perfectly and three songs are specially well known. The opening two overflow with youthful confidence, and the piano brings on the excitement of anticipation in the seventh, *Ungeduld* (Impatience), with the work's most familiar phrase, in one translation:

I'd like to carve your name in every tree.

Schubert had barely five more years to live: very prolific years considering his health, and including several masterpieces, to become one of the greatest and most influential of European composers.

3 *The Onset of Romanticism: to 1850*

At the start of one chapter in BBC TV's classic series, *Civilisation*, Kenneth Clark is standing in an elegant library in the finest 18th century style. This he uses to symbolise the Enlightenment, a refinement of human thought: Western Europe's neo-Classicism in the creative arts, most familiar in the music of Mozart. Its style was, as Clark says, symmetrical, balanced, consistent and enclosed. This he uses to symbolise the Enlightenment at that time; to nine tenths of European citizens toiling in poverty until an early death, this elegance and wisdom was meaningless. Yet the writings of enlightened men seeking just, reasoned solutions to society's problems would lead to a cataclysm, the overthrowing of the feudal world, so that 'modern history' is said to start with the French Revolution, leading into the 19th century.

Earlier in this series on *Civilisation*, Clark had praised symmetry and consistency in the arts, but he recognises they are the enemy of movement, for which mankind has an irresistible urge. Some will see the enclosed world as a prison from which to break free. Those who wrote about it around 1800 were the early Romantics.

From the library, Clark hears a challenging call to action. It is the freedom theme for the political prisoners in Beethoven's opera, *Fidelio*. He walks into the next room, opens a door, stepping out into a splendid Classical portico, to be confronted by a turbulent sea. The Romantics were to be inspired by nature, the sea being dynamic manifestation, often to be felt in the works of 19th and especially 20th century composers.

Classicism was cosmopolitan, designed for European aristocracies. With some exceptions, 19th century composers increasingly became independent of the courts and of royal patronage. Their new audiences were more familiar with popular and folk music and dancing, which would influence Romantic expression. Franz Schubert had no connection with the Viennese court and his style would develop under the influence of his native Austria's folk idiom. He moved

instinctively away from the sharply defined melody of the
Classical period to a smoother line, and more flexible rhythms.
He also belonged to the first generation brought up with the
advantage of composing on what we hear as a 'modern' piano,
with its capacity for *legato*.[4] If the piano was the most spectacular, other instruments were being given wide opportunities
for virtuosity, specially the violin which had performed a valuable solo role in folk music.

The improved instrument with its sustaining pedal increased
harmonic possibilities, so it served for what had always been
lacking: the ideal accompaniment to the voice. Schubert often
exploited the piano to perfection, heightening the emotive
power and Romanticism's fashionable themes, love, nature and
death, were prominent. The words were no longer just a pre-
text for a good tune, the lyrics matching closely to the melody.
This effectively created a new genre of distinguished art songs
(*Lieder*) and song cycles and many German composers would
follow: Schumann, Brahms, Wolf, Richard Strauss and others: a
repertoire of many thousand songs.

Schubert scarcely revised his work, and he used the terms
impromptus and musical moments for short compositions.
Later composers would use titles such as prelude, study,
intermezzo, ballade or those describing dances.[5] Even the
early compositions of Liszt, Schumann and Chopin seemed to
inhabit a totally different sound world from that of two decades earlier, freer in structure. Composing on the improved
pianos, they experimented with chords and harmonies in ways
previously not possible. Chopin never completed a score
without including piano, whatever the combination of instruments, and his music beyond expressing a mood or atmosphere was always abstract in conception. By contrast, Liszt and
Schumann favoured an expressed 'programme', mainly literary, a new trend which became fashionable. Schumann
composed great song cycles and his most characteristic piano
work was *Carnaval*, invoking characters out of his own fantasies. This was related to his being also a literary spokesman for
the 'new German music'. Except for one by Schubert, he
initiated a musical form, the piano quintet, combining piano
with string quartet. This was successfully followed by Brahms,
Dvorak, Franck, the American Dora Beach, Elgar and several
others.

Rubato is a technique dependent on the sensibility of the performer, the slight delaying (or precipitation) of a note, which can be very emotive[6]. This was most apparent in the piano playing of Liszt and Chopin, but also in the virtuoso conducting of orchestras, too large by the 1830s to be led as previously by the principal violinist.

Thanks to the dominance of Vienna in instrumental music, Mozart had known most of his leading musical contemporaries, and their compositions tended to sound similar in style. Half a century later, the musical personalities of the younger composers were developing in very distinct ways, increasingly easy to identify. This trend was part of Romanticism's cult of the individual. It had reached its first peak by the 1850s, by which time Mendelssohn, Chopin and Schumann were deceased. In opera and concert hall, its development as far as our own times will occupy the chapters of this book. Its most sophisticated medium has been the symphony orchestra whose development has been miraculous.

For much of history, playing instruments simultaneously would have sounded an excruciating noise. New inventions and technical improvements gradually led to combinations which were pleasing. By 1750 that could include strings, percussion, flutes, oboes, bassoons and, restricted without valves, trumpets and horns. It later acquired clarinets, trombones, tubas, bass drum, harps and improved trumpets and horns. Some composers have since the late 19th century added saxophone, celeste, piano or other instruments for special effects. With its power, its depth, multi-coloured sound and range, the modern symphony orchestra has had a major role in spreading a unique melodic and harmonic system into the New World, then to societies which have their own distinctive musical traditions. Smaller bands with less variety of instruments have played a part, especially for popular forms of music. As Kenneth Clark concluded, Romanticism's exciting journey continues and we don't know exactly where it will lead.

4 *Berlioz, Fantasy and Literature*

Hector Berlioz (1803–69) might have been a caricature of how one century ago insular Britons imagined a typical Frenchman. Far more than most, his passionate nature was reflected in the range of his compositions. Very difficult to work with, his sense of isolation from much of France's musical society was in part because of the excesses of his imagination. His second world, that of literature and the theatre, was so important that he would, or did, sacrifice most of his private life in serving it. A skilled writer and critic, his devotion to the works of Shakespeare and other writers in English, and some of the greatest of European classics, fired most of his best work. He would willingly have chosen poverty before the legal profession his father intended.

As a composer, he could not play the piano or any other instrument, other than strumming a guitar, and this added to an idiosyncratic style. Many would call this a disadvantage, leading to a hit-or-miss approach to harmony and its theory. His obsessions led him musically in unprecedented directions especially programme music beyond the scope of drama.

Absolute music is an end in itself, having no need to relate to other art forms; programme music relates to other ideas, such as in description or telling a story. Since pre-history, humans may have tried to give musical imitations of nature, but the results have been negligible; conversely, drama had been an outstanding achievement of civilisation. Songs and opera are linked to texts and other externals, so the distinction between absolute or pure and programme music is often blurred. Yet during the 19th century, this issue became of much importance. Programme music was to be an essential path forward in Romantic expression.

At 24, Berlioz became infatuated with a woman who raised his enthusiasm with her interpretation of Shakespeare: in the persona of Ophelia, the Irish actress, Harriet Smithson. For at least two years, she rejected him and he took refuge in a more real if turbulent love affair with Camille Moke, later a distinguished pianist. Once that passion was subsiding, he realised Harriet's career was in decline just as his was rising. So pity for her as she sank into financial problems began to play on his chivalrous nature, leading to their disastrous marriage and eventual separation many years later.

Goethe's *Faust* was another work which had fascinated him whilst young when he wrote eight scenes for concert performance, increasing them later to the size of an evening's concert, often performed now staged. Its *Walpurgis Night* revelries suggested another scenario which would externalise his feelings for Harriet; the outcome was both astonishing and historic: his *Symphonie Fantastique*. It was the first work known to use the device, an *idée fixe*, a musical phrase as recurring motif in this case present Harriet of the protagonist's fevered imagination, the indifferent then unforgiving spirit of the beloved. It was to appear in varied guises in each of the five movements, at first becalmed, feminine, sometimes elusive, but unwittingly arousing the lover from dreams to near frenzy. Then follows a ball scene, but this is a phantom waltz for her imagined with a rival. Nature might be consoling, so the lover takes to the pastoral life, only be left isolated in a storm. The combining of cor anglais and oboe to suggest the countryside was an inspired innovation in timbre.

Guilty of killing his love, to a march, triumphant but not for him, he is hastened to the scaffold. Guillotined, he returns as one of the ghouls to a witches' sabbath. These two sequences which occupy the last two movements of five reached what sounded like the wild extremities of musical expression. The *Walpurgis* (All Hallows Night) finale had the loved one present to celebrate the lover's demise.

No concert audience in 1830 had ever heard such a frenetic sound emerging from the woodwind section, with a grotesque variant of the motif on a screaming clarinet. Fugues had much dignity, but not the one heard near the climax, and in a mocking spirit. At a stroke, Berlioz was challenging Europe's musical tradition with a work calculated to shock. Its fierce tonal contrasts, the irregular rhythms, unfamiliar melodic style and harmonies repelled some, as it attracted others, younger musical students being much impressed.

By the following year, Berlioz intended to perform the work with a sequel, originally called 'an artist's return to life' (later

Lélio) in which he rejects his unrequited love in favour of a
'natural' one for Mlle Moke. Not that having planned a murder
through jealousy over Camille could be called 'normal'; but
Berlioz wrote that those feelings had inspired the sequel's final
part of the evening, a fantasy on Shakespeare's *Tempest.*

Lélio was to be the second half of an orchestral entertainment, a dramatic monologue in six parts with music referring
to his two *amours.* It was well received, but the whole conception was unwieldy, the interest ephemeral. *Lélio* still exists, to be
performed occasionally as a curiosity, with the melodrama
toned down. Franz Liszt favoured it, using it as a perhaps more
interesting orchestral fantasia with piano.

The symphony, despite its rude arrival, was a seminal masterpiece at the onset of a new musical age. Largely misunder-
stood then, its influence as programme music was to be lasting,
impressing Liszt, Wagner and another musical fantasist, Mahler.

By the 1820s, Europe's youthful intelligentsia regarded Lord
Byron's poetry as of the greatest relevance. He died in 1824, a
casualty through visiting Greece to support the resistance to
Turkish occupation and tyranny. He had opposed in writings
the injustices of British society and came to be seen as a fugitive
wandering in Europe, whilst enjoying its classical culture. As a
result, he became the model of a Romantic hero, the term
Byronic acquiring its historic associations.

Berlioz could hardly fail in part to identify with him, and
putting dramatic episodes from his poems into purely orchestral music occupied him more than once. The *Symphonie Fantastique* was followed by another one with a similar structure,
reinforcing the concept of the programme symphony. This was
Harold in Italy, (1834), inspired by Byron's *Childe Harold's
Pilgrimage:*

On with the dance! Let joy be unconfined.
No sleep till morn when Youth and Pleasure meet
To chase the glowing Hours with flying feet.

It reflected his own love of Italy's countryside, but not its
music, except that of the Abruzzi peasants. Harold is represented by a viola obbligato intended for performance by
Paganini. The instrument is rarely used solo, but its tone deeper than the violin could be suited to a more reflective role,
since Harold was to be an observer to a colourful four movement scenario of pilgrims, mountaineers and brigands. It was

an orchestral *tour de force,* a dramatic extension of concerto form.

Berlioz' *Memoires* are of great interest. He reveals a general dislike of Italian opera, and was appalled at the mangling of *Romeo & Juliet* in an Italian libretto by the supposedly distinguished Romani. Yet he was moved by the duet Bellini wrote here for the lovers, whilst wondering why Romeo should be a female role. Even so, he made the same decision when he fulfilled his debt to Shakespeare in what he termed a 'dramatic symphony', *Romeo & Juliet* (1839), for chorus and soloists. Curiously, the love scene was given to the orchestra alone on the grounds that the human voice could not fully express it. There is a dreamy lyricism chromatic enough to influence Wagner years before he set off in that direction with *Tristan.*

Berlioz also led the way in what nearly everyone else considered wild extravagance. He alone would have directed and financed the premiere, with some 200 musicians, a size which he did not regard as excessive, even in cost. Such enterprise did not reap its just rewards, and Berlioz would suffer decades of frustration. Yet at the height of his despair, in 1862, he could charm on a modest scale with wit and lightness of touch in a comic opera, *Beatrice & Benedict,* based on *Much Ado about Nothing.* He composed concert overtures to *King Lear,* and what must have appealed to his temperament, Byron's *Corsair,* and Walter Scott's *Rob Roy* and *Waverley.*

His melodies sounded very modern for the 1830–40s. To some ears, they seemed to wander, often very fast and with unexpected melodic shapes, making them difficult to follow. They disturbed many who were used to the light, airy style of the popular French operas of Adam and Auber. That was one reason Berlioz moved so many works based on literary themes from the theatre to the concert hall.

His most ambitious music drama was *The Trojans* based upon Virgil's *Aeneid.* Like Wagner, he composed his own libretto for the epic which he revered, It was exceptionally lengthy so that it was only performed split into two parts, the action at Troy and Carthage. This frustrated Berlioz' intention, and he did not live to witness its integrated triumphs. There are three commanding roles which few singers even today would presume to take: Cassandra in the Trojan episodes and Dido, Queen of Carthage. Her suicide is the climax of the drama when her lover

Aeneas deserts her to fulfil his historic mission, to found Rome. Berlioz was not troubled that the Aeneas role had a range most tenors could not manage.

The Trojans now stands as an operatic masterpiece, though Berlioz is more popular in Britain than France. This is partly because we British enjoy wild, Romantic drama, in the tradition of Shakespeare, whereas the French prefer classic restraint in the theatre.

5 *Meyerbeer & the Rise of Parisian Grand Opera*

Opera, the ninth and youngest of the muses, was conceived around 1600 in Italy, the intention to put tales of Greek and Roman gods and heroes to song in dramatic form. This led to a new art form with the term 'classical', and those early works were so successful as to be performed and imitated subsequently in the more refined courts of Europe. For their aristocracies, over two centuries opera in Italian became an attractive diversion alongside ballet.

It had wider popularity in Italy, with top singers, especially those most theatrical of celebrities, the *castrati*,[7] earning prodigious sums, many vain enough, often adding their own choice or replacing the prescribed melodies at will. Inferior music was being supplied cheaply as fodder for their virtuoso skills, but old favourites were available if public dissatisfaction led to a serious protest.

The drift into bad taste would be resisted in the late 18th century by composers of integrity. Outside Italy there were stirrings of opposition to Italianate music, with its language, which only the privileged favoured. The young Mozart was by nature inclined towards a private rebellion for which he could have suffered financially and politically. In great operas he had shown ways forward, such as use of the German language, before his life was cut off so tragically when relatively young.

The main impetus for reform came from musicians, in particular the talent of Weber, inspired by German folk music. They used a popular theatre form, the *Singspiel*, a play interspersed with songs. From this, Weber progressed to compose the first great German Romantic opera, *Freischütz* (1821), a world of magic in which love overcame evil. Yet by 1826, the ailing Weber was dead, and the great national cause would have to wait some years for its deliverer, Richard Wagner.

When Vienna reacted coolly to his early German opera, Jakob Meyerbeer (1791–1864), born in Berlin, went to live and study in Italy, and his colleague Weber resented his desertion. Rossini's sixth opera *Tancredi* (1813) written when he was only 21 had immense appeal abroad and Byron even referred to its most popular aria in his *Don Juan.* Such works had drawn Meyerbeer away, to perfect his skill in composing *bel canto,* the pure, long flowing melody which had become an Italian speciality. A comparable attraction was the coloratura technique, elaborate vocal and instrumental decoration, most thrilling when reaching up to the highest vocal peaks in sopranos who were destined eventually to replace in popularity the *castrati.* Yet after composing six Italian operas by 1825, he worked hard for several years planning new material which was so original that it escaped the dominance of *bel canto* and coloratura. This was the start of a revolution in singing technique; to compensate, Meyerbeer offered unprecedented power and startling rhythmic appeal.

His *Crusader in Egypt* won approval at Paris in 1825, but at this world centre for large-scale opera, conditions were at a low ebb and Rossini was brought from Italy in hopes of improvements. The French Revolution had brought artistic enlightenment to much of Europe, when large audiences were encouraged to gather at theatres for demonstrations of the power and glory of the new regime. Opera was no longer the plaything for the effete aristocracy, but an instrument of revolution, in support of great causes. Military choruses and rhythms were having strong appeal. The Italian Spontini became very popular in France and Germany composing works such as *Fernando Cortes* on an epic scale.

The rising middle classes would be its new patrons. An opera evening would also be a place for conducting business, and for some, just to be seen. For those who could not concentrate on the music, great spectacles were an essential diversion.

For singers, impresarios and composers, opera was the place to make money and in Paris, rather than writing symphonies. There were attractive operas by 1830 from French composers such as Auber and Herold. Their works are scarcely performed complete in our times, though well remembered now for their overtures which succeeded in advertising their best tunes.

Opera plots tended to questions of family relations and honour, enforced betrothals and love triangles, spiced with jealousy. A favourite type of melody consisted of short phrases, repeated and slightly varied, a simple pattern easy on the ear. Rossini followed this more vigorously and with a glorious succession of melodies. He struck a blow against cheap commercialism in Italy by composing in a way too complex to be taken liberties with. His larger orchestras and choruses could better compete with the singers. He had turned to his advantage a highly formalised tradition of opera with its flamboyant use of melisma, in which several notes are attached to one syllable. On the death of Beethoven in 1828, Rossini was widely considered the greatest living composer.

Romantic melody would discard melisma, which had dated back centuries to religious music, and trills would become old-fashioned. The new trend was more like the folk style, easier for more natural declamation and acting. In Italy, Bellini displayed a unique gift for *bel canto*, often nostalgic. He had achieved operatic excellence with *Norma* and other works by 1836 and his early death.

After the mid-1820s, Rossini was creatively troubled by the changing styles, but by 1829, when he had composed two works in the French language, he was supreme in Paris' operatic world. His *Count Ory* was probably his greatest work in the old manner, but *William Tell* appeared to move towards the new Romanticism in melodic style, more lyrical, less ornamental, and was critically praised as his finest work. Its over-popular overture is the perfect Rossini model with its imaginative use of instruments and startling crescendos but it does not reveal what was different in his new style. Yet Rossini stopped short of leading European grand opera into a new era.

He then walked away from triumph and the challenge of younger composers. At the age of 37, *Count Ory* and *William Tell* were to be his last operas, and the latter was too 'modern' to entrance most of his traditional fans. Its superlative Act II was often performed alone in the following years, partly because of the opera's 'excessive' length.

Daniel Auber's grand opera, *Masianello*, had immediate success with its 'patriotic' march tunes, one performance in Brussels (1830) having the impact to set off a successful revolution. That may have alarmed Auber so much that he decided to revert to lighter, less political subjects.

Who would replace Rossini to become the protagonist of the new trend, and to succeed him at the Paris opera? Some have greatness thrust upon them. Meyerbeer was one of the first generation of Jews who brought a fresh impact to European music. He wore a coat of many colours, carrying a large bag of cosmopolitan skills. Then fate helped; the new Opera director, Louis Veron, would support him throughout with the most lavish of resources.

Opera had been very formal and static, and the writer who could add vitality was Frenchman Eugene Scribe, creator of ingenious, well-constructed plots, leading up to spectacular climaxes. Since he went on to write some 400 plays, it was almost inevitable that he would be called formulaic. Liszt said it was irrational that he should be criticised for his unique successes.

Meyerbeer's *Robert the Devil* proved to be the ultimate melodrama, astonishing for the year 1831, or even today with the power of its singing and orchestral scoring, making *Masianello's* jaunty rhythms sound old-fashioned. It had the new, extravagant Romantic imagery like Weber's *Freischütz*, and an absurd plot in deserted locations with underworld creatures. Both works have scenes for which even today the music sounds intimidating, and such as a discriminating film director might use. Not all critics thought *Robert* a masterpiece[8] but the prototype for grand opera had arrived in Paris, or as they might say, *grand guignol*. Louis Herold's *Zampa* (1832) was in similar style, much performed throughout that century. He is best known for its imposing overture and the ballet, *La fille mal gardée*.

The sensation in *Robert* was a mock-religious ballet of defrocked nuns returning briefly from Hell to perform in the Devil's interests. This novelty may not have reached the highest aesthetic tones, but neither is Hell and most of the audience were thrilled. Meyerbeer was right to choose such ladies in preference to the alternative, an insipid crew of water nymphs, who along with sylphs had become stage chichés. The music is atmospheric though the nuns sound less vitriolic than the witches in Verdi's *Macbeth* two decades later. Even so, large numbers of women must have swooned in that Paris opera house, and the ballet was subsequently danced often by the century's two most famous ballerinas, Taglioni and Ellsler. *Robert* was a sensation as far as South America, making even Rossini's scores sound as if belonging to the past. During the

1830s, it was performed in nearly 2,000 theatres. For those who could not witness it, or desired the experience to be transferred to the concert lounge, Franz Liszt was soon preparing his piano version.

Meyerbeer had laboured very long, until he was nearly 40 years old, to emerge as master of a new operatic sound. *Robert* and his next works were much in advance technically of other 1830s composers', and the scores were given meticulous attention. He made audacious use of solo instruments and the larger orchestras made heavy demands on the voices. The melodies tended to be strident, their most distinguishing feature being an 'heroic' style, most apparent after the five years preparing his next success, *The Huguenots* (1834). It centred on a confrontation of rival forces, Catholic and Protestant, each fanatical within a realistic plot whereas in *Robert*, there had been a naive contest of good against evil. It was calculated to make the largest of all operatic impacts, staging the most infamous coup in French history, the massacre of Protestant notables in Paris on Saint Bartholomew's Day, 1572,

Audiences expected a traditionally decorative overture. Meyerbeer replaced this with a prelude: one majestic set of variations on a single theme, and what less suitable for treatment than Martin Luther's solemn hymn? It broke an operatic convention to avoid familiar religious melodies, in this case one sacred to German Protestants. As a dramatic device, such as setting the atmosphere for the first scene, preludes would eventually displace overtures, starting with Wagner.

This impassive movement is immediately followed by a swinging chorus of confident, fun-loving Catholic soldiers. During a military truce, Protestant guests include the main character, Raoul, who expresses love at first sight for a (presumably) Catholic girl. This angers his retainer, Marcel, a fanatic, who shows hatred for all of them (*We'll blow them away*), an aria in like terms, jerky and venomous, not quite what was expected in any opera house.

In order to secure lasting tolerance, the Princess Marguerite de Valois invites Raoul to her palace for discussions in the leisurely surround of a (ladies only) swimming pool. This is an opportunity for some lighter entertainment and coloratura singing, notably by the Princess, which is absent in the rest of the work. Meyerbeer creates the device of an attractive page, a

high soprano role, to announce Raoul's arrival with embel-
lishments, a seductive waltz. The Act ends with a chorus in
headlong rhythms of the kind which had made him popular.

Only Hector Berlioz could then write theatre music of such
startling effect, but he was not broadly accepted by the opera
public. Yet he praised his rival's exceptional dramatic skills,
writing in 1842 of a performance with the composer conducting:

> *orchestral playing superb in its beauty and refinement. The chorus
> was equally remarkable. The rapid runs, the antiphonal double
> choruses, the entries in imitation, the sudden transitions from forte to
> piano, and all the gradations ... an uncommon warmth of feelings
> and a sense of dramatic expression which is even rarer. The stretto*
> (accelerating section) *in the* Blessing of the Daggers *was an
> overwhelming moment; it was some time before I recovered from it. ...
> The richness of texture in the Pré-aux clercs scene, with the women
> quarrelling, the Catholics intoning the prayer to the Virgin, and the
> Huguenots bawling out the* rataplan *was extraordinary[9] ... Yet the
> ear could follow it with such ease that every strand in the composer's
> complex thought was apparent.*

Berlioz stated that in this opera, Meyerbeer had enough
ideas for ten. Act III would suffice for one opera, though one
modern 'approved' recording cuts it down to just one hour. As
planned, it included a septet (a rarity), military stands-offs, two
processions, with one for a wedding, separate male and female
choruses, ballet sequences, on-stage band. A recent London-
Berlin collaboration was given a 20th century Ulster setting.
The conspiracy (daggers) scene and the final love duet, when
the girl prefers to die with Raoul as the planned massacre
unfurls, is often specially praised. Opportunities to test *The
Huguenots* as a fully accomplished work of art on the largest
stages are now limited by excessive costs. These were once seen
as excellent publicity, such as being billed in New York as *the
Night of the Seven Stars,* one of the first uses of a term now sadly
devalued.

The Prophet once more concerned religious fanaticism, the
fate of West Germany's Anabaptist heretics in the 1640s. It
arrived after Meyerbeer had laboured for 13 years more with
the last of his grand operas to be performed in his lifetime,
confirming but without raising the composer's reputation.[10] It
was the first opera to enjoy electric lighting, and the photo-
graphic pioneer, Daguerre, was by then available to provide

wondrous scenic illusions. Permanent evidence of the opera's musical qualities is available in a recording with one of the 20th century's greatest singers, Marilyn Horne, in the formidable mezzo role, Fides the protagonist's mother.

It has one of the most spectacular coronation scenes in opera, and with solemn religious associations. For the second time, a Jew had used Christian intolerance as his operatic theme. Some resented this, but the majority were enthusiastic to see such great historic events unfurl, presented in the most lavish manner, staged in the largest theatres, with at least 200 participants. The action was to be leisurely stretched out over five Acts, five hours or more, and not excluding many charming digressions.

Dance being a major attraction at the Paris opera, Meyerbeer decided *The Prophet* should have a ballet score with a very light touch. This appears in an Act III skating rink scene, another improbable location within any opera. Yet the music's excellence ensures that today it has a second existence as a ballet, *Les patineurs*. That and the coronation march are often heard at popular orchestral concerts.

When on its first Parisian appearance in 1861 Wagner dared to place a ballet in the first Act of his *Tannhäuser,* the young bloods arrived too late for the dancers, so they created a noisy demonstration which has gone down in history as infuriating him.

In the luxurious five Act format, grand opera was most prestigious into the 20th century, state sponsored. With hindsight, Meyerbeer's many critics might say he was a crowd-pleaser with concoctions which anticipated the excesses of Hollywood. In fact, some Europeans with memories of opera's splendour emigrated, ending up in Hollywood as producers, and applied its most spectacular visual features, curiously to the 'silent' cinema.

Verdi's maturing style was incisive and fast-flowing, Italian operas being less than three hours in length. When agreeing to compose in French *Sicilian Vespers* for Paris (1855), he was obliged to provide five Acts of music, and follow the Meyerbeer formula overall, irritated by having to compose a lengthy ballet score. The critics pronounced the *Vespers* a partial failure, yet still by 1867, his epic *Don Carlos* showed even more evidence of his being influenced by Meyerbeer's music and dramatic techniques.

The main problem with such operas is now a practical one; apart from excessive expense, they have to be severely cut to enable audiences to leave the performances before midnight. *Don Carlos, The Huguenots* and Wagner's *Rienzi* are often treated in this way. There is now a tendency to regard such works as dinosaurs, and a modern composer hardly dares to compete.

There was a second tradition in France, *opera comique*, plots not without happy ending and spoken dialogue but not 'comical' in our sense. Its main Parisian home was and still is the building so-named. Meyerbeer composed two 'comic operas' and invaded their territory successfully.

The Star of the North was about the Russian Tsar Peter II, and it had a second life in Berlin as *A Camp in Silesia*, the hero changed to Prussia's Frederick II. This has added historical interest because Meyerbeer was for long also appointed to the Prussian court, sharing his duties between there and Paris. *Dinorah* was hardly for export, a French pastoral, based on a folk story, but for continuous beauty of sound, probably exceeding anything else he wrote; the heroic style gives place to a lyrical one. It now stands just as a reminder of his melodic gifts but in its time a show- piece, almost a parody of his own style. Its *Shadow* song, breath-taking coloratura, might now be thought too long and over-the-top, like a mad scene in an Italian opera. In contrast, its overture is specially imperious, so Germanic that it might be mistaken for an excerpt from *Rienzi*. Yet the naive plot works severely against it being much performed now.

Meyerbeer's perfectionism caused him to worry over his final grand opera, not quite living to see its first performance in 1865, 27 years after Scribe had handed over the libretto. It was (eventually) the story of a Hindu queen, wrongly designated as *L'Africaine*, who sacrifices herself for love of the explorer, Vasco Da Gama.[11] It concerns Portuguese navigation politics involving the Grand Inquisitor, and includes an on-stage ship wreck which allegedly caused much sea-sickness among at least one early audience. This 6-hour work[12] was favourably received, though markedly different in style from previous ones, more lyrical with a sombre beauty, long-flowing melodies rarely broken up by the action. The interest is centred on the characters, a love triangle, with a glowing role for the doomed heroine, the finale a quiet fade-out untypical of Meyerbeer. By

1865, interest in exotic places was becoming fashionable in Paris, but for its colourful ballet the sound is totally 'European', the one obvious defect. Meyerbeer was not quite up with the times.

Despite his prolific gifts, to our times Meyerbeer remains a controversial figure, if not as a musician, and no definitive book on his work or status is now available in English. The main charge against him is showmanship, placing audience appeal before artistic integrity. Yet his influence on those who followed, from Verdi and Wagner to Tchaikovsky, is apparent.

Some of the most popular works we still hear as *opera comique* were soon adapted as grand opera, such as Gounod's *Faust* (1869) but the composers of *Carmen* and *Tales of Hofmann* were no longer alive to object. The changes did not guarantee improvement, possibly weighed down with extra ballet, and other trappings such as sung dialogue (recitative). Today they are produced nearer to their original forms.

By the 1870s, when Paris' new home for (grand) National Opera, the Garnier, was completed, new styles were emerging. Commercial theatres were competing with productions on a smaller scale. The beneficiary was lyric opera, an appealing option in the many works of Jules Massenet and others.

6 *The Younger Liszt*

T he Hungarian cimbalom is a gong-like dulcimer in folk bands, with clarinet and strings. Sacheverell Sitwell in his biography of Franz Liszt (1811–86), wrote:

The tapping and rattling of the cimbalom is embodied in Liszt's Hungarian Rhapsodies, *equally with the chorus of violins and the solos of its leader ... all the effects of a gipsy band, with extraordinary success. In its day, those rhapsodies must have been of immense originality; since then, they have carried the fame of Hungarian music from end to end of the world.*

A few of the first 15 transcriptions, or at least one, has become overplayed because of its excessive popularity, obscuring most of the others[13]. They were unlike anything ever heard on a solo piano, technically astounding, rising in the style of a *czardas*, from a relaxed tempo to the wildest exhilaration.

Scientific research into such areas of folklore did not exist in Liszt's time, so the precise music of the Hungarian peasants would have to wait two more generations for its annotation through musicologists. Liszt relied on music popular in the towns as performed mainly by gipsies, who had often embellished the material. How much was original gipsy music is less important than the fact it gave him a fund of beautiful melodies and exciting rhythms. His skills in transcribing them were such that on hearing the orchestral version of the one numbered two, one might think it unplayable on the piano.

It was from childhood memories of them that Franz Liszt's work on their music originated, and his later art song, *The three Gipsies,* is a moving tribute to their culture. He was born in 1811 of Austrian parents. His father worked on the Esterhazy estate which had been linked with a major phase in Haydn's career, on the other side of the Austro-Hungarian border when that was not a political frontier. He never mastered the language, but was proud of being thought Hungarian.

By adolescence, he was living in Paris thanks to prodigious talent at the piano. His witnessing the first world-famous violinist Paganini was a decisive event as he determined to work hard enough to become a great virtuoso. Paganini's skills were such that once when he played on just one string, the Devil was alongside giving a helping hand. That at least was the witness of a journalist he had probably bribed.

Perhaps one million people believed it. Paganini's compositions were of their kind uniquely difficult to play, and Liszt spent much time transcribing them. In particular, he was the first of many Romantics including Brahms and Rakhmaninov to be fascinated by the melodic potential of Paganini's Caprice no XXIV. He would make the piano rival the violin in speed of note repetition with breath-taking effect. As both men were unusually gaunt, the tag of diabolism was often attached to both by way of explaining their expertise. But Liszt was no charlatan.

His *Liebestraum no. 3* was once probably the best known love song in Western Europe, thought to be the very idealisation of love. Yet Liszt did not choose to repeat his popular successes. The *Consolation no.3* has some melodic similarity, but none of that ecstatic feeling, and is nearer to Chopin's style. Liszt admired him greatly but did not imitate; when Chopin died young, Liszt used some of his valuable time to write a book about him. Great composers were not known to pay this kind of compliment, but Liszt was very generous towards others. Chopin was not inclined to return the compliments about Liszt's creativity.

Being born at a time of the greatest change in music, Liszt was quick to discover what lay beyond, moving away from traditional forms. He led the way in piano music inspired by artistic and literary themes, an approach new for the mid-1830s, leading to *Years of Pilgrimage, Year I, Switzerland.* This was completed by the age of 25, with impressionistic pieces such as *The Bells of Geneva.*

Clearly written by the composer of that *Liebestraum,* the impassioned *Petrarch Sonnet no. 104*[14] is a piece he revised with much care over the years. On the theme of love's anxieties, he produced several versions for male or female voice, and as a piano solo. It is marked by brief, pregnant phrases, with much note repetition, sighs, highly emotive gestures, forms of instrumental recitative. An early version has the added beauty of the soprano voice, and the later solo piano variant is a fine virtuoso piece. It appeared one decade later in a set, *Years of*

Pilgrimage,Year II, Italy, with two other interpretations of Petrarch sonnets, combining *bel canto* melody and the operatic style of the 1830–40s with his new techniques. Its companion piece, *Petrarch Sonnet no. 123*, relates to spiritual love and may have inspired Strauss' Italianate aria in *Rosenkavalier,*

Years of Pilgrimage, Year II, Italy was inspired by works of the Italian Renaissance, with his *Dante* Sonata forming the largest item. Dramatic episodes in Dante's *Inferno* called for unprecedented expressive power on the piano, such as double octaves in a description of Hell.The chord of the diminished fourth dominates the opening, the so-called Devil's Interval, once banned by the Church from all music because of its disturbing sound. There is a poignant interlude in the love story of Paolo and Francesca suffering in Hell.

Raphael's *Sposalizia*, the betrothal of Mary and Joseph, depicted a sacred event whose tenderness was translated in what Liszt termed a 'psychic sketch' or 'poetic counterpart'. As an afterthought, he added three short works with melodies by other composers, one from Rossini's *Otello*, all developed for brilliant virtuosic effect, called *Venice and Naples*. The gondoliers' song by Ponchini has a compelling local feeling *in the noctural dying-away chords*, according to Kentner. He is specially impressed with the Neopolitan tarantella, the opening *swaggering*, the theme later transforming to the sound of distant guitars, ending with *a paroxysm of gaiety*.

Liszt took two classic Spanish tunes, *La Folia* and the *Jota Aragonesa*,[15] placing them in brilliant contrast for his *Spanish Rhapsody*. Pianist John Ogdon writes that it has one of the finest of all his cadenzas.

In the days before recorded music, the piano and its transcriptions led to unprecedented sales of sheet music, ensuring that families and friends could enjoy operatic drama in their homes, and Liszt's versions are classics. Exceptional demands had been made on his time as soloist, across Europe from Spain to Russia. He was the first great virtuoso to benefit whilst young from the development of railways.

The age of the public concert hall and larger orchestras encouraged him to create on a larger canvas themes depicting ideas, history and legends. His friend Berlioz' works on literary subjects had pointed the way, but Liszt's innovation was what he termed the symphonic poem. This is a single-movement composition not tied down by the strict rules of symphonic structure but growing mainly from one main theme. From 1849, and within a decade, he had created 12 of these lasting some 15 minutes or longer. The form of each work was to be influenced by its subject matter, subjecting his melodies to transformation and integration.

The Preludes' melodic appeal has always made it the most popular of his larger works. That and its rhetoric put it high among several of Liszt's works which many critics find vulgar. Some of the other symphonic poems have interesting cross-references, such as *Héroïde funèbre* (Heroic Funeral March). Like Berlioz' *Triumphal Funeral Symphony*, it was intended to pay honour to the victims of the 1830 Paris uprising. Liszt developed it over several years and after he had lived through Europe's revolutionary year 1848, he took a broader political view of the suffering of citizens. So he eventually planned a symphony to commemorate all the dead but it got no further than this one movement.

Other works in the set were from poems, history or classic stories. Sitwell specially admired: *Hungaria* which he likens to the style of the later Chabrier, with its immediate appeal: *Festive Sounds* was to celebrate his intended marriage to the Polish Carolyne von Sayn-Wittgenstein, *timpani and fanfares, part Meyerbeer, part Rimsky-Korsakov*, as Sitwell commented. Finest of all for him, *The Battle of the Huns*, unique, its opening *magnificent and terrifying*, the final chorale, bell-like, anticipating Mussorgsky's *Great Gate of Kiev*. Sitwell understands why *Mazeppa* was a theme which attracted Liszt as well as Tchaikovsky, but believes he gave this violent piece of history a shallow interpretation.

The first *Mephisto Waltz* published separately from his symphonic poems described an episode from the original *Faust* legend. Its orchestral version brought eroticism into the concert hall, a tale of seduction and gratification during a wild country dance with Mephisto as the demon fiddler. Liszt worked long on this fairly short piece, and on his *Faust Symphony* (1854). Its three movements are studies of the drama's main characters, the one inhuman. As Mephisto keeps reinventing himself, his personality was ideal for thematic transformation. It is like three linked symphonic poems and Sitwell regarded it as Liszt's masterpiece, describing the *Mephisto* movement:

*Wildness and hysterical excitement run riot; the (earlier) themes are
tortured and twisted, given sneering, sarcastic shape: are corrupted
and made evil: are presented in triumphant, exultant loudness: they
mock and imitate . . . (then) are recalled in their original forms, and
like the dispersal of the ghosts at cockcrow, the whole atmosphere
changes; and the magnificent choral ending brings the* Faust
Symphony *to a close.*

The form of the symphonic poem would be taken up by
many composers, especially in the following half century.

Liszt's fame among audiences promoted the spreading of the
solo piano recital and the media phenomenon of 'Lisztoma-
nia'. The adulation he received as a performer was often
extreme, thought some thought him an exhibitionist all
his life. As a young man, he could not resist showing off
and might break several wooden pianos, but only through
energetic use. He rebuked Tsar Nicholas I neatly for speaking
whilst he was playing. Strange stories, even bedroom farce,
related to the behaviour of certain women admirers, such as
Lola Montes.

Aged 37, he moved away from temptation, even standing by
his resolution no longer to give paid performances. He would
dedicate himself to composition, also performing others'
works; he concerned himself least with commercial advantage.

He was one of the first performers to attempt to heal with
music the sick and mentally disadvantaged. This approach was
warmly approved by his friend, Pope Pius IX, though he tired
of hearing Liszt's confessions about carnal intercourse, with the
words:. *I've heard enough. Go and tell your sins to the piano.*

Liszt had reason to fear his father's prediction that women
would be his ruin. He may have been saved through a lengthy,
adulterous affair with Carolyne which was stable and supported
his creative spirit. This coincided with his being music director
(1848–59) at the court of Weimar where his patron provided
him with an orchestra and facilities to create a music centre,
away from the distractions of the great capitals. His promotion
of operas by contemporaries, notably Wagner and Berlioz, was
very important.

His proposed marriage to Carolyne fell through in 1861,
forbidden by the Church. He sought refuge in religion, his
composing gradually turning further in that direction, and to
partial residence in Rome.

Remarkably for those times, he lived openly with women regardless of his patrons' and societies' feelings. From an earlier liaison with Marie d'Agoult, he had three children including a daughter, Cosima, who would become the wife of Richard Wagner, though the most important relationship between the two men was musical. Wagner was in the broad sense not a generous man, and unlikely to admit the extent of Liszt's influence.

As a pianist, Liszt was the most famous of the 19th century, and by repute an authentic interpreter of Beethoven's sonatas. The severe English critic, Henry Chorley, disapproved of his playing others' new works, yet grudgingly as an early witness, he applauded Liszt's incomparable tonal range:

> ... *the real instrumentalist among many charlatans (in Paris). He can make the strings whisper with an aerial delicacy or utter voices as clear and as tiny as the very finest harp notes. Sometimes the piano becomes a trumpet and a sound is extracted as piercing and as nasal as the tone of a clarion: the power of interweaving the richest, most fantastic accompaniments with a steadily moving melody: fire, poignancy, in flights of octaves and in chromatic succession of chords.*

Liszt's had a reputation for 'flying fingers'; previously pianists bent them over the keys. He exploited certain known techniques to added effect, such as *rubato* which became a major feature of Romantic expression and some pianists were tempted to exaggerate. As a composer, he had a liking for the chord of the diminished seventh[16] which in earlier times had been frowned upon as 'sensationalist'. Repeated several times in rapid succession, this can raise tension dramatically. His sonata (not the *Dante*) was admired by pianist Louis Kentner:

> *In a short introduction, he introduces three seemingly incongruous elements, then proceeds to demonstrate how these can be welded into a unity of such compactness, such compelling power ... he twists and bends them, rhythmically reshaped to fit into the musical design. Here, the purpose was purely musical, but elsewhere, it could be dramatic.*

Kentner refers to Schubert's *Wanderer Fantasy*, which had intrigued Liszt because of its originality in developing one theme over a whole composition. Liszt adapted the work under the same title, expanding it for piano and orchestra, and covering a wider range of emotional experience.

His songs with piano are generally less admired in Britain than those of Brahms and Schumann, but many of them are very passionate, masculine but eloquent. This may point towards opera which apart from a juvenile effort he avoided. His melodic style was subject to far more influences than his contemporaries'. Yet Liszt's musical personality was very individual; typical of his lyrical side were the main themes of his symphonic poems, *Orpheus* and *The Preludes.*

He is one of only a handful of composers whose music has been compiled in recent decades for a ballet. Kenneth Macmillan's *Mayerling* was about a suicide pact at a hunting lodge in 1882 of two lovers, one the heir to the Austrian throne, four years before Liszt's death.

Throughout his life he had explored new ideas in melody and harmony, and the final verdict on his place and influence in music has yet to be made. For example, in a passionate song he used perhaps the most significant phrase in modern music, the *Tristan* motif[17]. Yet Richard Wagner would accept the entire credit for this and Liszt was modest enough to acquiesce.

Around the age of 50, Liszt entered a new phase which was to take in the final third of his life. He was turning to matters spiritual, taking minor Holy Orders as an Abbé, which was symbolised by normally wearing a cassock. His composing reflected these changes, increasingly austere and experimental in technique: 'continuing to throw a spear into the future', as Carolyne said.

The younger Liszt remains a controversial figure as a composer, in part unfairly because of the suggestions of showmanship in him. Yet no-one was more broadly dedicated to music, helping where possible the finest compositions of others. Like most, his works were unequal in quality, but the term 'music of the future' was very widely used in his years, and it applied very significantly to his work.

Those who thought Liszt spread his talents too wide were denied by Bela Bartok, who said there was no work in which the greatness of Liszt's creative power can be doubted. He might have been speaking of himself when he said:

What Liszt touched was first crushed to a pulp, then moulded together and so completely reconstructed that his individuality was indelibly stamped on it, as though it had been his original idea.

7   Waltz and 3/4 Time

ongress dances!! That was the slogan which first circulated in the German language. The year was 1815. The international peace congress was spending its evenings dancing the waltz! Most of the rulers of Europe were rumoured to be doing so, having come to Vienna, capital of the Habsburg Empire. The waltz had at last achieved respectability.

$\frac{3}{4}$ timing, three beats in a bar, had always been an option, and there were examples in refined ballets of the 18th century. The concern, which some thought scandalous, was that 'country dances' being performed in alpine South Germany and Austria included body contact, even embracing. The excitement of 'whirling around' could have an appalling effect on the men and if it was fast, the females would be obliged to cling to their partners. Many thought it a display of sensuality in which men might even throw their partners into the air: a shocking place for any woman to be.

Best known in $\frac{3}{4}$ time was the Austrian Ländler, a stamping dance at moderate pace with the accent on the first of three beats in each bar. Franz Schubert added a distinctive, smoother touch to sets for piano: graceful, often sad, using a minor key and full of rhythmic ingenuity.

French revolutionaries wanted to overthrow the minuet and other aristocratic fashions, so introduced a whirling dance to Paris by 1800. They later developed an important waltz style differing from the Viennese. Resistance across the waters took longer to break down: in 1817, Lord Byron was disapproving of the waltz, a case of sour grapes. With his limp, he could hardly have impressed the ladies in a ballroom. By the 1820s, such places in Britain and the U.S.A. had added the waltz and the more boisterous polka to the fashionable quadrille, there to dominate for nearly a century.

From the open air hopping and stamping of the peasant Ländler, the ballroom waltz developed indoors with lighter shoes gliding across the floor, and speeded up by about half. A variant missing out the middle of each three steps, called the

Langaus, required couples to dance the length of the room at speed several times until exhausted. This resulted in so many casualties that it was eventually banned.

Viennese musicians tended to advance the second beat of their authentic waltz slightly, giving an illusion of permanent acceleration. It was and should be danced on the heels, in a non-stop clockwise spin. This is so strenuous that in modern times, social dancers 'cheat', such as turning anti-clockwise. There were normally two or more melodies for each piece, a speeding-up in the second or final one. The Parisian version from the early 19th century included leaping and was danced on the toes. That was imitated with the incoming style of Romantic ballet.

Viennese waltz dominance was complete by the 1820s with rival bands under the violin virtuosi, Josef Lanner and Johann Strauss. Between them they composed in the major keys about 500 dances, as well as putting Rossini and other operatic favourites into waltz time. To prevent boredom setting in with the dominant $^3/_4$, they used cross-rhythms, syncopation and slight pauses. Rossini's exciting use of the orchestra was a model, but pressure of speed caused some falling off in quality. Interest abroad was so great that even before the railways, Strauss took some of his 200 musicians by stagecoaches on the long road to Paris.

The Czech polka was very prominent alongside the waltz. Other $^3/_4$ time dances came from Poland. The elegant polonaise was processional and had been favoured by the upper classes, and the mazurka had a more martial flavour, such as in their patriotic song, *Dombrowski,* now the national anthem. The second beat was emphasized, especially with the stamping of boots. Most of the early Romantic composers from Central Europe wrote piano pieces for one or more of these dances.

The perfection of the Strauss waltz came through his sons. Josef wrote over 200, often movingly in the minor keys, but he died young, not before instructing his youngest brother Edouard to destroy all his unpublished works. When the father died in 1849, it was oldest son Johann II who was to become for decades one of the world's most famous names. Continuing to play and conduct nightly before perhaps over 5,000 dancers, he was influenced by other cultures within the Empire, notably Hungarian and gipsy musicians drawn to the capital. As a virtuoso he could play on the emotions through the use of rubato, though he had to avoid disorienting the dancers' rhythm with it.

He perfected the lengthy concert or showcase dance, each subtly unified through a chain of contrasting tunes. He would increase the excitement up to the end, in the manner of a symphonic movement. His introductions could be inspired, such as the evocative appeal of a solo zither in the *Tales from the Vienna Woods*, followed immediately by full orchestra. The *Emperor Waltz* came to be thought as symbolizing the ceremonial aspects of the Empire.

Strauss was also master of the polka, gallop and the slow, swaying waltz. Specially seductive ones are heard in two of his operettas, *A Night in Venice* and *The Dancer, Fanny Elssler*. That artiste had become world famous during Johann's youth, taking the new style of ballet as far as Washington D.C. where her appearance in 1842 led to Congress deciding to adjourn early.

Strauss took his band to the Paris Exhibition of 1867 and was a prodigious success, also with the new *Blue Danube*. Similar enthusiasm greeted him in New York and Boston after a passage on one of the earliest steamships. For twelve successive seasons, he was pressed to visit the Russian capital where there was a very different tradition in dance.

Hector Berlioz was an enthusiast, introducing a waltz suggesting the intoxication of love into a symphony. $^3/_4$ time entered opera, its glorious sweep providing numerous great arias and underlying whole scenes, certainly by the time young Verdi was heard. Later, the lengthy Romantic ballets would include at least one spectacular waltz, and it had pride of place in 19th century operettas. The French variety drew many great ones from Offenbach, and Waldteufel whose waltzes included the perennial *Skaters*.

Brahms regretted he could not presume to compete, but in a very distinct, relaxed style, he wrote two sets of *Love Song Waltzes* for vocal quartet. One century later, these inspired a clever imitation of operetta, *A Little Night Music* by Sondheim, who also had in mind Ravel's elegant set of waltzes inscribed as *noble and sentimental*.

As if in final tribute to the dying waltz culture, the Bavarian Richard Strauss gave it place in three of the most important of the 20th century's music dramas. Waltz tempo and the spirit of operetta took command for most of Act III of his *Rosenkavalier*. Curiously, the action takes place in upper class Vienna of the 1740s, which makes too early by at least 60 years. His penalty remains that lesser informed persons assume he was just another one of the Viennese family.

Both in popular and art music, the waltz had been a major accomplice of Romanticism for almost a century, right up to the first world war. By then its dominance was being challenged in Western music by the exciting rhythms of North and South America. Subsequently, the Viennese style was associated often ironically as a symbol of the 'good old days' which for most people had never existed. So it had been used in a satirical manner by such composers as Mahler, Shostakovitch, Prokofief and Stravinsky.

In the realm of light music, it has come to play a very subsidiary role. On both sides of the Atlantic, the quality of the later 20th century waltzes has generally been sub-standard, whilst the finest lyrical melodies tended to go to the slow fox-trot; the slow waltz has often had to carry over-sentimental lyrics. Yet at least two faster 'Viennese-American' ones have achieved distinction: from Richard Rodgers' musicals, *Carousel* and *Oklahoma*. *Out of my Dreams* was for long a signature tune for the American Forces Network in Europe.

8 *Excelsior & Marble Halls*

There was only one world premiere of a Verdi opera in England, and it was to be conducted by him at Her Majesty's Theatre, London: *The Robbers* in 1847. After the first performance, he handed over the baton to an accomplished Dublin-born conductor. This was Michael Balfe (1808–70) who in the previous decade had been admired as an operatic baritone on the Continent, once singing *La Sonnambula* with the now legendary Malibran at Venice. Over his unusually versatile musical career, he came to know many composers from Rossini to Massenet, and may have had more experience on the Continent than any other British musician of his stature in the 19th century. He had the achievement of composing 27 operas over 30 years which were played, many in European cities and all the capitals where his fame once rivalled that of Donizetti and Bellini. A famous team of leading Italian singers were prepared to perform with him in their own language his operas as far as St Petersburg, and in London his *Falstaff.* Unlike most English singers at that time, they tended to know the works they were about to sing.

A handful of Balfe's melodies were to become over-familiar and one or two are recognized still by millions who do not know his name. His neglect must be one of the least deserved in British music, so a rare opportunity to reassess his importance is due now in his bicentenary year.

Sir Thomas Beecham had called him the most interesting British musician of his century. It was partly on his recommendation that for Britain's 1951 Festival, Balfe's *Bohemian Girl* was selected as the most representative British opera. It had known more popularity than any other, and its loss of status had been a result of the overall decline of opera's popularity in Britain during the first half of the 20th century.

Comparison with Arthur Sullivan serves no purpose; he was of the previous generation, and their best works are in differing musical genres. *The Bohemian Girl's* long popularity was based on several fine melodies: three in particular had deeply

nostalgic associations. *I dreamt I dwelt in marble Halls* is still
familiar out of context and worthy of the best in Bellini. *The
Heart bowed down* is sensitively matched with its lyric:

> *To long departed years extend*
> *its visions with them flown;*
> *for mem'ry is the only friend*
> *that grief can call its own.*

and the tender *When other Lips* was one of the reasons Bernard
Shaw stated that Balfe was a finer composer of ballads than
Tchaikovsky.

The Bohemian Girl of 1843 had a lightweight story, an aristocrat's daughter abducted by gipsies falling for one who is
eventually revealed as of noble birth. The gipsy idiom as we
understand it was then unknown in England's enclosed society,
and Balfe did not even try to imitate it, though he gave them
two flowing theme-songs for pleasurable make-believe. The
Gipsy Queen's solo, *The Lady Moon,* is one of his finest arias,
moving without being too sentimental. Despite the lack of
genuine 'local colour', the opera's success raised curiosity
about gipsy life, just as four decades later the *Mikado* brought a
cult of things Japanese.

Apart from his foreign language works, Balfe was expected to
follow the requirements of the English, century-old ballad
opera, with its songs separated by dialogue. *The Bohemian Girl*
succeeded beyond that, as perhaps several of Balfe's lesser
known ones did, such as with integrated crowd scenes. Its Act
III sent its audience home fired by a happy ending, a fine trio
and for its times a very dramatic quartet.

Greater operas would appear in the following decade outside
Britain; but it stood high for the warmth of its melodic appeal.
So the 1951 production was a useful testing time. The Times
critic said that *The Bohemian Girl* sustained its charm after a
century, but he was irritated by an excess of *arpeggi*[18] which had
been very pleasing once to singers and audience alike.

■   ■   ■

Several outstanding composers have written upwards of 20
operas including Rossini, Donizetti, Verdi, Massenet, Mascagni
and Lehar. If they were prolific, one every year or two was
possible without serious decline in quality. Were their lesser-
known operas less deserving, and if so, why?

Most composers were not free to chart their own courses. Impresarios, other interested parties and public taste were commercial factors, and working to time schedules could be at the expense of inspiration. In Balfe's earlier years the popular demands in opera were specific: show-stopping solos for the four or more principal singers: duets which made dramatic sense: stirring ensembles. Fine instrumentation was not so important but British publishers wanted ballads to be prominent so they could also be printed in piano versions for separate sale, perhaps earning more income than the operas. Rossini could space his best arias out among a rapid output of operas, but pressures sometimes caused hurry, notably in the case of the accomplished Donizetti, who wrote over 60, quality often suffering as a result.

Balfe's *Maid of Artois* was one of the works which caused Rossini to express special admiration for him as a melodist. It arrived at the height of the *bel canto* vogue, 1836, a work of early maturity which rivalled some of Donizetti's abroad.

In Paris, Balfe had sung duets with Maria Malibran, once with Liszt and Chopin in the audience. She had promised to perform for Balfe, and the opportunity in *The Maid of Artois* was the only one because she died tragically young within months. The aria, *The Moon o'er the Mountains,* proved unpopular and she had it withdrawn, but modern audiences should find it intriguing, with a Weber-like appeal. The need to gratify distinguished singers could be a disadvantage, and including an inferior *cavatina* for the villainous Marquis. The hero's *cavatina* was of the kind which Sullivan parodied in his Savoy operas. Yet the ballad, *The Light of other Days* was guaranteed a success, the nostalgia to please Victorian tastes, especially with a warm cornet solo as introduction.

This sad note is promptly dispelled with the lively Act II finale; one can't have the villain setting the tone, and the original intention to have a tragic ending was replaced with an added Act III, its waltz being specially popular abroad. The work, unequal in quality, was served by an inadequate libretto from Alfred Bunn, then a very influential figure in the London theatre. It was a version of the much-used *Manon Lescaut* story but Bunn spoilt it by purifying Manon's character. Nor would treating slavery as a light, teacher-pupil relation be acceptable in a modern performance.

The numerous attempts to found a national opera in that century had perhaps the best chance with a new opera from Balfe in 1857. Though *The Rose of Castile* was acclaimed and held centre stage in London for some three years, the national project failed through lack of government support and had to wait almost another century for fulfilment.

At present, there is in performance almost no opportunity to evaluate the other operas, and only the highest standard would suffice for revivals. The early *Siege of Rochelle* was successfully performed in London a few years ago including the exquisite aria, *The First Kiss.*

The 1885 biographer, W.A. Barrett, wrote of Balfe's developing techniques over the following 30 years in line with other trends, such as the selective repeat of motifs and through-composed (no dialogue) scores. He argued without analysis – which in those days was scarce – that *The Talisman,* based on Scott's novel, was the greatest of Balfe's operas, as performed, Paris 1874, in Italian. Barrett wrote of its great success in the U.S.A., despite *a vulgar finale which was impertinently concocted by the conductor and performers.* That was typical of risks in the opera world then which he might have avoided by accepting invitations to America. Lack of copyright laws also prevented Balfe enjoying the royalties from unapproved performances.

Barrett recommended the cantata, *Mazeppa,* on the much-used Cossack story, for its fine arias. That Balfe could compose in ultra-heroic style was evident from one of the most extraordinary short pieces originally composed for a salon audience. As a dramatic *scena* with piano, it was to a poem *Excelsior* by the American, Longfellow about a youth determined to scale a mountain pass regardless of the threat from an avalanche. He even spurns the invitation to lay his weary head overnight on a maiden's breast. Despite the warnings from monks, he proceeds only to be found the following day buried, not alive but clutching the mystical banner inscribed with the word *Excelsior,* onwards and upwards!

It has immediacy and panache, the voices, as if in the mountains, in full power with uplifting melodies to match. The orchestral version up-sizes Gounod and turns it into a mini-drama whilst its implicitly religious feeling would have set Victorian audiences alight. How it has declined in fame to become a museum piece is ironic and related to social history.

Fascinating as music, was it unlike anything else in Balfe's output? We no longer live in heroic times; the youth would now be admired for resting the night and living to become a celebrity.

Excelsior was one of six poems with Balfe's interpretation, helping to increase Longfellow's popularity. His poems are now much less known except for *Hiawatha*, which in the 1930s was a much performed oratorio by Coleridge-Taylor. Tennyson's *Maude* was destined also to receive a passionate interpretation, not to say excessive publicity for which it is still known. Two ballads reveal other sides of Balfe's musical personality: his tribute to *Killarney*, and the witty *Trust her not*.

9 *Verdi and Comedy*

W hilst still only 21, Rossini had adapted Beaumarchais' comedy *The Barber of Seville* to make an historic opera. Its success was related to a lively plot with two young would-be lovers outwitting foolish opposition from an elderly Pantaloon character. It was essentially an Italian Harlequinade, a spirit that had passed into musical comedy-farce, *opera buffa*. In *The Barber,* it was spiced with such diversions as a graphic presentation of a rumour and singing lesson given by a young lover incognito.

Rossini had a unique talent for extending jokes in musical terms. In *Cinderella,* the girl's family face the world astounded by her elevation to Princess, and in *The Italian Girl in Algiers* the entire Turkish court are outwitted by one woman. With all the characters on stage deluded or in a state of total confusion, the translating with clarity into an ensemble for upwards of six singers was a heavy challenge. Rossini often rose to it, creating breath-taking musical climaxes and some of the funniest scenes in all opera.

Giuseppi Verdi (1813–1901) greatly admired Rossini but, planning his own career in the late 1830s, had no wish to emulate what in other hands could have turned complexity into a farrago. He also perceived that with Rossini retired, the comic genre was in decline and he should be looking for serious, tragic themes. He could not have predicted that after many years, he would develop to great effect his own style of musical humour.

He found the proffered libretti weak and hidebound, so very reluctantly he agreed to write as his second opera, *King for a Day.* The plot was comic but trifling, just enough to provide a setting for four lead singers to fit the roles of two couples overcoming love difficulties. Each had a solo aria, with a slow section leading to a fast-paced climax *(cabaletta)* and duets for two sets of lovers.

In conventional pattern, the action opens with two comic basses (each a *basso buffo*), celebrating with chorus an intended marriage. In a later scene, they quarrel when one reneges on this. It is speculative that Verdi realized he had two vivacious tunes at hand with broad appeal somewhat in the Rossini manner. These could climax two amusing episodes in the plot, otherwise he might have rejected the whole project. The overture is a model of youthful hilarity.

The first *scena* for soprano conforms to what audiences expected: leisurely *bel canto*, coloratura technique, trills, *arpeggi*, an exciting bridge passage within an exhilaringly fast *cabaletta*. It is followed by a spiky chorus (with 'dotted notes'), a rhythm anticipating more familiar Verdi which would contribute decades later to a barrel-organ mania. In common with some more famous operas, there is a vigorous quintet in which some talk of love, others of business, and Verdi crowns it with a soaring soprano melody.

Recitative was a traditional device, conversation to a 'dry' harpsichord background, which many listeners today would find tiresome. Verdi was to use it here for the only time; he would gradually merge recitative and aria into his own style of *arioso*. The work had climaxes in the style of Rossini, and lyrical moments worthy of Bellini and Donizetti almost at their best. Yet because these composers were so established, their fans were not necessarily keen to recognise the emergence of a young rival. In our musically sad times, *King for a Day* sounds very spirited. Leaving aside the feeble scenario, the music can still offer a most pleasurable evening's entertainment, though it was not at all to Verdi's satisfaction. Despite subject matter for which he had no empathy, this was objectively a most promising start in comic opera. Verdi had worked through this despite a depression which had struck him on the natural deaths of his young wife and two daughters.

Unfavourable public reaction turned Verdi not only away from comic opera, but briefly from composing. He was later presented with numerous tragic stories which moved him. With 13 more operas over the following decade, he achieved a strong dramatic sensibility climaxing in quick succession around 1850 with three operas, *Trovatore, Rigoletto* and *Traviata*. These are the masterpieces with which he reached a peak of his so-called middle period, before he was 40 years old. Genial humour did not feature in these works.

It was prominent in his first great Italian success after that, in

1859, *Un Ballo in maschera* (A Masked Ball), an affective if
inaccurate account of the political assassination of King Gustav
III of Sweden in 1792. The plot by France's prolific librettist
Eugene Scribe was one of his best, having already been used for
three operas. Verdi's exceptional skill in stagecraft had him
advising his Italian librettist, Somma, how it could be adapted
for Italian tastes. There was to be a new emphasis, moving away
from crude melodrama towards those operas, very few, interesting enough on stage to be performed even without music.
Verdi had reached the point where he could dramatise perfectly in music the human comedy. The hero is innocent,
remaining optimistic in the face of danger until struck down
through jealousy.

The royalist government at Naples would not tolerate a play
staging the killing of a monarch, and despite Verdi's resistance,
it was eventually agreed, the victim should neither be royalty
nor located in Europe: instead, one Riccardo, British governor
of Boston a century earlier. Despite enforced changes and
recent attempts to reinstate the Swedish King, Somma's Italian
version was excellent whilst the compromise New England
setting is still favoured.

Nearly half the action has the spirit of comic opera. Riccardo's sense of humour sometimes makes light of his official
duties and he often shares jokes with a minor figure whom he
likes to have around. This is a carefree young page, Oskar, as in
The Huguenots, a soprano role adding much to the gaiety. He/
she provides a light, decorative note in a powerful quintet of
otherwise opposing forces and in coloratura arias anticipates
the pleasures of a court ball. At the end of Act I, the two of
them join an ensemble so skittish that some critics accused
Verdi of straying into Offenbach territory. Yet at the masked
ball, Oskar unwittingly betrays Riccardo's disguise to a supposedly loyal subject. This leads directly to the assassination.

In Act II, Verdi handles dramatic irony in ways anticipated in
Rigoletto, but more extended and comical. Riccardo is curious
about an allegedly wicked witch, so he turns up in disguise to
'investigate' her and in a laughing song ridicules the superstitions affecting the large crowd being manipulated. This
drives the witch to a fury and there is a sparkling ensemble of
conflicting emotions. She performs in a spooky location,
invoking the Devil, exorcising a girl and predicting wealth for a

passing sailor. Riccardo whimsically gives him enough money to fulfil her claim, but he is not so amused when she says he will be killed by the next man who greets him; which turns out to be a close friend.

The gradual move from emphasis on solo arias to ensembles typifies changes in Verdi's work, from the egotism of obsessed individuals such as in the earlier *Ernani* and *Trovatore*, to the tragedy of those who are rational and socially responsible.

This would hardly apply to the action of *The Force of Destiny* (1862), based on a revenge drama by the Spaniard Duke of Rivas. It is described as an Italian four-Act opera, but in terms of scene changes, it has far more. These are necessary for a kaleidoscope of a plot ranging through diverse parts of Europe. It starts with a young woman witnessing the accidental killing of her father by her lover. Such a melodramatic staging some opera-goers found improbable if not farcical. Remorseful, he seeks repose in Holy Orders, and the girl becomes a hermit. This doom-laden scenario is completed when fate brings him into contact with her brother who intends to kill him.

In the ceremonial church scenes Verdi excels himself musically. That should also have appealed to the citizens of Holy Russia, for which the opera was first prepared. Yet Verdi had by then a fine sense of dramatic balance, and he visualised what became virtually a second sub-plot. Of his production team, he was the master laying out the broad conception. For the first time, he relished portraying a surging mass of common folk with at least two large scenes to themselves, much more imposing than conventional light relief. These were drawn from the better-known play, *Wallenstein's Camp* by Schiller. There are dramatic scenes in and near the battles supported by the tumult and variety of their music.

So characters not relevant to the main action are introduced, most attractively Preziosilla, a gipsy living on her charms and wits, one of the many present hoping to become war profiteers. She takes centre stage three times: first in a tavern as an informal recruiting officer promoting a struggle against the 'German oppressors'. Later she tries to lift the soldiers' spirits, then following them to the battle area, where she leads the singing to the ultimate drum roll, a *rataplan*. This is a device illuminating (in Meyerbeer) or ridiculing (in operetta) the martial spirit, and Verdi was very comfortable briefly composing in either of these modes. A vivacious fortune-teller, Preziosilla is a mezzo-soprano, almost ranging from the commanding music of the *Masked Ball's* clairvoyant to the high notes of its page Oskar. She gives colour to the opera, preceding *Carmen* by 13 years.

Verdi includes an uncouth, quarrelsome friar, Melitone, who makes himself the butt of soldiers and citizens alike. His is the *buffo* role, given a mock-serious song when he deplores public morals and behaviour; whether he is knave or fool depends partly upon interpretation.

The opera's breadth, vigour and spectacle by chance were on a scale comparable with those which the new school of Russian composers would within a few years be presenting. Yet perhaps it was fortunate *The Force of Destiny* had been written for St Petersburg. A Parisian or Italian audience may have reacted less politely, to judge from the rapid alterations made before it was shown elsewhere. Today, it is recognised as masterly but flawed.

It was 28 more years before Verdi surprised the world with his final opera, realizing the privilege of old men to look back on life with some detachment. This was his second straight comedy, *Falstaff*, where he put aside themes of war, heroism, rebellion and passion in order to portray human action in the domestic field. It is a conflict of people of property, and those hoping to steal it: the diplomacy of the boudoire, the urge for revenge, and the naïve idealism of the young.

Verdi was confident of the special skills of his final librettist, Arrigo Boito, who prepared an admirable Italian version from one of Shakespeare's most untidy plays. Titled *Falstaff*, it gave an inspired sketch of Sir John Falstaff, the Shakespeare favourite as seen in three plays, but mainly in *The Merry Wives of Windsor*. Once debonaire but now debauched, Falstaff needs money, so venturing into cheating and other desperate remedies.

Hoping to trade on his noble title, he conspires with his gang of petty thieves to defraud two married couples. He sends identical love letters to each of the 'merry wives', so that from the moment they compare notes, the plot becomes a joke in reverse. On the way to public humiliation, Falstaff is hidden in a laundry basket, then thrown into the Thames.

The Merry Wives of Windsor was written casually by Shakespeare under protest at the request of Queen Elizabeth. Verdi excelled him by far, serving up his most sophisticated score with incomparable musical wit. Aged 80, he was capable of stating in a phrase what most composers put into a whole aria. His melodies might flow through at a pace and there were no repeats. Verdi was smiling at himself, at opera, and his years of dedication, in an affectionate farewell to the world.

He initiates his own form of realism, using the orchestra to express ideas and gestures, such as in Falstaff's speech on honour, taken from another play, *Henry IV*. Instrumental trills describe the effects of wine passing through his body and the pleasure of fresh intoxication.

He reflects on the style and idiosyncrasies of Italian opera he had worked within over the full half century, with moments of self-parody and in-jokes. There is a section which recalls ghostly and comical moments in *The Masked Ball*. The most subtle burlesque occurs when tactical differences between the men and women pursuing Falstaff come to the fore. Verdi reduces the spectacular choruses of grand opera to comic dialogue led on by conflicting rhythms: the mocking, measured tread of the women and the accelerating fury of the men. It is here that he really competes with Offenbach.

King for a Day in modern perspective is full of good tunes, light and as enjoyable as first class operetta of later date. *Falstaff* might almost have been by a different composer. In it, Verdi completes the break with the traditional Italian solo aria, its repeats and compulsory change to fast tempo. In the sub-plot, there are no extended love songs, just brief, affectionate phrases exchanged; and Falstaff's gratifying aria of nostalgia for his boyhood at court lasts only half a minute. This precision of expression marks the furthest point of his development and without any melodic decline in a unique stage work which more than does justice to a routine Shakespeare play.

10 Dies Irae, *Secular and Romantic*

The Grim Reaper was the medieval personification of death, in black cloak and carrying a large scythe. He appears now mainly in comic sketches, but features respectfully in a symbolic chess-playing role in Ingmar Bergman's *Seventh Seal*, a film epic of Europe's 14th century plague. A revered musical equivalent was for the first time used facetiously in the year 1830. The melody dated back to the 13th century, the *Dies Irae*, giving terrifying warning of the day of wrath, when God will descent to judge all humanity. Whilst Western Christianity was united, all believers feared it, and until recently, when the melody was withdrawn from the Church liturgy, most Catholics were familiar with it.

With the solemn, unchanging plainsong chant, it starts with the notes CBCABGAA, one of the most inspired and imposing in all music. The words have been present in the Requiem masses of numerous composers, and Hector Berlioz had used them in his. Familiarity may bring contempt, so he seized an agnostic's chance to make a sophisticated joke. He composed a freakish version of the plainsong to be used in a Hellish context, the hallucinatory scene which forms the finale to his *Symphonie Fantastique*.

Here, an impish revelry of witches is interrupted to church bells by the *Dies Irae* at first solemn, then often changing shape and pace, briefly into a fast satanic dance alongside the work's main theme also transformed. This is the protagonist's ultimate degradation, Walpurgis Night being the occasion, never so incongruously celebrated. So far from regarding it a blasphemous, Franz Liszt was impressed by his older friend's burlesque and by the age of 22 had given the whole work one of his many piano transcriptions.

Liszt had an artistic curiosity about the underworld and its imagery, and remained fascinated by the great dirge. He would later convert it into a virtuoso piece for piano and orchestra, spending time over years to perfecting it as a set of variations. Liszt was inspired by having seen the Italian fresco *The Triumph of Death,* with the Grim Reaper performing his task digging up corpses for dispatching in one of two directions. It is called a dance of death, *Totentanz,* the theme on full orchestra in the bass, alongside crashing chords on the piano, spellbinding. The variations affect differing moods; Judgment Day does not preclude redemption. There are fiercely sustained passages, *ostinati,* glaring contrasts, marked syncopation, cross rhythms and using hemiola, what half a century later would be called 'jazzing it up'. There is speculation whether a second plainsong also treated to variation is not just a serene version of the *Dies Irae.*

Camille Saint-Saens used the chant's first five notes as part of the climactic theme in his Third Symphony, the first successful work of its kind to introduce a triumphant melody at full power on an organ. As a composer, Saint-Saens was exceptionally versatile, and had a special gift for musical humour, which was then a cult in Paris. He gives the *Dies Irae* a brief, facetious appearance in his orchestral fantasy, *Danse macabre,* where his skeletons dance frantically until silenced by the crowing of the cock. An orchestra catches the scene and atmosphere of this intriguing ritual, but for listeners who prefer a narrative, there is a very funny sung version which spares a tear for the ghouls' final moments.

Very many Romantic composers were tempted to use the theme, in part or whole, conscious of its downward-sliding symbolizing doom. The male duet in Bizet's *Pearl Fishers* uses that opening five-note pattern, but with a changed rhythm, and fate themes, such as that heard at the start and end of *Carmen,* sound like reminders.

Brazilian Impressions was a work influenced by Debussy's use of orchestral colour. Before composing it, Italian Ottorino Respighi spent some time on a visit to a snake farm outside Sao Paulo. The work's slow movement suggests the writhing of these creatures, the rhythm eventually masked by an extended high note on the strings. The tension breaks with a leisurely version of the *Dies Irae,* which merges smoothly into a sensuous rhythmic pattern. An awesome stillness follows, then a single note on the church bell enlivens with the invitation for the congregation to attend the dance, a samba.

The melody was not part of the liturgy of the Russian Orthodox Church, probably known there simply as a great tune. This seems how two Russians approached it: Glazunov for a collection of medieval songs, and Tchaikovsky in an orchestral suite. Secular but solemn, it was used by two leading Soviet composers. Nicolai Miaskovsky's Sixth Symphony was his largest and most impassioned, with several distant allusions, including two of the French Revolution's most inspiring songs, *Ça ira* and *La Carmagnole.* The sacrifice of human lives is expressed in its later movements with the *Dies Irae.*

Shostakovich had a tendency to make diffuse musical allusions in his scores. Quotes from Wagner and Rossini in his final 15th Symphony suggest the greatness both of comic and grand opera, but the appearance of the *Dies Irae* at the start may be related to his concern with ill health by the year 1971. A bleak version of the theme opens a short section by him, death without resurrection, as part of an earlier symphonic suite from music for a renowned Russian film of *Hamlet.*

Sergei Rakhmaninov wove the plainsong into parts of his dynamic First Symphony. He developed a morbid fascination with death, and its appearance was predictable in his symphonic poem, *The Isle of the Dead,* where it is placed alongside a theme in his warmly Romantic style. In his late *Symphonic Dances* there is no nostalgia for Russia, and their vigorous pace suggests the New World. Here, the *Dies Irae* does not inhibit but joins in the celebrations of what was to be his final work of any significance.

The intriguing rhythm of Paganini's *Caprice* no.*XXIV* drew Rakhmaninov to compose a set of variations, a *Rhapsody* for piano and orchestra. Having found that one melodic inversion produces the *Dies Irae,* he uses it in many guises, sometimes in syncopated passages suggesting modern city life. That he intended the *Rhapsody* as a study of Paganini's inner self is a theory which does not trouble most admirers of this exceptionally popular work, both lyrical and extrovert.

In our times, diminishing numbers of music lovers know the *Dies Irae,* and the references are therefore becoming esoteric, but its subliminal force remains. Bernard Herrman wrote a fine score for the film, *Citizen Kane,* the theme gently stated during the enigmatic *Rosebud* episode. Its integration into *The Ballad of Sweeney Todd* by Stephen Sondheim is ingenious, another of his witty cultural allusions.

11 *Romantic Opera*

I n those decades of *bel canto* from the 1820–50s, the melodies were easy to take in, stirring, euphoric or occasionally
sad. The Italian style was near to Neapolitan folk singing,
though G.B. Shaw complained that in opera it was exaggerated
to the *lacrimosa*, tearful. The French style was lighter, more
balletic; the German reflected the folk idiom in *Singspiel*, songs
interspaced with dialogue. The three cultures had numerous
popular composers: such as respectively Bellini and Donizetti:
Auber and Hérold: Nicolai and Marschner. Their operas were
breaking away from the Classical 18th century pattern. Donizetti was prolific, with masterpieces such as *Lucia di Lammermoor*
and *Don Pasquale*. Hérold and Bellini had even greater potential, cut short by early deaths.

In one of Auber's best operas, *Manon Lescaut (1856)*, a
reckless love affair's youthful thrill was felt through the vivacity
of music which could however have fitted countless scenes.
Massenet's *Manon* was a model of a new, sophisticated style,
analysing two complex people with their foibles and anxieties,
tragi-comedy. From the opening scene when the heroine
Manon introduces herself, the music expresses her personality.

Massenet was born two generations after Auber, and his
music sounds it, though only 28 years separated these operas.
What had come between such contrasting compositions and
changed opera so radically relates firstly to two names: Wagner
and Verdi.

Wagner was moved by Bellini's inspired use of *bel canto*, and
thought the lightness and vitality of contemporaneous French
opera was also a model, with which the Germans should com-
bine their own inimitable musicality. He exemplified this with
his first major opera, *Rienzi*, greatly influenced by Meyerbeer's
Paris successes, and an auspicious landmark for 1842. Wagner
then shrugged off his Meyerbeer phase with the three following
operas concerning fatefully driven heroes and abandoned
women. There he found his mature style, what could be called
his middle period, as far as the solemn, extended melodies of

Lohengrin, the first model for his conception, German grand opera.

Wagner, as political revolutionary in 1848, influenced Wagner the composer, with a new aesthetic and a program which absorbed him over three decades. This was a fusion of opera and symphony, the comprehensive work of art, music drama: conception, plot, lyrics and music by one man, himself. His gigantic *Ring of the Nibelungen* was concerned with the triumph of mankind and morality over the gods, expressed in four music dramas. Characters, objects and concepts were to be given distinct motifs, *Leitmotive,* from the shortest of phrases to full melodies, reappearing whenever relevant and being developed within the drama. Many Wagnerites would learn to identify as many as one hundred of these. The result was a vast symphonic canvas; a scaled down or piano version would be unthinkable. Like Verdi, he would also eliminate the distinction of recitative and aria.

Between the *Ring* creations, Wagner composed a noble comedy on the largest scale, *The Mastersingers of Nuremburg,* a tribute to his national culture and traditional German music-making. The melodies seemed simple, clear-cut whereas those in the following work were strangely chromatic. *Tristan and Isolde* was a tragic legend of forbidden and as a result doomed love. That was symbolized by the wood-wind chord first heard in the fourth bar of the prelude preceded slowly by cellos, and moving upwards to an orchestral climax, but there is no resolution. The harmonies were not resolved until the work's final scene, the Love Death (*Liebestod*)[19]. This was a new concept, unending melody. Experiencing this disturbed many, pleased others, but it was inevitable in music's history. Wagner's discovery of the *Tristan* chord opened up new possibilities for the extension of chromaticism and harmony. The impact upon the musical world of this work and the *Ring* cycle was one of the most significant developments in the 19th century. Music drama became an alternative to traditional opera, though few composers could undertake it, with its need for vast resources, even if they had the imagination.

Verdi was his contemporary with a comparable potential to change the face of opera, unwilling to live with all the conventions as he gained status. By chance, the popularity of his earlier operas pushed his music into becoming a symbol of the call for Italian reunification (*Risorgimento*). These were the years of his melodramas, climaxing with *Trovatore*, but he was set on moving to more realistic plays with deep human interest. *La Traviata* (1853) doubly shocked many as a (for us) sympathetic tale of a 'fallen woman' which Verdi dared to set in modern dress.

He was by then master of his own projects. With exceptional feel for drama, he could direct his librettists towards several masterworks with *Don Carlos* (1867), and *Aida* (1870). The audiences were more than just spectators, but increasingly involved emotionally in response to greater characterization. That left Verdi still with time to compose great interpretations for Shakespeare's *Otello* and *Falstaff.*

Bizet's early death was a severe loss for the opera world. *Carmen* (1875) had an exceptionally fine libretto about the fate of two lovers, one drawing the other into crime. Two such 'heroes' were unprecedented, the plot considered scandalous, breaking the mould of conventional good taste. The opera won through for the portrayal of a *femme fatale*, its realism and vibrant melodies. Even though *Carmen* may have remained unique had he lived, Bizet' genius and dramatic flair would surely have continued to flourish.

Bizet was quoted as predicting that Massenet would 'beat them all'. He had first succeeded in the fashion for mock-Oriental themes with *The King of Lahore*, which had come after Bizet's *Pearl Fishers* and Delibes' *Lakmé*. Following in the Gounod tradition, Massenet went on to become most prolific in lyric opera, where he resolved the problem of merging dialogue and song in his unique style.

His selection of subject matter seemed infallible, a fine sensibility. His versatile skills earnt him the criticism if not the envy of others. Was he just a crowd pleaser? His *Werther* and *Esclarmonde* were considered Wagnerian: *Herodiade*, a version of the Salome legend, and *Thais*, in the words of Debussy, were 'discreetly erotic': *The Jongleur of Notre Dame* an evocation of the Medieval spirit: *The Navarraise* a noisy imitation of Italian realism. He was composing until his death in 1912, but one century later, the vogue of his earlier works continues after a brief lapse.

By the turn of the century, European literature was being subjected to new cults, the main post-Verdi development being

verismo, Italian realism, heralded by two melodramas. Leonca-
vallo's *Pagliacci* climaxed with the most graphic on-stage murder based on a case in which the judge had been the
composer's father; Mascagni's *Cavalleria rusticana* was a tragedy
of Sicilian jealousy. Both were so popular that these titles are
never translated and they are short enough whilst still in such
demand as to be performed on one evening normally together
as *Pag &Cav.*

Though neither composer could repeat this extraordinary
success, Puccini followed rapidly with several most successful
verismo operas, mainly concerning ordinary citizens with whom
modern audiences could readily identify. The most typical was
La Bohème (1896), a story of poverty among Paris' artists and
demi-monde.

All three operas had rare appeal, inspired songs and mod-
ern-sounding harmonies. Puccini's languid melodies were
erotic, as one critic said, like a love call; when he wrote a version
of *Manon Lescaut,* he joked about an Italian showing the French
(Auber and Massenet) the meaning of passion. Like Richard
Strauss, he created musical portraits of several alluring females,
and his chosen plots were stark and direct. Exceptions were the
broad humour of *Gianni Schicchi,* and the operetta-like delicacy
of *La Rondine.* With his death in 1924 the masterly *Turandot* was
not quite completed.

Opera as an expression of passion peaked in the first decades
of the 20th century with him, and certain of the works of
Richard Strauss, who, some said, moved music drama as far as
neurosis. The emotional range of Romantic opera and the
exceptional number of successes give it the greatest prominence in the history of the genre, but there was eventually a
reaction.

It was among the following generation of composers that
some began to move against what they considered 'overheated'
music. Three in particular created large-scale operatic signposts
intended to obscure the entire Romantic landscape: Debussy
made the start with *Pelleas and Melisande,* whilst Stravinsky's
Rake's Progress and Weill's *Mahagonny,* both intent on distancing
the audience from the emotions of the action, reversed the
previous century's overall trend.

Mainstream opera engaged many composers in the 20th
century, but no others with the impact of Strauss and Puccini.

Prokofief's *Love for three Oranges* was a masterly burlesque, a perfect operatic send-up; and his *War and Peace* perhaps the last successful grand epic. In 1952, Neville Cardus wrote what now reads like an obituary for the genre: *In contemporary opera the characters are supposed to possess psychological reality and speak in the language of everyday argument . . . close attention to words and visual movement. Music is often hardly needed.*

He speculates that beautiful voices may cease to be the priority for certain works. Opera may revert to its 17th century purpose, a background to dramatic action, such as by underlining rises and fall in speech.

∎ ∎ ∎

Britain was ill-equipped throughout the 19th century for the widening interest in opera on the Continent. Performing seasons were short, few and erratically financed; nor was the demand excessive. London produced fine home-grown operas, admittedly by Irishmen Richard Balfe and Vincent Wallace (*Maritana, 1845*). Paris had two state-subsidised opera houses, London none. Yet Drury Lane theatre had an orchestra of 70 by the 1840s, and the most famous quartet of Italian singers came to London specially for Balfe's opera, *Falstaff,* in their language. British audiences preferred it that way; it was perhaps more enjoyable simply to hear what could not be understood, considering the poverty of English libretti. That was a by-product of the appallingly low standards in the kind of play served up in the early to mid-Victorian age.

This inadequacy could be target for ridicule on stage: came the situation, came the men. It was the achievement of Gilbert and Sullivan to parody, especially the Italian musical style and English (Victorian) melodrama. Yet because G&S are now an 'institution' and were a source of very familiar melodies for decades, their original functions such as satire and burlesque have become obscured. The wider audiences hear the *Mikado, Patience* and *Iolanthe* today simply as classics in their own right and without reference to their original targets.

London developed forms of English burlesque strong on improvisation, especially at the Gaiety theatre, with zany music to parodies of popular operas, plays and legends. Melodies banned by copyright, such as from *Faust* and *Carmen,* were substituted. The French offered more substantial if light musical theatre, and the vast Alhambra theatre in Leicester Square produced nine Offenbach operettas during the 1870s. Classical operetta, with its sensual flair, spectacle and risqué plays remained in great demand. After 1900, it would take second place to a new fashion, Romantic operetta, which started in Vienna and rapidly took European and U.S. cities by storm. Its melodic appeal was infectious, and the rhythms adapted well to the ballrooms, though for practical reasons, the 1914–18 war sadly reduced its currency[20]. The English musical became a pale reflection of the Continental versions; there were countless new productions but hardly any have survived into our times.

That would have been the case even if the American musical had not made such a big impact in the mid-20th century, taking over London's most suitable theatres, such as Drury Lane, for years at a time. Whilst continuing the Romantic tradition, its popular appeal was reinforced by two advantages it had over traditional opera. It used 'modern', everyday stories; more importantly, its melodies had one syllable to one note, making lyrics easier to hear. A fine melodist, Richard Rodgers, created such long-running shows as *Oklahoma* and *The Sound of Music.*

The early gramophone around 1900 had given a selection of operatic arias unprecedented popularity, but divorced from their own works. Names which became very familiar included Caruso and Melba: *On with the Motley,* Flotow's *Marta,* Balfe's *I dreamt I dwelt in Marble Halls* and a few Verdi arias. The cinema simply ignored opera, and Hollywood gave operetta a bad name by misusing or truncating some of the second-rate ones. *The Bohemian Girl* and Auber's *Fra Diavolo,* or parts of them, shared films with Laurel and Hardy. 1930s Hollywood thrillers used themes from Wagner and Liszt, before incidental music became a speciality for U.S. composers, such as Alfred Newman and Max Steiner, both in rich melodic vein.

Opera's fresh popularity in Britain gradually surfaced during the later decades of the 20th century, thanks partly to the establishment of large, nationally subsidized companies, at least five full-time. Mozart and Britten apart, Romantic opera has had by far the greatest drawing-power.

12 *Johann Strauss II: Challenge and Competition*

Built in 1801 and still open, the Theater an der Wien was intended as a large, popular venue for drama and as far as light musicals. Its founder had been Emmanuel Schikaneder, now remembered outside Austria more for having written the text of *The Magic Flute*. Inclining towards fantasy and farce, even he could not have guessed the scope and international fame that the theatre would gain by 1870, many decades after his death. By then, its director and the wife of the most popular musician in the world were planning to persuade the great man to compose for it.

Johann Strauss II was most reluctant to go outside his proven creative gifts, his reputation was established, and he was committed for life to the world of dance entertainment which the family name had come to symbolise. He did not want to risk failure in what would be a sideline. Fortunately, his first wife had been a distinguished singer and brought musical insight to their marriage. Raiding his cupboard, she let a few musicians from the theatre turn some of his compositions into song; when played back to him, he was agreeably surprised. With a nod in Shakespeare's direction, he prepared a musical, *The Merry Wives of Vienna;* but it was never performed. Nothing less than a great star would suffice to launch the work, and the leading soprano of the day preferred to sing Offenbach at the rival Carltheater.

The two theatres had been carrying the traditional German musical, the *Singspiel*, comedy with songs regularly interspersed. The theatres' competition had improved quality of production, as well as introducing a much more sophisticated form of musical, classical operetta, brought over by Offenbach from Paris. *Nach Pariser Art,* Parisian fashion was taking over among the moneyed classes.

Franz von Suppé was of Strauss' age, could equal him in writing marches, and had been composing the best musicals in

Viennese style on show over two decades. Born in Dalmatia and brought up to assimilate Italian as well as South Slav music, he spoke German with a foreign accent yet as a composer of 'Viennese' songs, he was a local favourite. In our times, except for his lively overtures which Elgar so admired, he is under-performed, but his *Requiem* might in parts be mistaken for Verdi's.

Suppé was an exceptional musical parodist, like Arthur Sullivan, an added attraction for operetta. He showed this in *Ten Maidens without a Man* where the ten multi-national girls each perform in their diverse national styles. By the time the work reached the Vienna State Opera, it had been enlarged for 25 singers. Vilem Tausky, a conductor of BBC fame, arranged it as *Ten Belles without a Ring* for London Guildhall in the 1980s.

Suppé first wrote a 3-Act work in 1847 for the Theater an der Wien and the more impressive *Girls Boarding-school* was of operatic strength but not length. He wrote a 'military' operetta for male voices only, *Light Cavalry,* still heard in its galloping overture, and a send-up of Wagner's *Tannhäuser.* Yet he persisted with small-scale entertainments, even when he wrote an excellent piece in the Offenbach manner, *Beautiful Galathea,* on the Pygmalion theme.

Offenbach is said to have called Vienna his 'bank'; his native language being German, he regarded Vienna as a permanent theatre option, especially as others would finance the productions there, whereas in Paris he often spent until he became insolvent. His operettas, specially written or translated, were the sensation of Vienna in the 1860s, setting the new genre and style. Suppé could have entered into competition but was making good money conducting, and was inclined to creative laziness.

With Offenbach in France suffering the turmoil of war, 1870–71, fate may have determined Strauss' entering the field of operetta briefly unopposed at the top level. On the Ali Baba story, *Indigo and the 40 Thieves* was as spectacular and successful as the overpriced tickets demanded. Nearly three hours of music, singers of operatic strength, and ballet, it includes the slow waltz, *Night Slumber,* and other songs in his best vein. Despite a commonplace libretto, it was then highly praised by the influential Hanslick. Its warmth and vitality deserved the 1906 revision, *1001 Nights.*

Drawing on current French plays was then common and Victorien Sardou, who wrote the play *Tosca,* was the originator of the next success. It became *The Carnival in Rome*, and Strauss added Italian touches.

Meilhac and Halévy are permanently associated with texts for Offenbach, and one of their plots centring on a spectacular party was adapted for *Die Fledermaus*, or the Revenge of the Bat. He is an idle young man about town known for his nocturnal habits and plays an elaborate joke at the expense of the spendthrift Eisenstein, whose glamorous wife he uses as a decoy. Not that the Bat could foot the bill, but a rich, decadent young Prinz Orlovsky was always prepared to pay high in hopes of relieving his boredom, in this case for a fancy dress ball. In Act I, Eisenstein is absent when the Law calls to arrest him as a debtor. His wife's operatic lover, serenading her with a few Verdi arias, is caught wearing Eisenstein's dressing-gown; *noblesse oblige*, he does not resist a stay in jail. This leaves husband and wife free to attend the masked ball, she disguised as a mysterious Hungarian aristocrat, whilst the housemaid Adele also accepts the Bat's secret invitation. Eisenstein attempts to seduce each of these masked ladies in turn with the tried techniques of a philanderer. It is a perfectly crafted farce where all the main party guests are pretending to be who they are not.

Strauss had seen it as a straight play in Paris, realising its stage potential and for once giving it his maximum concentration. Prinz Orlovsky would be played by a light soprano, the wife would be a dramatic one and the maid a soubrette; they and the three leading male roles, a drunken jailor and some others would need acting skills. Strauss wrote more music for it than was needed or used now for one performance, such as five items in 'foreign' style. The masked ball Act II is an all-round masterpiece. In it, among the best known songs are the *Champagne* ensemble, *the czardas*, Orlovsky's permissive *Chacun à son goût*, and *My dear Marquis* in which Adele's fiercely denies she is a chambermaid. Perhaps because the plot ridiculed the rich at a time of stock exchange collapses, two generations had to pass before the locals recognised the great qualities of *Die Fledermaus*, and it has since become one of the three most performed of all operettas between Vienna and Sydney.

Though often distracted from the theatre, Strauss did not abandon ambitions once started. He was fortunate to be offered the *Fledermaus* text because he was a negligent judge of these and could even be fobbed off with inferior ones. He had a weakness for 'foreign' themes, such as an Italian con man in *Cagliostro in Vienna* which succeeded because of the emergence of two outstanding performers, soprano Marie Geistinger and Alexander Girardi. The first setback came with the play, *Prince Methusalem,* which was in a facetious French spirit that Offenbach might have brought off. It disappointed because although Strauss' music had wit, he was not a 'comical' composer.

Over-confidence meant he was not giving sufficient thought to a play's complexities, and tended to compose the music first. His worst failure was *Blind Man's Bluff,* and the libretto was so bad that he confessed he had not read it (other of course than the lyrics) whilst composing. The lesson learnt, he went on to two more successes, either of which would seem to deserve a revival now.

Girardi started with youthful parts, but as the versatile lead singer, he became the popular choice for character or comic roles, so that his personality had to be considered in creating every new work. For the next one, he insisted upon added couplets, and as the *Nature* song, it became a big success. *The Merry War* had an amusingly eccentric plot for those times: one of the armies is all-women, but hostilities are avoided. It had a witty libretto, romance, several excellent sung marches, and the alluring waltz, *Bel Ami.*

The Austrian (German) and Hungarian (*Magyar*) cultural links during the 19th century, and the influence of gipsy musicians inspired Strauss' *Gipsy Baron,* which in parts has a seriousness to match the sentiments of its original, *Saffi,* a famous novel. This had been written to support the land claims of the poorer people of the Hungarian part of the Habsburg Empire. Strauss could brilliantly assimilate the gipsy musical style and as elsewhere, the Hungarian national dance, the *czardas.* One aria which asserts gipsy rites, such as couples living together without wedding ceremony, was destined for worldwide fame. It even entered the portals of Hollywood some six decades later to be equipped with more 'respectable' new lyrics, *One Day when we were young.* The heroine, Saffi, was a strong role and Girardi played a greedy landowner.The play was slanted to present a warm relationship, reconciling the dignity of its *Magyar* and gipsy characters with the family aspect of the Empire.[21] Many regard it as Strauss' finest achievement in the theatre.

Suppé had the first option on *The Queen's Lace Handkerchief,* but was preoccupied. So Strauss composed what became exceptionally popular in the U.S.A., a fictitious story of Columbus and the Portuguese Queen. Its finest melodies are recalled in the composite waltz, *Roses from the South,* with its gastronomic *Truffle* song.

Suppé had finally stirred himself to write a large-scale adventure, *Fatinitsa,* which was perfectly timed for the oncoming Russo-Turkish war up to 1878. A Russian officer enjoys dressing in drag to entertain colleagues; so he is given the chance to spy as a woman on the Turks. The text was by Vienna's best writing team, Zell and Genée, giving opportunities for marches with outlandish instrumentation, a Turkish shadow play, parody and much comic confusion in the enemy camp. It had the first-ever rapid cross-Continental 'hit', a tearaway title march which Vienna adopted as its own. New York quickly had five productions, but the following work was to be the most popular operetta of all during the 19th century.

This was a Florentine story of adulteries, partly based on the 14th century writer Boccaccio's experiences; after publicising them, the author often had to flee the city. One rumbustious tale from the *Decameron* had a cooper banging nails into a barrel whilst his wife makes love nearby. Suppé's *Boccaccio* of 1879 would outlast in popularity *Donna Juanita* which followed, attractive for an Hispanic setting. Its Peninsular war plot resembled that of *Fatinitsa;* but his later works, such as *Africa Journey,* had only briefer successes.

Two Suppé masterworks were more than enough competition for Strauss on the Viennese stage. As a widower he made a regrettable new marriage, and when the young wife eloped with Steiner's son, he transferred the premiere of *A Night in Venice* to Berlin where he conducted. Certain Berliners, not being partisan, ridiculed a specially inept libretto during the performance. A quick revision was necessary for Vienna, and it is more performed now than *The Merry War,* which for decades was more popular than *Fledermaus.* These three were all with scripts by Zell and Genée, so their respective fortunes were incalculable.

This pair also provided a superlative libretto in the *Beggar Student,* for which Karl Millöcker's music became the 'hit' of 1882. There were other rivals deserving long-term success, but this left Strauss with a further ambition to fulfil what others would not, a straight opera. Following Wagner's example, he wanted it to be related to German folk culture. One familiar legend concerned a character living during the Thirty Years War, *Simplizius.* In a story of virtue and innocence rewarded, it resembled that of *Parsifal.* Yet whereas Wagner could treat such themes in full solemnity, Strauss' lightness of touch was inappropriate, and *Simplizius* failed.

Perhaps thinking of *Tristan,* Strauss was persuaded that jealousy between a knight and his king could be expanded into his most ambitious work. *Ritter Passman* was prepared for the Imperial Opera, music in the Hungarian style, heroic with swagger, grand opera. The ballet sequences were exceptionally fine and varied, and certain critics thought them the better part of the whole work, so damning it with faint praise. Though praising the orchestration greatly, Hanslick wrote that Strauss was weak in large ensembles, dramatic characterisation and expressing passionate feeling:

His nature reacted against the dull, conventional plot, sentimental situations.

Strauss' Viennese audiences had become committed over 20 years to his inimitable style of light musical and were unprepared for such a change. They were not too concerned with the plot or even the décor; above all, they just wanted the waltzes and Girardi, then at the height of popularity. Strauss had to face disappointment, but another Empire theme beckoned after his being impressed with Smetana's *Bartered Bride.* He planned to compliment the neighbouring South Slavs with *Jabuka,* a comparable folk opera. It started well but external factors helped to decide its fate one decade later, a sudden deterioration in Austro-Serbian political relations which climaxed in the 1914 war.

Approaching 70, Strauss may have been past his best in the theatre, and no outstanding project revived him. *Princess Ninetta* is now most remembered for the *Pizzicato Polka,* and *Waldmeister* for its overture. He had second thoughts about his final operetta because it tried to make light of a theme related to the French Revolution, *The Goddess of Reason.* Strauss tried to withdraw until threatened with court action, an ironic ending to a remarkable association with the theatre. In 1899, ill health made him decide to participate in selecting some of his most popular melodies for inclusion in a new operetta, *Viennese Blood*. Despite its tame play, it is in the permanent repertoire of the Viennese Volksoper.

His stage works rivalled Offenbach's for popularity in the German- speaking countries, but elsewhere much less so in the long run. Offenbach's fleet-footed operettas had more rhythmic variety, and better libretti. The Viennese style had great charm and spectacle, but was more sentimental. Operetta composing had encouraged Strauss to exercise a special skill, taking the waltz away from the ballroom and giving it inventive variations of pace. Song-writing became easy for him, and some of these arias, if occasionally now heard just within orchestral pieces, seem to lack the extra dimension. His first wife's initiative had been proved right.

Strauss had been prodigiously successful in what was probably the finest of all styles of light musical: the glamorous Viennese 'Golden Age' (c. 1840–1900). Though it preceded the arrival of recording and broadcasting, the sensuous appeal of his songs ensured their being familiar 'on the streets', in the inns and cafes.

13 *Souvenirs of Covent Garden*

Covent Garden theatre hosted Strauss operettas, but Johann's *Souvenirs of Covent Garden* was a medley in tribute to British popular song and specially the music hall whose heyday spanned slightly more than the maestro's adult lifetime. He gave the waltzes immense panache and charm, superbly orchestrated, raising the status of several modest songs to what sounds like a front-rank Strauss concert waltz.

With a brief introduction which suggests dancing round a maypole, he fires off melodies in rapid succession, ten for the price of one. All this in seven minutes, a generosity that would disturb any modern commercial music promoter.

Of the tens of thousands of songs heard at music halls over 70 years, most of us might be able to sing a mere handful, even without words; our younger generations may have heard of one or two. Perhaps scarcely more than two dozen written deserve to be remembered as classics, for that is the way of 'fashion'.

Of the finest, Johann did not hesitate to give pride of place to what above all others commemorates the spirit of music hall, the institution which declined rapidly when the laws banned alcohol:

Champagne Charlie is my name,
Champagne drinking is the game,
I'm the idol of the barmaids,
For Champagne Charlie is my name.

Champagne Charlie is a euphoric piece ideally suited for converting into a Viennese waltz with a compelling beat on the first note. None of the other nine tunes admirably selected come round for a second time. Words and music were credited to George Leybourne, stand-up comic and ballad singer who died of too much Champagne aged 44 in 1884. Half a century later, he was played by Tommy Trinder in an historic film called *Champagne Charlie* directed by Cavalcanti. Words and music were credited to George who had been one of the Lions Comique, special music hall favourites. They had started the habit of changing suits, very posh, not just hats, between acts and were all 'swells' supposedly passing their days drinking and pleasing 'the ladies'. His name is remembered with that of his rival, The Great Vance, who barely outlived him. *Up in a Balloon, Boys* was also by Leybourne and sounds like it, very bouncy and almost as popular with its praise of the era's most exciting venture before flying arrived. Yet even Strauss could not have converted that into a waltz.

Frenchman Jules Leotard of ballet fame appeared at London's Alhambra in 1861. He was celebrated in *That daring young Man on the Flying Trapeze*, words by Leybourne, popular even when many people still living were young. Most thought he also composed the music, but it was from Offenbach's *Papillon*.

It took second place in the *Souvenirs* and the remaining melodies are scarcely known today, with one notorious exception. The last item was the largest surprise; only Strauss could have breathed life into Henry Bishop's old Victorian war-horse, *Home, sweet Home.*

14 *Brahms' larger Choral Works.*

Except for opera which he did not attempt, Johannes Brahms composed great works in all the main forms of art music, and what was inferior is difficult to find because he did not leave it lying around. He was the leading musical architect after J.S. Bach and as such is now most famed for his symphonies and large-scale chamber and piano works. So his reputation as a melodist and songster appears to take second place, though he could excel in these areas. He combined a lyricism with classical restraint in composing, developing beautiful themes rather than looking for extra ones to sustain interest.

Before he was forty, his larger choral works brought him widespread fame, though he could be very rude to strangers who treated him as a celebrity. For nations guided by Christian beliefs in the second half of the 19th century, grand statements about life and death were fashionably made and listened to; the oratorios of Bach, Handel, Mendelssohn, Gounod and others were a major attraction and thoroughly elevating. Though they did not wipe away sin, congregations certainly emerged from church feeling better.

Brahms was one for grand statements, and not for small talk. This was reflected musically as he was the first Romantic to dispense largely with formal introductions, a point rarely made. In his *German Requiem*, he straightaway moves with full chorus to sympathy for those who are left to mourn; this was a main theme. He was not a practicing Christian but a pessimist who did not believe in an afterlife. He used choral music also to commemorate people and professionally to improve his techniques in large-scale composition. Those major works were complete before he even dared to publish his first symphony. One such abandoned item was inspired enough to be used for the funeral march of that *Requiem*, the movement *All Flesh is as the Grass*. This is one of his most noble statements and characteristic of the best in his music.

He worked on this masterpiece over several years up to 1868

when he was only 35, though his music had matured early. Its contents were unlike that of any comparable work and he had selected from Luther's texts which he knew so well, just as he pleased. Following his own logic, there is no prayer for the deceased. The emphasis was on the living afflicted by the certainty of death and the incidence of others' passing. The third movement with baritone solo relates to humanity's confusion, building up to an imposing fugue with female chorus most prominent. Many have noted a touch of Mendelssohn in the following 'interlude', *How lovely is thy Dwelling*; then there is an idyllically beautiful song in tribute to his deceased mother on very high soprano notes accompanied by serene wood-wind passages. The last stages draw on the *Book of Revelations,* the climax in the sixth movement with the end of the world (*Death, where is thy sting?*) having the grandeur of Bach's oratorios that Brahms so much admired. The finale returns to the spirit of the beginning, *Blessed are the Dead*, remembered for their works on earth.

Six of the seven movements were first heard at a very distinguished gathering (Bremen, April 1868], the German-speaking world attaching much importance to this confirmation of Brahms' greatness when he was barely 35 year old. Typically, one movement was not prepared to his satisfaction until 10 months later when the complete work was heard in Leipzig with that soprano solo. The *Requiem* finally enabled him to put poverty well behind him.

Of the other choral compositions, *Schicksalslied* (Song of Destiny) comes close to the *Requiem* in inspiration. It contrasts the idealised life of the Greek gods with the suffering of humans. Though the Greeks' experience under centuries of Turkish oppression is related, the tone of the music concentrates on the gods, and the work is uplifting. Its title might therefore be confused with another one, the *Triumphlied*, 8-part and on the largest scale which Brahms wrote to celebrate the Prussian victory over the French in 1871. As such, it is not performed in Britain despite its musical excellence.

Gesang der Parzen (Song of the Furies) relates to the pleasures and sports of the gods, like the *Schicksalslied*, but the treatment is very different. It is taken from a Goethe poem in which the appalling curse laid upon Agamemnon and his descendants is explained by a nurse to his daughter Iphigenia. The Furies were the creatures sent by the gods to inflict mental torture on the family, and the music reaches depths of anguish.

Nänie was a Schiller poem lamenting the death of beauty, and with it Brahms commemorated a friend, the painter Feuerbach. It opens with an arresting theme unusually on a solo oboe, and this fairly short work is most gratifying for singers with its smooth flow.

The *Alto Rhapsody* is a perfect medium for a solo contralto in rhetorical style. The subtle rhythmic effects and late entry of a muted chorus ends the tension with a melody disarming in its calm beauty. An unusual work for Brahms, it is more often heard in the concert halls than the other choral works. Its text was by Goethe who had travelled to the Harz Mountains to comfort one of the many people who were driven to depression or suicide by reading his novel on the suicide of a fictitious young lover named Werther. This curious scandal among educated people was the 18th century's equivalent of the worst aspects of today's youth scandals. The novel became the theme of a Massenet opera.

Brahms would have had scarce sympathy with Werther and his kind, being of a stoical nature. By those who did not know him, he was assumed to be a misogynist, though he greatly admired those women whose talents he perceived. He had often enjoyed conducting two women's choirs and written much for the lower female vocal range.

Rinaldo was for Brahms an unusual venture, a large narrative cantata; in it, a warrior finally puts his duty before his love of a woman. Though it might have symbolised the composer's creative life, it did not inspire his finest music. Its main interest is that it was the nearest he came to an operatic style of writing.

15   *Five Romantic Suites*

Incidental music was a response to the growing popularity of 19th century theatre. It was needed for classic or new texts to be played as background to the action or during the intervals. Movements lasted only a few minutes, providing atmosphere but not taking centre stage, unlike in opera. Composers could use some of their most appealing material such as dances not needed for symphonic treatment.

Orchestral suites had been common in the 18th century, but not for the theatre, and Beethoven was one of the first to take the idea seriously. A dance theme from his *Prometheus* was later transformed into a set of variations for the finale of his *Eroica Symphony*. His sense of fun which can be heard in his arrangements of songs of the British Isles took over when composing an eccentric march for the Turkish enemy in *The Ruins of Athens*.

Suites with instant appeal of a lighter kind continued to appear well into the 20th century, an opportunity for composers to show an unusual and diverting side of their art. For plays in English Vaughan Williams treated Aristophanes in boisterous 'country' style, Holst treated a magic tale as farce, Delius took 'the golden road to Samarkand' for a glowing score to the 1920s play, *Hassan*. Elgar was inspired by a whimsical play in which the roles of children and adults were reversed. He wrote a lengthy score with exceptional charm and humour *The Starlight Express*, a title more recently used for another musical.

The expense of orchestras in commercial theatres almost brought the practice to an end. So the best loved of this music is now mostly heard in the concert hall, suites conveniently arranged for orchestra in cohesive movements and occasionally in ballets.

■   ■   ■

From Felix Mendelssohn's cultured family he gained an early love of Shakespeare, leading to an inspired composition when aged only 17, an overture to *A Midsummer Night's Dream*. It is unlikely he could have been familiar with Weber's English opera *Oberon* because it was first performed in the same year, 1826, but it has some affinity. The overture relates to those parts of the story where the magic spell operates, solemn wood-wind chords, fairy music on high strings, the boisterous fun following, even the braying of a donkey. A descending four-note motif ends the magic spells, bringing harmony to the courtiers and Queen Titania who have been victims of Ober-on's elaborate joke.

The overture was admired for years before the Prussian King asked Mendelssohn to compose more music for the play, and this was sensitively integrated. The solemnity of the opening court scene has no musical accompaniment, which is mainly provided for interludes. Mendelssohn's scherzos were unique in their lightness of touch, and this one introduces the second Act and its frivolity. Excellent scene-painting, the sopranos' fairy song, *You spotted snakes,* is his most inspired duet. Sinister music accompanies the spell Oberon places on Titania, to become infatuated with the first creature she sees:

What thou see'st when thou dost wake, Do it for thy true love take.

She is awoken to an embracing nocturne for horn, the young lovers having been soothed to sleep through the night. Whilst recovering their senses, they witness a makeshift play put on by clownish workers. Its funeral march suggests a grotesque mockery, a plodding clarinet out of rhythm with a gloomy bassoon. Touched by magic, the chorus of fairies, *Though the house give glimmering Light,* ends the play.

The bridal march has become over-familiar because its greatness has induced the world to take it to its own. One of the most joyous moments in all music, it lies ahead even of the great wedding marches from operas by Wagner and Mozart, and the proud, restrained beauty of its second melody com-plements the sweep of the first. The music is still often per-formed ideally with the text and had the advantage of reaching the mass media in 1936, when Max Reinhardt directed the work in an authentic, much admired Hollywood film of the play.

■ ■ ■

Henrik Ibsen wrote about fallen men, anti-heroes, and one of his least redeeming characters was the subject of his only verse drama, *Peer Gynt*. He was keen for Norway's leading composer to write incidental music but Grieg was reluctant, though admiring its fine poetry. A protagonist who has negative relations with the whole of society would be more suited to our times than his. A prodigal son and model of self-delusion, Peer's morality at best leans on platitudes:

A man's duty is to be himself, without reserve, and to his own concerns. I've had to fight for it but I've always won the honours.

There is a synthetic gaiety in a wedding march touching the reality of Peer's marriage to Ingrid, his wilful nature expressed in a short, impatient motif such as when confronted by his new wife's regret at their grief-stricken marriage. He escapes to the mountains where he encounters his first troll women whose witch-like addiction to evil attracts him. Their princess entices him in a sinuous dance, grotesque to most humans, and taking him to their kingdom. In the Mountain King's hall, he is drawn into a pagan ritual until his lecherous behaviour forces him to flee from her brothers' rage.

He loves only his mother, but she has been an early victim of his neglect and a moving elegy accompanies her death. The freshness of *Morning Mood* might suggest the North, though it introduces the second part of the play in Morocco. By middle age, Peer's unfeeling existence has been the price of acquiring wealth and a set of false values. He has spurned love and womankind, a hypocrite selling slaves to Carolina, idols and missionaries to China. Yet he feels the degradation of having traded himself, his humanity, to become a troll. His serenade is as devoid of real joy, hardly changing pitch, ungenerous. After a Moroccan chorus with piccolo and drums, a Bedouin, Anitra, performs a graceful dance, flattering his pretence of being a new prophet the easier to steal his money.

Ageing, it is time for him to sail home, living through a storm, when he lives by sacrificing the only other survivor. As in Norwegian myth, he has a preparatory meeting with Death and is challenged to prove he is fit to live on. Yet he finds one who has always loved and awaits him. The most lyrical episode involves Solveig, fulfilling her destiny as his saviour to the consoling background of the Whitsun choir.

The orchestral suite lives in a Romantic glow in contrast to the spirit of this perverse morality play. For this, Grieg could

hardly have escaped criticism, though in the long run the
music wins out because it is characteristic of his finest style.

■   ■   ■

Rimsky-Korsakov was an expert on orchestration, gifted with a
form of synaesthesia, associating specific colours with musical
keys. Stories from the *1001 Arabian Nights* familiar to Russian
children were ideal for him. *Sheherezade,* a four-movement work,
was for the year 1888 an astounding venture into story-telling
giving a picture postcard impression of the East. In those days
pre-broadcasting, it conjured up an exoticism which had no
musical equal in the popular European imagination.

A concubine virtually condemned to execution, Sheherezade
has a sinuous, ingratiating violin solo which appears in subtle
guises as she tells her stories in the hopes of staying alive. The
tyrannical one-man audience is her Sultan sketched in a fierce,
impatient orchestral phrase which will eventually be transformed for the reconciliation between the two. Before then,
this theme is heard in variations, suggesting the heaving of
Sinbad's sea voyage and more humorous episodes, a swirling
ballet of changing rhythms. Romance, in the sloth and opulence of court life, is introduced with a languorous theme,
typically Russian. Often shipwrecked, Sinbad meets with hostile
civilisations and monstrous cannibals, calling for desperate
actions. The helter-skelter music has since been adapted for
backgrounds often to suggest convulsive terror, especially in
radio drama.

In more recent times, *Sheherezade* has to share its deserved
fame with another Russian *tour de force,* Mussorgsky's *Pictures at
an Exhibition* in Ravel's rich orchestration. The two works make
interesting contrast at the opposite ends of descriptive composition: *Sheherezade* interprets a fantasy whereas Mussorgsky
sketches lifelike musical portraits. Yet these were at first criticised as 'discordant' piano pieces concerned with the grotesque or commonplace. Decades later their potential had
been realised with this vivid transcription to instruments.

The first item takes off with a brassy shock, a nutcracker,
gnome-like, evil of eye, clumsy in gait: a wood-wind ballet of
chicks breaking from their nests, followed by playful snatches
of melody for children with their nurses in the Tuileries: a
nimble scherzo of Limoges women arguing in a market place.

There is tragi-comic contrast in the sketches of two Jews, one rich, fat and gruff, the other poor, thin and obsequious, corpulent orchestral tones against a solitary trumpet. An eerie saxophone spans the ages for a minstrel song against slowly rising strings, once upon a time in a castle setting. The stridency of the Promenade theme which accompanies the exhibition visitors is checked by the oppressive subterranean brass during a catacomb scene.

These movements are based mostly on naturalistic pictures by Mussorgsky's friend Hartmann duly exhibited in his honour posthumously. They were reputedly modest in subjects and quality, but Mussorgsky dignified them with an innovative music technique. He was dedicated to furthering Russian consciousness, and with brilliant strokes gave Hartmann longer fame than he expected.

Folk history was sacred to Mussorgsky who had a radical attitude to social reform. A trundling ox-cart is dignified with the deep sound of trombones, the driver heaving like a Volga boatman. Two of Hartmann's ingenuous fantasies are highlighted to give the work an imposing climax. *Baba-Yaga*, the witch who frightened naughty Russian children, searches for human bones, not on broomstick but in a hut. At a furious pace, she cavorts through the skies unchecked until seeming to collide, though only musically, with the *Great Gate of Kiev*. This construction has never existed beyond Hartmann's imagination, but significantly Mussorgsky chooses to idealise it with full ceremonial music.

■　■　■

In the era of silent movies, the young Dimitri Shostakovich at times worked as a pianist-accompanist. That disciplined him to subdue his musical personality to the needs of composing for films, and he developed a flair for light theatre music. This side of his personality has encouraged a growing international interest in his many cinema scores played as symphonic suites.

The Gadfly, a film about a fighter for Italian unification, required a colourful pastiche, the music suggesting the early 19th century. Beyond that, atmosphere is more important than period, and the Italian scenario is not apparent in the 12-movement suite. This music is often nearer to that of French café-concert and Russian dance.

The 19th century's fast ballroom dance, the *galop*, which once reached the music halls as the can-can, is here played at a pace which only youthful limbs could follow. Then there is a *contradance* suggesting the leisurely aristocratic society pre-1800, and the waltz sounding less ballroom than a dream straight out of the *Nutcracker*. Shostakovich had a facility for sensuous parodies and there are hints of Tchaikovsky throughout such as of the *Swan Lake* motif in the penultimate scene. The *romance* is the emotive highlight, a glowing melody starting with a violin solo. Its rapture is balanced with another theme, disturbing, leading to the hero's death. Elsewhere, dramatic events are accompanied with music which recalls moments of Shostakovich's symphonies.

16   *The French and Romanticism (music with orchestra)*

The classical sonata form, as developed also for symphonic and chamber music, is traditionally associated with Vienna, and the Germanic culture which strongly influenced musicians of neighbouring countries. This applied much less to the French, who were so committed to opera with its powerful social status. One man outside the French musical establishment was a prophet not accepted in his times. He would make a unique contribution, in effect combining the symphonic and operatic approach. Some of Hector Berlioz' structures were so original that he found new ways of describing them; his operatic *Damnation of Faust* he termed a dramatic cantata and his oratorio-like *Romeo and Juliet,* a dramatic symphony. He impoverished himself paying for what was needed to perform compositions, some conceived on a vast scale but which would have more influence upon other composers after his death in 1869.

Works for soloists, chorus and orchestra gained increasing attention in Paris by the 1870s. Among those very well known for oratorio were by Gounod, Franck, Saint-Saens, Massenet and Fauré.

By the 1880s, Paris with two permanent orchestras was better equipped than London, and Wagner's achievements had increased interest in symphonic composition. Cesar Franck was an admirer, an unobtrusive organist whose late attachment to composer Augusta Holmes may have inspired a late flowering and the most uplifting of French symphonies in which he is credited with applying Liszt's cyclical method of construction.[22] Other outstanding works included the *Symphonic Variations* and the symphonic poem, *Cupid & Psyche.* They were harmonically so original that they attracted many disciples.

Camille Saint-Saens embracing all the traditional forms was unusually versatile and seemed when young to be destined for the highest role. He worked to bring French music more into the European mainstream, but his efforts spread phenomenal talents too wide to satisfy many of his critics such as G. B. Shaw[23]. More interested in Bach than Wagner, his contribution to the repertoire was admirable, with ten concertos and the only French non-programme symphony, his third, to join Franck's in wide international acclaim. Living until 1921, he came to represent France's classic past.

France had a ballet tradition going back centuries associated with the court. In style, technique and even language, it had dominant influence in ballet schools abroad. Its earliest large-scale work to retain favour into our times was Adolphe Adam's *Giselle,* 1841, with a quaint scenario. Offenbach's *Papillon* was one of the century's greatest ballet scores but because it set out to ridicule *Giselle,* it is not performed in France except as a concert piece. In the following generation, Leon Delibes led the way in *Sylvia* and *Coppelia,* with its multi-national dance scenes; they influenced Tchaikovsky's future ballet scores. Edouard Lalo's *Namouna* was similarly successful, and some of his orchestral works displayed an attractive Spanish influence.

Franck's pupil, Vincent d'Indy, wanted Frenchmen to study their musical roots, setting up a major school of composition. He was one of many who thought the influence of foreign composers had been too great over at least half a century. His style reflected the countryside and more restrained styles of beauty, such as the austerity of medieval Church music. Ironically, he will certainly be remembered, if not for his theories but for a youthful work (1886), an invigorating symphony on a Cevegnol folk tune, with a very strident piano role which might have astonished Liszt if he had not just died.

Among those that admired Wagner but thought music was becoming 'over-heated' was Claude Debussy. He worked towards new combinations of sound. Associating with great Impressionist painters of the 1880s, his aim was to match their revolutionary approach to shade, colour and outline with a delicate application of fresh tones and harmonies. Though his famed *Clair de lune* is an exemplary Romantic piano piece, his later melodies are generally less clearly defined, elusive, emotion expressed in subtle timbres. His musical personality was suited to piano and chamber works, like water colours, such as in describing a flaxen-haired girl or a submerged cathedral. As if painting in oil, his orchestral Impressionism reached to clouds, the surge of the sea, a festive procession, and the spirit of Spanish dance. He displayed interest in exotic scales and styles, as far as Javanese, and his *Gollywog's Cakewalk* was an early jazz parody

Maurice Ravel's music has some parallel traits. Both sought new instrumental colouring; yet he used a more brilliant canvas and pronounced rhythms. Like Debussy, he avoided the strict symphonic forms and composed fine miniatures, notably for the piano. Born near the frontier in Basque territory, he was influenced by the colours and rhythms of Spanish music, and his *Spanish Rhapsody* typifies his unique mastery of orchestration. His style often has a distinct modal feeling[24] more remote in time or place, with some delicate imitations of Asian music. Most talked about were his fashionable works, *La Valse* and *Bolero*. This with its solitary theme he used to ridicule for its repetitive, 'non-musical' aspect, which partly explains its continued popularity.

The four years of the 1914–18 war were to give France the worst culture shock anyone could remember. Romanticism in all the arts had been a casualty. How would it be transformed or would it be superseded? That country's creative *monde* would hope to be in the vanguard of progress.

The Ballets Russes added to the appeal of Paris as the centre of European culture through the 1910s and 1920s, when many of the younger French composers were invited to contribute new works, notably Poulenc and Milhaud. Georges Auric following success in ballet revealed a talent for popular songs. Being a communist he was turning from what he called 'elitist music', finally reaching mass audiences by composing for films, many of which have become classics, such as the 1950 *Moulin Rouge*.

Several of the younger composers were criticising Debussy as 'lifeless' and Ravel as too refined. They wanted a link with popular cabaret and music of the streets, and Eric Satie's idiosyncratic, piano style charmed them. Behind the artistry, there is a sense of freedom and in his best known *Gymnopédies*, an unusual sense of relaxation. He influenced a youthful group called 'the Six', a loose association of 1920s composers including Poulenc, Milhaud and Auric.

One who faced both ways was Arthur Honegger, also inspired by earlier European and Church music, pre-Romantic. *Pacific*

231 was once thought very modern with clashing chords and fragmented themes in a symphonic poem describing the acceleration of a railway engine. His oratorio, *Joan of Arc at the Stake,* combined several of the performing arts, and became well known in the West, with famous actresses in the spoken role.

Francois Poulenc merged features of the two previous centuries' music into his style, graced with French wit and elegance. His Christian beliefs inspired the opera, *The Dialogue of the Carmelites;* his *Gloria* had pronounced rhythms which brought success as a new departure in ballet. He wrote four concertos, and was a distinguished performer of the two for piano. Poulenc was one of several who took the harpsichord out of the cupboard to which the 19th century had condemned it, exploiting its clarity and vitality in a solo concerto.

Swiss Frank Martin's scores were more radical, finding beautiful melody outside the familiar tonal system. His *Petite symphonie concertante* is a masterpiece in this style, and brilliantly exploits the differing sonorities of harpsichord, piano and harp, respectively exuberant, dramatic and languid. It is typical of his works, finding unique appeal in the merging of pre-Romantic and modern.

Darius Milhaud's style spanned a similar era, but to very different sound effects, rather dry. He had spent a few years in Brazil, which is apparent in some of his most popular works, such as *Scaramouche* and *Boeuf sur le toit* (Ox on the Roof). A visit to hear jazz at London's Palais de Danse in 1919 resulted in *La création du monde* (1923), a modern concerto grosso and perhaps nearer to symphonic jazz than anyone else achieved. He composed terse miniatures far from Romantic spaciousness, very brief operas and symphonies and helped to create a passing fashion in the use of polytonality, using two or more keys simultaneously.

17 *Gounod: Rise and Decline*

How you come down after that I do not know. Maybe you come down a notch or two. ...

A U.K.Classic FM radio announcer suggested this one early morning in March 2006, referring to the impact of a melody seemingly from another age, ennobling, with a grandiose beauty. Perhaps he found it most inspiring. Or was he simply astounded? It was composed by 1885 and if radio had existed then, the comment would have been in a more devotional spirit. It was widely thought to be one of the most inspired melodies to come out of that century. Not many would have disagreed.

Its audiences at the time had come to expect such grandeur from the oratorios of Charles Gounod. It had deep religious significance for millions of French and English speaking Christians. It was the *Judex* from *Mors et Vita,* concerned with divine judgment in a sequence of religious works including the other giant oratorio, *Redemption* (1882),[25] both premiered at Birmingham festivals.

By 1885, Gounod's last opera *The Tribute of Zamora* had known moderate success with some 50 performances but was to disappear from the stage whereas his *Faust* of 1859 was then probably the most performed of all operas. One cannot measure now whether stage or concert was the greater general appeal for his music, but he enjoyed a fame others could only hope for. It was one which would decline steadily into the following centuries.

As a youth, Charles Gounod (1818–93) heard the great soprano, Malibran, singing Rossini, and later had an affair with her sister, Pauline Viardot, who was the last of a distinguished musical family. She had premiered *The Prophet* in 1849 and had helped to place in a commercial Parisian theatre Gounod's first opera, *Sapho* (1851). It was to be as a virtuoso piece for Viardot, who however was reaching the end of her career.

In the spirit of a classic Greek pastorale, it relates to the desertion of the poetess from Lesbos by her male lover. It

showed in the finale the young Gounod's gift for a beautifully
restrained lyricism. For dramatic interest, it uses the well-tried
device of a song contest; here the male rival sings a martial
verse, losing out to Sapho.

There is a triangular love intrigue which would become
familiar in Gounod's operas of which he wrote eleven more.
Three were comedies on a modest scale, but most of the
others were spectacular productions. *La nonne sanglante*
(Bleeding Nun, not translated) was a melodrama which several
composers had rejected, by Scribe in the manner of *Robert the
Devil.* Meyerbeer was impressed, not knowing if he had a fol-
lower or a rival. Yet already established successfully in Church
music, Gounod was not in sympathy with sinister underworld
imagery, and this failed to inspire his best music. Berlioz had
started on the same play by Scribe, until it was clear he could
not get it performed in Paris; it would have suited his style
better.

Gounod needed more lyrical subjects which explains why he
later abandoned sketches for *Ivan the Terrible.* One sequence
ended up in the fine Act I finale of a later opera, *The Queen of
Sheba* (1862), for her legendary arrival[26] at King Solomon's
court. The French Emperor objected to aspects of this play,
specially the Queen rejecting Solomon for a commoner. In a
London production, the plot and its characters were soon
being changed. Gounod was depressed by the apparent failure
of this most ambitious work, and it probably does not deserve
the neglect which continues until now. It would make interesting comparison with Karl Goldmark's 1875 opera of the
same title.

Before that, in 1859, Gounod had his greatest operatic success, *Faust.* The story of a male seducer, his victim and the
surrogate Devil would intrigue us much less today, but through
much of the 19th century, it seized the Romantic imagination
like no other. By the 1850s, it was well known in the Parisian
music theatres, not least in several burlesques. It led to an
earlier work by Hector Berlioz (1847) which makes for interesting contrast, with its more detached, classical approach.

Gounod had found an expressive power which went well
beyond opera purely as a collection of beautiful melodies. It
enabled him to achieve a break-through, then overdue in Paris,
towards a more naturalistic operatic style. This was perhaps

helped because unusually, the plot had no heroes, just two characters briefly enjoying then suffering through a common human experience. In the intimacy of the lovers' feelings, Gounod achieved a fusion of words and music to a degree most of his French predecessors had not reached.

Coloratura singing may be very exciting, but can hold up the drama, and Gounod reduced it in *Faust*, except in the much admired jewel song. He also showed skills in dramatising the crowd scenes, such as at the ball where Professor Faust and a young girl Margarite first see each other; and a soldiers' homecoming including her brother.

The Professor, ageing and bored with the intellectual life, is susceptible to the offer of returning to his youth, acquiring a girl of his choice, and enjoying magically bestowed powers. The price to be paid is surrendering his soul to the Devil.

Legends are often concerned with life's deepest values and decisions, and *Faust* symbolises those humans who have made fatal choices. The Devil's emissary is Mephisto, who restores Faust's youth and provides the casket of jewels with which Faust will seduce Margarite. He soon tires of her to embark on wondrous adventures with his benefactor

Mephisto is one of the most attractive villains in all opera, engaging many composers' interest. Gounod gives him perhaps the best of all laughing serenades, alongside Mozart's in *Don Gionanni*. Audiences were delighted with music which had Mephisto presenting specious arguments, telling funny stories, impersonating a holy man, flirting with a widow and performing miracles on wine. This talent for musical humour is a rare facility which Gounod used in his three modest but successful comic operas.

Margarite is left pregnant and has a child; but Mephisto is not finished with her. The Devil now wants her soul and she is driven to temporary insanity. She recovers to seek God's help, and has a final confrontation with the two men before Mephisto casts Faust down to hell. This powerful trio is the climax and her salvation is accompanied with music in the elevated style of Gounod's oratorios.

His original version of *Faust* was seen in a commercial theatre, but unlike Verdi, Gounod had some defects in his judgment of dramatic suitability. He was under the influence of impresario Carvalho and his prima donna of a wife, who might have deflected his dramatic intentions in several operas. Fortunately, he was persuaded to move a soldiers' chorus from his unperformed *Ivan the Terrible* to *Faust* where it had an immense impact. It became so popular along with the waltz that they soon were being played by bands right across Europe.

To render *Faust* suitable for the state-subsidised National Opera, it had to be converted into grand opera. That included a substantial ballet sequence, which drew on extra literary material, Faust being transported by Mephisto to ancient Greece and a meeting with Helen of Troy. Its melodious ballet music became in turn a popular classic; yet in modern productions it is mainly truncated or eliminated as unnecessary for the main plot. This is an obvious way for saving costs. The original medieval scenario is now often replaced by one in the 19th century. A recent Welsh Opera version has citizens in crinolins and stove-pipe hats, which enhances the effect of bourgeois condemnation of sexual 'immorality' in the 1860s. That is of the greatest relevance because Gounod had to please his audience, notably by retrieving Margarite from the status of a 'fallen woman', deceived by the Devil's magic.

Faust shows tender feelings for her which are absent in the original play where Mephisto had felt free to mock his carnal interest. Precisely until fighting the war of 1859 in Italy, France's popular conception of war had been for decades one of Napoleonic glamour, whereas the real horror of every battlefield was then to be brought home, infamously at Magenta in Italy. Contemporary versions may have many of the soldiers returning from the war on crutches or stretchers, but to the triumphant music.

Margarite evolves from naïve girlhood to disillusioned mother, and Faust is transformed by magic from elderly, reflective professor to irresponsible young man. These changes have to be reflected in the singing styles, along with Mephisto's devilish physical transformations and magical acts. As a result, in Europe's great opera houses, *Faust* needed the finest and most versatile of Europe's singers, and this contributed to its unprecedented fame over decades.

Yet since sex is today considered an enjoyable option and the Devil has died, modern conceptions of the opera's theme, as distinct from Goethe's philosophical play, have been devalued, and with it the opera's reputation. *Carmen* is now preferred and admired as a realistic tragedy, though Bizet was once a youthful *Faust* enthusiast. Nor is Gounod's historic position in French opera so widely appreciated, though his stylistic development paralleled that Verdi had applied to Italian opera one decade previously. It would seem the process went no further, as Gounod could not repeat the success of *Faust*. It will survive on at least its wealth of fine melodies.

Mireille (1864) has a story similar as far as a love affair which society disapproves to fatal results. The opera has the pure lyricism evident in *Sapho,* and is now valued as highly as *Faust,* being performed in its original form since 1939. The overture and girls' opening chorus express the happiness of carefree youth, and the early scenes, Mireille's lust for life. Local songs of the Midi added to the work's sunny appeal and were enthusiastically received. Yet the girl's life is to be destroyed because she intends to marry a young man without property. The music's warmth must have suggested to Carvalho that the tragic end should be avoided, which reduced the poignancy of the drama. The original plan with Mireille's death from sunstroke is now restored in the dramatic church scene.

If *Mireille* had strong appeal in evoking the South of France, *Romeo & Juliet* (1867) had an obvious appeal, and it did not disappoint. The composer responded ideally to the love theme and the libretto by Michel Carré and Jules Barbier, It respected the original text as far as possible, bringing the important ballroom scene which set off the violence even nearer to the beginning.

While innocent of future unhappiness, Juliet sings a waltz song which was to become almost as familiar away from theatres as Margarite's jewel song. There are an exceptional number of fine duets for the lovers, four. Years later for the grand opera version, there was the compulsory ballet for Act III, very well received but no longer used, though unfortunately the recitative has tended to stick.

It was eight years before Gounod attempted another grand opera. Three more were to come, but are now rarely performed and not known to English speakers. Gounod was attracted by the theme of Christian martyrdom when he chose *Polyeucte*, but its 17th century classical text by Corneille was the opposite of what can be associated with Romanticism. After that, he lost the services of his long-serving librettists, Carré and Barbier.

Marie de Bovet wrote a sensitive book on Gounod shortly before his death, and dismissed the first of these operas about a king's favourite, *Cinq-Mars* (1877), as hastily written and not worthy of further remarks. She commented on *The Tribute of Zamora*:

> *Sombre without being dramatic, monotonous and incoherent, with no really interesting character. ... Gounod has lost himself in a confusion of styles.*

She did praise a war chant, the ballet and a mad scene. A melodrama, its vigour seemed to suggest renewed inspiration. But the year was 1881, thirty years after Gounod's first essay, and critical opinion would soon conclude there was much repetition in these works of ideas from earlier successes. Gounod tried no further in opera.

The 1870 war and siege of Paris had proved a watershed in the theatre and new styles were emerging. Massenet by the 1880s was sustaining a consistently high level in his operas with exceptional variations of theme and even style. He had admired and learnt from Gounod and his melodies sometimes have a striking affinity but uses more artifice and to great effect. Whereas he was more of a detached observer who could rise to sudden heights of passionate declamation, Gounod was sentimental and needed more space to sustain his lyricism. This helps to explain why *Faust, Mireille* and *Romeo & Juliet* are considered the most durable of Gounod.

18 *Dvorak and Brahms' Influence*

Bohemian is a word with mixed associations in our language. The *Bohemian Girl* was about a girl brought up by gipsies, Puccini's were poor artists and girls of the Parisian *demi-monde*. Any association between our use of the term and the Czech folk idiom is obscure, though from the Middle Ages, Bohemia was so rich in musicians that many travelled abroad for work. Antonin Dvorak was born there not long after its capital, Prague, had been a bilingual city, and he grew up with keen awareness of Czech and German culture. If performances and teaching tied him to towns, his preference was to compose in a quaint country dwelling near the voice of nature. This is heard in some of his greatest works such as the Eighth Symphony.

He had the gift of spontaneity, so notable in his instrumental works; in this and other ways, there was an affinity with Schubert. He was one of the century's great melodists, the dominant influence being the Czech folk idiom, in particular the *dumky* rhythms, alternating slow and fast like the czardas, but often in nostalgic mood. He once wrote a complete Piano Trio around them used in all six movements. By inclination, his style was rhapsodic and he often threw in more melodies than needed, especially in his chamber music. He was not inhibited from writing what some called 'cafe music', relaxing with instant lyrical appeal, such as his opus 97 Quintet, in that sense like Schubert's lightest works.

Born in 1841 to relative poverty, Dvorak was grateful for the Church's role in his musical education. He became skilled, playing violin or viola in a professional orchestra and while very young composed symphonic and choral works. There was much to absorb from established styles and techniques, especially Italian and Viennese. This, close at hand, he respected and, as he understood, it helped him to impose more discipline on his compositions. Fairly prolific from the start, he was aged 36 at the time he was befriended by Johannes Brahms, eight years older.

Brahms' Romantic side and attachment to the German folk style are revealed in many of his more intimate works, and his songs nowhere more obviously than in his famous *Lullaby*. Yet the most famous quote about his music in general has been:
Emotion recalled in tranquillity.
His symphonies display this, having great strength with internal tensions, the fulfilment of a Classical tradition. He had imitators, but no authorised school of followers.

There were enigmatic sides to Brahms's nature, belying his outer personality which tended to conceal emotions. Born in Hamburg, he had known poverty and whilst very young his family needed the money earned from his playing piano in disreputable places of entertainment. He may have had a taste for music at a distance away from the kind he would compose.

By maturity, he admired many different music styles, and after a concert tour accompanying a Hungarian violinist, Remenyi, was introduced to a more famous one, Joachim with whom he remained life friends. Brahms specially liked Goldmark's *Rustic Wedding Symphony*, leading to part of a creative interest in Hungarian music. This might surface surprisingly in compositions, such as whole movements in his Violin Concerto and opus 25 Piano Quartet.

It was a novel idea to compose a set of *Hungarian Dances*, musically letting his hair down. As many as 16 were based on what he assumed to be authentic melodic sources, and the last five probably his own. Arranged four-handed for pianos they would be a treat for music students, especially when compared with typically 'boring teaching exercises' for middle-class daughters to practice in the home. By any standards, they were earthy, brief and very exciting. In the 1860s, they set a new fashion. Brahms' personality was apparent within them, but he enjoyed this brief holiday from four-square German rhythms. He was interested in the popular forms of Bohemian and other Slavonic music and even edited Dvorak's *dumky* Piano Trio and other of his works for publication.

Dvorak was of the second generation of Romantic composers who could not fail to be impressed by Wagner's work, so that Brahms was to become a valuable counter-weight. Unlike most composers of his time, Dvorak was devout, essentially a family man, unsophisticated and determined to remain close to his peasant roots. Brahms, a city man, intellectual and agnostic, could seem insensitive, even falling asleep when Liszt was playing. Aloof but no snob, he treated the talented Dvorak as friend and protégé for the remaining twenty years of his life. The empathy between them was instant, and being a bachelor, he wanted Dvorak to come and live in Vienna, so that he could enjoy life with a large family.

Brahms had migrated to Vienna where he disliked being lionised by musicians as their leader, or by public admirers. He was at pains to choose his own friends and first met Dvorak whilst on a committee of music judges. Dvorak's *Moravian Duets* had first impressed Brahms who then took his work to the Berlin publisher Simrock. This was a decisive event for the younger man who had enough spare material for several composers, or so Brahms thought. Later he introduced Dvorak to the Hungarian Josef Joachim who advised both men on their respective violin concertos.

The popularity of Brahms' *Hungarian Dances* resulted in Dvorak orchestrating some, and Simrock suggested his following with comparable sets of *Slavonic Dances*. These quickly became his best-known compilation; of the 16, half were Bohemian in style. They were longer, more elaborated than Brahms' and Dvorak used his own melodies entirely. Both men also composed original works in the manner of gipsy songs.

Dvorak from the start of his career specially revered Brahms who had greatly impressed Schumann with taut, disciplined instrumental music whilst still a very young man in the 1850s. In contrast Dvorak's approach to composition was very spontaneous, discursive, Slavonic. Brahms' attachment to folk music was more apparent in his songs than in his symphonies.

Dvorak had already composed five symphonies, the early ones tending to ramble, by 1876 when he met Brahms, who had none published. This was because, as he said, he felt in the shadow of Beethoven. Eventually the critics assumed that his second had influenced Dvorak's numbered six. They are both very lyrical but the Dvorak, dispensing with an introduction, builds up with a great sweep which was unique. The third movement has a Czech rhythm, a *furiant* of rare pace, leading to the most satisfactory conclusion he had reached. Until then, endings had been his particular symphonic problem. Resemblances to Brahms' were superficial.

Brahms' symphonies were very tightly structured, suspenseful.

Dvorak was aware he stood to gain much by studying the formidable techniques of his friend. Resemblances to Brahms' style are most striking in three subsequent works: his opus 65 Piano Trio, melodically and in the percussive use of the piano, and perhaps the greatest of his chamber works, the opus 81 Piano Quintet. His Seventh Symphony was composed in years of unusual personal stress, more impassioned, reflective, with some melodies which might be mistaken for Brahms'. Critical opinion often praised it for being more 'profound' but it is now regarded just as an interesting departure in style, none the less valuable for that.

Composing a cello concerto presents a problem of the instrument's pitch, much lower than the violin's, against the orchestral sound. Dvorak overcame this, and Brahms recognising its inspiration said he would have done likewise if he had realised it was possible. That was modest because some years previously, he had composed a work for violin and cello, probably the greatest double concerto of the century.

Both men wrote distinguished choral works and Dvorak's *Stabat Mater* reflected his own family bereavements. By the time Brahms died in 1897, Dvorak had ceased to compose non-programme music, symphonies and instrumental, to concentrate on symphonic poems and opera, none of which Brahms had written.

19   *Bizet through to Carmen*

During the 33rd performance of the first production of *Carmen*, the singer playing the title role had a presentiment and fainted as she left the stage, resuming later. Her interpretation was excellent by report but that was the night in 1875 Georges Bizet died aged only 37, suffering from angina and complications. The opera's world-wide popularity make it appear to stand alone as Bizet's masterpiece, so there is curiosity about Bizet's other stage works, especially with the scope for recording the previously unknown.

A Parisian born to musical parents, his composing and pianistic talents were so great that it took years for him be sure of his destined path, which was opera.

Because he had been composing for 20 years, the amount of music is considerable: including some 40 songs with piano, two early operettas, two other operas which are often performed in our times, and some others which exist in manuscript. His biographer Winton Dean had studied Bizet's little known and incomplete works in great detail during the 1940s so made an expert commentary in the Master Musicians' series of books.

In an apprentice competition composing for a farce, *Doctor Miracle*, Bizet had shared first prize with Charles Lecoq who went on to excel in operetta. His next stage work, *Don Procopio*, had a similar plot to Donizetti's *Don Pasquale*, and its music was in suitably comic spirit. He had often contributed to the musical jokes and dressing up which were a feature of soirées with his colleagues when Offenbach imitated animals on his cello. Striking evidence of this lighter touch are his *Children's Games* written as piano pieces, the most popular ones later orchestrated.

In his 20s Bizet had started several compositions, then partly destroyed or recycled them. Valuable material reappeared in the posthumous 16 songs. An earlier one, *The Arab Hostess' Farewell*, is of special interest. Indecision came from lack of confidence, anxiety about the number and strength of influences which bore upon his style when young, such as the

Germans Meyerbeer, Wagner and Weber. Nor could he decide
about concentrating on symphonic or operatic writing. In the
first category, *Roma* and *Patrie* clearly involved national sentiments which, like religious ones, were not Bizet's strength, and
eventually he realised the musical stage was his destiny. Yet a
symphony written when he was barely 17 was not discovered
until 1935. Schubertian, it is now admired more than he could
ever have expected.

France's gaining territories in North Africa led to the notion
that 'Oriental' music was what simply one might associate with
the southern and eastern coasts of the Mediterranean. Yet it
was a convenient starting point for popular understanding. In
melody the pronounced sliding between close musical notes
gave rise to the term *arabesque*, less used now. Pleasing imitation
Asian melodies and rhythms would come from several French
composers. Bizet did not need to travel abroad but a valuable
stage in his development came through studying foreign and
oriental melodic styles from travelling musicians in Paris. He
took the opportunity of the 1867 International Exhibition
which helped to promote new cults and fashions.

Before that. aged 24 he had composed a large, complex
opera, *The Pearl Fishers* (1863), a tale of friendship and religious
inhibitions. The male duet has become specially liked through
the spread of broadcasting along with a romance for the tenor.
A duet for the lovers and a *cavatina* for the soprano also gave
the work distinction. The story relates to India, most closely felt
in a choral hymn to Brahma, though he might not be so
pleased by a ritual dance nearer to first-class operetta. Nearly all
the soloists' music sounds European and Gounod's influence
was strong. The friendship theme is heard in the male duet and
elsewhere, though Dean thought it not strong enough for a
motif, unlike the fate theme in *Carmen*. He was less impressed
by the ritual music and the final trio because he thought its
heroic sentiments did not suit Bizet's style.

Bizet remained enthusiastic about Gounod's work and soon
after the older man broke off working on *Ivan the Terrible,* he
prepared his own score then later discarded it. Probably like
Gounod, he felt the subject was not sufficiently lyrical but the
work was reassembled in Germany and performed in 1946. *The
Fair Maid of Perth* (1866) suited Bizet better, a comic opera
based on Walter Scott's novel. It had a wretched libretto he was

contracted to accept, though the characters are more rounded than in his earlier works. Musically there is no trace of Scotland in it, but Dean welcomes the absence of Meyerbeer's influence to be replaced by that of *Rigoletto* and *Mireille*, two operas which he says Bizet specially admired.

There are humorous episodes such as a failed seduction scene backed by music of great delicacy. The lilting serenade was composed when Bizet was nearly 21. It is exceptional enough to be used several times, finally for the balcony scene of lovers' reconciliation after the feckless Maid Catherine had suffered operatic madness. An amorous gipsy woman provides the opposition, such as entering disguised into a bed intended for another. Her wild *Bohemian dance* is now so familiar that many assume it comes from *Carmen* in which it would be well worthy of a place.

There is a jealous witch who wreaks havoc in *King Thule's Cup*, a half-finished opera of which parts were published separately. Dean specially admired the prelude, considering the work would have shown a big advance in tragic expression. Bizet was at his best inspired by conflicts between couples where just one or both are emotionally distressed; his treatment of idyllic love is less impressive.

The following stage work had the slightest of stories; a court official plots unsuccessfully to acquire a girl from a harem. Namouna had been a slave in a 1829 Musset poem, the subject of a ballet by the French composer, Edouard Lalo. Her name was changed to *Djamileh* for Bizet's one-Act opera in which her master takes a time to decide he desires her. Interest centres on her anxieties, and these are most sensitively expressed in Bizet's finest 'Oriental' score. Dean thought Bizet had gained maturity with it. About her dance he comments:

> *Djamileh's dance is rhythmically reminiscent of the Bohemian dance in* The Fair Maid of Perth; *it is in the same melodic variation form but the exotic colouring is much more pronounced. Its sinuous melody, half in the minor key, winding its way through combinations of voices and instruments accompanied by a syncopated rhythm, gives an effect of seductive languor ... The exotic element is never unpleasantly obtrusive, never mere titillation of the ear. It is always subservient to the dramatic purpose ... The music is as fresh today as in 1872.*

Bizet wrote incidental music for a dramatisation of Daudet's tragic novel, *L'Arlésienne*. The French term *mélodrame* bears no relation to our *melodrama*. It is music providing ambience or more for on-stage speech or action, quite different from a traditional operatic aria; composers such as Massenet and Lehar used it selectively to good effect. In *L'Arlésienne* he uses it to extend his dramatising skills, but the finished product was excellent. It was to be with *Carmen* his finest achievement in the few years left. The minimal chances of seeing *L'Arlésienne* as a play with music are compensated partly by two orchestrated suites made from substantial extracts.

The girl from Arles never appears in the play, nor in the opera composed soon afterwards by the Italian, Francisco Cilea. Though this is intended in the original to add to her mystique, her absence is regrettable as she might have inspired Bizet further. The lover commits suicide through jealousy on the eve of his wedding to another girl. This pathos is reflected early in the suite by a melody strangely enhanced by the (then) unfamiliar sound of a saxophone.

The King's March was a local song selected by Bizet, elemental, imposing itself above the human tragedy. It is heard at the start of the prelude of the suite, its excitement prolonged in a set of variations. Flute and drums are prominent later as it is in canon with the *farandole,* a stomping medieval dance. Bizet's carillon suggests the community, its curiosity about or indifference to personal tragedy.

Winton Dean referred to the *greater energy, flexibility and variety of his melodic line, not too symmetrical, and attractive for lasting slightly longer than expected.* He cites one theme from *L'Arlésienne* covering two octaves over 16 bars in slow time, suggesting a pathetic character who matures through the trauma of his brother's death. Much admired is a movement, the *adagietto,* suggesting the love of an elderly couple. A lighter charm is introduced with a conversation piece transcribed from *The fair Maid of Perth.*

Carmen was based on Prosper Merimée's short, brutish story of that title, but the credit for inspired stage adaptation goes to librettists, Meilhac and Halévy, and not least to the composer. The original plot was concerned almost exclusively with Carmen and Don José, but the opera gained dramatically with the early involvement of Carmen's work companions. Changes to the original text included a larger role for the Toreador, the

card game where Carmen's death is predicted, and her being
stabbed outside the stadium just as the crowd cheer his killing
the bull. The addition of a sub-plot brings relief, also musically.
This is the 'nice, homely girl', Michaela, who admires José and
could have been his escape from disaster. Merimée's account
has him handy with the knife, killing no fewer than three. But
most productions outside France have always had artificial
recitative added, so there is none of the original spoken dialogue to tell the full truth. José may gain more sympathy than
he deserves, though his vulnerability is shown at best in the
Flower song. His rival Escamillo the Toreador is as insensitive
and boastful as one might expect in a bull killer, Bizet craftily
makes his *Toreador* song similarly popular but crude. Carmen
cares little for him but enjoys his celebrity status.

The plot's ironies are perceived in advance by the lovers.
Don José asserts women are like cats who never come when
called; Carmen warns that love is a bird which cannot be tamed.
Soon afterwards she continues her game with a most alluring
gesture. This is a throw-away phrase but with enough musicality
for a whole aria, superbly displaying her defiant spirit in the
face of arrest. As much as the *habanera*, the *seguidilla* is a technically perfect piece of stagecraft, Carmen's characteristic
seduction song. As she flirts and dances, her interplay with José
reveals their personalities very early in the drama as the action
moves quickly forward. Much later, there is a fine quintet in
which the women are talked into a smuggling operation, to
their growing excitement.

The work was of historic significance, the first serious opera
to be concerned mainly with people of 'ordinary' status, short
of money or inclined to petty crime. Its treatment was realistic
but artistically refined, a perfect model. Within a decade or two,
the fashion for realism in opera would spread though not
always in such satisfactory ways. *Carmen* was at first not the
failure some presented it to be. Though the drama is centred
on Seville, the Spaniards have never accepted it as Spanish, nor
should they on account of its famed *habanera* and *seguidilla* or a
few melodies borrowed[27] and given greater appeal.

If Bizet had not died in 1875, the next work would have been
seen at Paris' newly opened building for grand opera. Whilst
planning *Carmen*, he was working on *Don Rodrigue*, the same
warrior as in Massenet's later classic French play, *Le Cid*. Bizet

had insisted on a more authentic Spanish version, less idealistic, but his largest and noisiest conception until then. Having examined its vocal score, Dean doubted it would be an advance, and specially deplored the inclusion of two items taken from *Ivan the Terrible* including *the dreadful march in all its saxophonic splendour.* He concluded that legendary heroes were beyond Bizet's scope, and he was about to write about real men and women, so making legends and adulation no longer fashionable. Moreover, *he could sink himself into his characters. Carmen* is utterly convincing as it shapes melody perfectly to the action. By 1875 the most vital French opera composer since Berlioz had arrived, to become straightaway a tragic loss for the music world.

20 *From Folk to Art Music*

U ntil the late 19th century, Italian, French and Austro-German musical traditions were dominant in Europe. In countries using other languages, the gradual expanse of education was bringing greater awareness of national identity. Over several decades, the vitality of their traditional folk song and dance would be recognised in influential circles, and new styles would emerge. Yet one man, seemingly alone, set an example well ahead of his time which was heeded because of his fame at the piano: Frederick Chopin with his Polish-inspired compositions.

The Russian Michael Glinka started his career imitating Western music, especially Italian, but aged only 38, he succeeded at a second attempt to write an all-through 'Eastern' opera. Its well-known overture gives no hint that, allowing for much that is conventional, *Ruslan and Ludmilla* broke the mould, as early as 1842 when nationalism was not even on the European map.

Melodies, harmonies and dance style were Russian, and what the first Court audiences disapproved more, there was a lengthy ballet imitating Caucasian and Persian music; this departure from the accepted Western fashions often had to be cut out in early performances.

Glinka had said that the Russian people were the composers, he the arranger. The following generation of composers took him and his final opera as a model on which to build. Five of them calling themselves the 'mighty handful' set up a free music school in Moscow far from the capital, Western-influenced St Petersburg. It was a principle for them that the Russian folk idiom was unsuitable for German-style symphonic development. With strong nationalist feeling they looked for traditional sources of inspiration which included the music of the Orthodox Church, and with it, much ringing of bells. That has woken up many of the audience in concert halls since then,

Of outside influences, at least they favoured the advanced techniques of Liszt, especially the idea of using themes integrated through a whole work, 'cyclical'. With Glinka's *Kamarinskaya* (1848) as the admired model, orchestral compositions, often short single movements with a strong rhythmic basis became common. Balakirev (1837–1910), the nominal leader, and Borodin (1833–87), showed the way with Russian-type symphonies; Borodin's knowledge of non-European melodies suggested the opening theme of his Second, 'barbaric', unlike any heard in such a work, and admirably taut.

The Russian Empire had expanded during the 19th century to take control of vast territories in central Asia. Both composers and some others were fascinated by its ancient culture and music; Balakirev's piano work *Islamei* was rhythmically dazzling and Borodin conjured up a seductive exoticism for the Polovtsian scenes in the opera, *Prince Igor. On the Steppes of Central Asia* was an orchestral sketch symbolising the meeting of cultures, an Asian caravan briefly protected by a troop of Russian soldiers in the desert. One melody is a slow march, the other a leisurely 'arabesque', to the rhythm of advancing camels.

Borodin's sophisticated approach had great appeal for European ears but Modeste Mussorgsky (1839–81) rejected it. He studied Russian speech patterns as a basis for melody, so that even his colleagues thought much of his work was crude. With hindsight, his own conceptions are critically admired as the authentic voice of Russia such as in the opera, *Boris Godunov.* Ideologically committed, Mussorgsky subdued his personality to the broad needs of his subject matter, one valued path for a perceptive dramatist.

His *Night on the bare Mountain* and the prelude to *Khovanshchina* were impressionistic movements of the kind which would take Russian music abroad and have an influence notably on some French composers. Several projects were left incomplete because of his chaotic lifestyle and early death, such as the boldly original *Pictures at an Exhibition.*

Rimsky-Korsakov's (1844–1908) own style was remote from Mussorgsky's, as fantasy differs from reality, highly mannered, enhanced by lush melodies and glittering orchestration. Their unfamiliar sounds inspired by his travels as a naval officer were prominent in several operas, and he experimented with intriguing scales. *Sheherezade* and *Antar*, another adventure, were his expressed notion of a Russian symphony.

Romanticism with its emphasis on individual sentiment had minimal impact on Russian culture or these composers. Their larger works were concerned with the people collectively and their relations with the rulers and the state. These men were deceased well before the Russian revolution, but musical nationalism always suited the Soviet pattern, partly because their 15 republics included some 100 different languages. Alexander Glazunov (1865–1936) was the last of the old school, holding an eminent post in the U.S.S.R. So the younger nationalists had the option to fit in, and of them, Reinhold Glière lived through until 1952. His best known ballet is the *Red Poppy* to a Chinese scenario but ending with a Russian sailor's dance. Of the nationalists known abroad, Khachaturian (1903–78) made a huge impact, the sinuous 'Eurasian', Armenian style being translated into exciting symphonic works in such ballets as *Spartacus*.

Bohemia was an ancient kingdom whose ruler was the Habsburg Emperor in Vienna. Its Slavonic (Czech) people being culturally advanced, it had strong nationalist feelings earlier than most. Bedric Smetana (1824–84) followed Glinka's example in Russian opera, expressing the Czech spirit in several successful ones, notably *The Bartered Bride* and *Libuse*. National symbols were themes for his set of six symphonic poems, *Ma Vlast* (My Country), one invoking Prague's river *Vltava* and two others the 15th century Protestant resistance to the Imperial forces, *The Hussites* and *Tabor*.

His fellow-countryman, Antonin Dvorak (1841–1904), likewise chose for operas and symphonic poems tales of traditional folklore. During a short residence in the U.S.A. he showed interest in native American melody, and met some who were striving with difficulty to promote it. This is thought to have inspired a few of his compositions, though he played down the suggestion in relation to his *New World Symphony*. Laos Janacek (1854–1928) followed a solitary musical path years after arranging folk music suites. He began to compose operas based upon speech-melody and his dedication was fully justified. Even those with the most eccentric themes are now very widely performed in foreign countries including the U.K.

Sweden's cultural influence had once spread to Norway and Western Finland, and there was a strong music tradition. A great folk song, the *Neckanspolska*, appeared as a motif in

Cordelia's mad scene from Ambroise Thomas' once-popular opera *Hamlet*, and an English composer, William Hurlstone, used it for a set of symphonic variations. It was left to a Swede, Hugo Alfven (1872–1960), to compose two short works which became well known abroad as the *Swedish Polka* and *Swedish Rhapsody*. He was one of several Swedish nationalists by around 1900, but earlier, Scandinavia had been less advanced than countries further south, their intelligentsia looking to Germany for leadership, and their musicians for advanced training.

Eduard Grieg (1843–1907) was among them but he came to admire an original cult of fiddle-playing in Norway, and to transcribe such works for the piano, stimulating foreign interest specially in the folk rhythms. They inspired polished sets of symphonic dances, and he used themes taken from dramas by his contemporaries, Björnson and Ibsen, his music such as for the play *Sigurd Jorsalfar* increasing national awareness.

Grieg acquired two unexpected English-speaking admirers looking for fresh musical inspiration. Frederick Delius (1863–1934) was spare in praising other composers, and he also used a Norwegian melody for his tone poem, *On hearing the first Cuckoo in Spring*. Australian Percy Grainger was a virtuoso pianist-composer who became well known for playing the Grieg Piano Concerto. He advocated an ambitious 'nordic' musical revival, but one not to be dominated by the Germans.

Grainger (1882–1961) had a preference for intensely rhythmic arrangements of English folk songs, his *Country Gardens* remaining unusually popular. He rediscovered a classic, *Brigg Fair*, on which Delius composed a glowing rhapsody. This was at a time around 1900 when musicologists were taking recording machines into country areas to find 'ordinary' people who remembered and could sing the traditional songs. Notating this authentic music was an invaluable contribution to folklore studies in many lands. Some took their task with extreme seriousness, such as Cyril Scott who tended to place folk above art music, notably when he converted his intended symphony into a set of dances.

Traditional English music tended to be modal, and Vaughan Williams (1872–1958) among others locked one, the Doric scale, into many of his melodies, giving them a distinctive personality. As a graduate historian, he knew the Church had always discouraged folk tunes being used in the liturgy lest men might sing 'rude words'. Not worrying about that, he used many by way of a much-needed revitalising of the English Hymnal. A fine symphonist, he also had time for curious instrumental combinations, not excluding harmonica, and his most important *English Folk Song Suite* was composed for military band. He used some of his own melodies to promote 'English country style', exuberantly linked to a disrespectful farce, Aristophanes' *Wasps*.

There had been some confusion about *Magyar* (Hungarian) and *Romany* (gipsy) music, and their distinct musical traditions were clarified by Zoltan Kodaly's (1882–1967) researches. He made hundreds of Hungarian song transcriptions, including an opera, *The Spinning Room*, uniquely with folk melodies: for his *Psalmus Hungaricus*, and one for an important set of symphonic variations, *The Peacock*. His music teaching methods are now world famous. Working well within the communist system, his reputation and the traditional folk culture continued to flourish there into our times.

His colleague, Bela Bartok (1881–1945), joined in the research before travelling far, working outside Hungary, with cosmopolitan sympathies for Balkan music. He also went further than Kodaly, researching even outside Europe, in breaking down folk music into its elements. This was on the way to constructing his own style, analysing then transmuting the Hungarian features. His final compositions often sound less like folk than art music, such as in his abstruse string quartets and *Music for Strings, Percussion and Celesta*. He, however, did merge his modernism with the more recent past in two very important works, the opera, *Duke Bluebeard's Castle* and the much later *Concerto for Orchestra*, which moves genially between the music styles of city and countryside. That rivalry has always been a feature of Hungarian musical entertainment.

In southern Spain, the Moors (Arabs) had made a strong cultural impact over centuries, and a *flamenco* (gipsy) style developed in Andalucia and beyond. Partly as a result, Spanish music had attracted much attention across Europe well before 1900 and the arrival of a nationalist school of composers. Manuel de Falla (1876–1946) earned international fame with *Seven popular Spanish Songs*, the ballet *The Three-cornered Hat* and the opera, *La Vida breve*, with its *flamenco* songs. Isaac Albeniz' (1860–1909) research led to important piano compilations, notably *Iberia,* a *Spanish suite,* and his one orchestral work, *Catalonia.*

In the U.S.A., European music styles dominated throughout the 19th century and there was no nationalist movement of note. Two men had followed solitary paths to create important compositions which are now critically admired. Louis Gottschalk was more a regional composer, arranging mainly as songs or for piano North and Latin American material. Scott Joplin composed a successful 'black' opera, *Tremonisha,* and was a pioneer of ragtime; his inspired 'classical' skills were discouraged socially because he was black. He has been well revived since the 1970s, his music accepted into high art with the ballet, *Elite Syncopations.*

Since the early 20th century, classically trained U.S. composers have searched for a national style in art music. Many of these were the sons of immigrants, such as Aaron Copland. He arranged traditional songs with a wide expressive range, and used a famous one for a symphonic work, *Appalachian Spring.* His ballets, *Rodeo* and *Billy the Kid,* became the prototype for film music suggesting the cowboy life and the Continent's wide expanses. Roy Harris was aiming for an American-style symphony in a series of 14, expansive, rugged and forthright. The Third (1943) in one movement caused a sensation, inspired by Sibelius' Seventh, but with a rare individuality, strident blocks of orchestral sound, and immense rhythmic vitality.

■ ■ ■

Sets of orchestrated national dances, mostly composed originally for piano, include:

Alfven: *Swedish Rhapsodies.*
Arnold: *English, Scottish and Cornish Dances.*
Brahms: *Hungarian Dances.*
Dvorak: *Slavonic Dances.*
Enescu: *Rumanian Rhapsodies.*
Grieg: *Norwegian Dances.*
Janacek: *Lacian Dances.*
Kodaly: *Dances of Galanta and Maroszek.*
Schubert: *German Dances.*
Skalkottas: *Greek Dances.*
Smetana: *Czech Dances.*
Svendsen: *Norwegian Dances.*

21 *Four Russian Operas*

T he historical irony of kingship in England no less than Russia is related to the ideal of the father and protector of his people; that the role passed to or was usurped so often by men too weak or evil to fulfil such responsibilities. Ivan IV, Duke of Muscovy, rebelled against the Tartars to become the first Russian Caesar or Tsar (1547–84), called 'the Terrible'. He acquired the name mainly because, as he might have said, he had to 'restore order' by crushing the greedy nobles, the boyars. To many of the common people that meant 'awesome', to be respected, even though to him might be attributed the practice of 'boiling in oil'. His private army, the *Oprichniki*, were also best avoided.

Both he and they were subjects of several operas. Alexander Pushkin's play *Boris Godunov* centred on a Tsar who determined to follow the policies of his friend and predecessor, Ivan. It is assumed he felt that Ivan's child heir should not be allowed to succeed and must be eliminated. Yet conscience left him haunted by the crime, eventually fearing for the fate of his own children.

Modeste Mussorgsky made a morality of this theme with a music drama (1869–74) originally based closely on Pushkin. Mussorgsky was the most uncompromising of the first generation of Russian nationalist composers. His operas were most innovative, disregarding the style and form of familiar Western models. He does follow one new trend, weaving motifs for the most important ideas into the melodic patterns. The structure is unusual: years pass between Acts: scenes often cut out: there are soliloquies of exceptional length. The music has a strength largely based on the folk idiom.

Emphasised from the start, the crowd, the people have a major role: volatile, gullible, cowed or high spirited. The Clerk of the Duma (Parliament) declares they are crying out for a strong ruler, and Boris Godunov must be persuaded to accept. A new and invigorating sound in opera, the pealing of bells announces his forthcoming coronation as Tsar. The scene is given added splendour in the completed version by Rimsky-Korsakov and dominated by the chorale *Slava* (Glory to the Tsar), which brings the prologue to an end.

In Chudovo monastery, the wise, pacific old monk, Pimen, recalls his violent youth, and how tsars had repented their misdeeds, even Ivan IV doing so in that very place. He refers to the murder of the 7-year old Tsarevitch 12 years previously: he would have been Grigory's age. The perpetrator had been the regent Boris Godunov.

Grigory, a young monk, listens intently. There had been rumours or superstitions that the child had not died, was free and would assert his rights. Grigory sees no obstacle to absconding and to become a Pretender, and left alone, he rips off his cowl. Time and distance pass before he is seen at an inn near the border of Lithuania, then linked politically to Poland. He endures the boasting of a disreputable monk, Varlaam, who has picked up strange-sounding Tartar songs on his travels and sings one. This is by way of begging for charity to keep him and a colleague in alcohol. The Tsar's agents arrive seeking a dangerous fugitive, a young 'heretic' monk, but because they are all illiterate, Gregory reads out their arrest warrant to make Varlaam fit the description. This gives him just time to escape, confident of fulfilling God's wrath on Boris.

Following a time lapse of five years Boris looks back to justify his rule in an impassioned monologue, *I have attained supreme power*, but like Macbeth he is overwhelmed by the vision of the murdered victim. By then there may be political and religious factions even at court supporting a Pretender to the Crown, assumed to be the missing heir, Dmitri.

Grigory's deception succeeds and in a few years he controls large areas of western Russia; certain nobles may be disloyal and in Moscow Boris complains of their treachery. His plans for his daughter's marriage fail through the death of the fiancé and she sings of her grief. He sees this as a blow to his dynastic ambitions.

Insurrection and famine continue. Symbolising his fractured relations with the people, a bizarre encounter comes through an old Russian tradition which tolerated village idiots, partly because they might speak truths not permitted to others. One is amusing the crowd who respond by stealing his solitary kopek. At this moment he recognises the approaching Tsar and asks him to kill the thief, since he has already committed one murder. Boris is disconcerted but orders his guards not to harm him.

Boris' responsibility for the murder is not historically proven and he is presented with some compassion. Fearing death, he shows sensitive traits in his final scene urging his youthful son, Alexei, to act with justice and firmness. Its tenderest moment comes when he tells Alexei to protect his sister. As he clutches the boy, his dying prayer is met with funeral bells and a choir. but this moving conclusion cannot be the end of the drama.

The first version had scenes of public dancing, charming ballads for Boris' children and other light relief, but Mussorgsky was persuaded to enhance the operatic appeal. This was with additions in an 1874 version of *Boris* with a new Act III to include the romance of Pushkin's garden scene when Grigory visits the Polish court at Sandomir.

This takes place in musical contrast to the style of Russia's modal[28] church and folk music, a change to a more Westernised style at court, artificial and smoothly underlined by the rhythm of the aristocratic polonaise. In the Pushkin play, Grigory, now widely recognised as the Pretender, has a brief encounter with a priest, rashly promising to return Russia to the Roman Church. Mussorgsky replaced this, installing a Jesuit plenipotentiary Ragnoni with decisive influence at the Polish court. He is to provide foreign help in the hope of prizing the Russian 'heretics' from their Orthodox beliefs.

A beautiful Polish princess is to be used as bait and Grigory, now 'Dmitri', is already enamoured of this Marina, as she is of becoming the Russian Tsarina. In successive scenes the Jesuit when not using flattery to play on their personal vanities has a keen battle of wits in turn with Gregory and Marina. A pretentious young lady, she looks askance at the courtiers dancing a stately mazurka. This leads to the garden scene, where her amorous posturing with Grigory is intriguing. She will only marry him and in Moscow when he is Tsar, an ambition which will succeed in history though not finalised in the opera.

The false Dmitri has led a polyglot army into Russia. In the Kromy forest scene also added for 1874 the crowd are seen celebrating a brief sense of freedom, the breakdown of law. The mob enjoy torturing a captured boyar, accused of being

Boris' 'henchman', but they will also turn on the foreigner. Two Catholic priests are seized and will be hanged, but Dmitri on arrival is not concerned with saving them.

He seems to have won the war, but his victory will be brief and there will be other pretenders. In scenes of confusion, the fool is a symbol of the people's suffering, having predicted starvation and *blood-soaked darkness*. The opera ends with a solitary dirge.

This second version and its sub-plot which broadens the political perspective remain favoured in modern productions. The main issue in *Boris* was crime and retribution, Mussorgsky presenting a psychological study of a ruler in decline. Not only Boris is guilty; personal ambitions of small-minded individuals cause whole nations to suffer.

The work as intended appealed to revolutionary elements, and its performance was discouraged by the regime. Its widespread recognition as Russia's greatest opera came in the 20th century. Mussorgsky later wrote his own script based upon history for a second epic, *Khovanshchina,* a term which refers to one boyar leading a plot against the Tsar. It presents the main characters treated evenly in musical terms, with a wide-ranging view of a specially violent phase in Russia.

In the opera, a hidden hand applies rough justice. Implicitly the force for good is Tsar Peter II, the Great, not seen in the opera, but managing a successful coup. More than a century after Boris lived, Peter was the all-powerful Westerniser who dragged Russia out of its ignorant, dark ages condition. In *Khovanshchina* he is opposed by disparate forces: the fanatical Old Believers and the para-military thugs, the Streltzy. These were the arm of the brutish Prince Kovansky, and the two factions were tactical allies in resistance to modernisation. The Old Believers are inclined to see any slight divergence from their thinking or behaviour as the work of the Devil, Beelzebub, and imagine themselves as future martyrs in an act of collective self-immolation by fire.

There is a heroine, Marfa, despite sharing their dogmas. She is troubled by her 'sinful' affair with Prince Kovansky's spoilt, cowardly son, Andrei, but catches him out as he is threatening to rape a Lutheran girl whose lover and family he has disposed of. The Tsar's first minister is Prince Golitsin. A temporiser, he is seen consulting a fortune-teller who reveals that he will soon be banished. When he tries to warn his ally Kovansky of the Tsar's intentions, the messenger is flogged. In Act III, in what will be his most eventful day, Kovansky relaxes to music, then his harem of Persian women severely wrapped in veils languorously dance for him. This has an erotic delicacy, but it is to be his final pleasure; he is murdered after a sudden intrusion by the Tsar's assassin.

Marfa tries to save her lover, who is implicated in his father's conspiracy. She now has a death wish, hoping he will join her in the mass religious suicide, which is becoming more likely as the Tsar is set upon destroying all opposition. The Streltsy are a drunken, pillaging gang whom only their wives and other women will stand up to. They are surprised but submissive when to brusque, secular fanfares the Tsar's men take to the streets and round them up. The opera ends with the Old Believers setting fires to their buildings and jumping into the conflagration.

Despite uncertainties about Mussorgsky's final intentions, both operas are well integrated. They were well in advance of their time, anticipating the realistic styles adopted in the 20th century. In 1874, many thought *Boris* 'unoperatic' and technically faulty and his friend Rimsky-Korsakov's more refined version is now most performed.

Kovanshchina's original material was not orchestrated or satisfactorily performed until 1911 after Diaghilev had commissioned Stravinsky's completion. It stands comparison with *Boris* as a great folk drama. In form, it is closer to traditional opera, such as in the Act I trio and the closing love duet. *Boris'* portrayal of artificial, courtly romance gives way to a more lyrical kind in the person of Marfa who carries the longest singing role in a work without male heroes.

■　■　■

Alexander Borodin was the son of a Caucasian prince which partly explains why *Prince Igor* was his priority. He had studied Caucasian music which has distinctive Georgian, Armenian and other sounds from those cultures lying at the fringe of Eastern Europe and Central Asia. His very small but distinguished musical output was the result of his being a full-time Professor of Chemistry and dying aged 54. Parts of *Prince Igor* had to be prepared by others but the loyalty of fellow nationalists ensured a faithful completion.

Its plot reflects the struggles between Russian and Tatar armies throughout the 12th century when Asian tribes were encroaching in the regions north of the Black Sea. The treatment of the warring parties is fairly even-handed, dramatically and musically. The defeat and humiliation of the Russian army is explicit in Act III, so that in many Soviet productions some of this was cut. The score had more genuinely exotic music than had ever been heard in any opera at the time of Borodin's death in 1887.

In a military expedition against the Tartars, Igor is captured but treated hospitably, as was the medieval way with valuable hostages whilst the common prisoners were tortured. Igor's Polovtsian (Tatar) captor, Konchak, is an ambivalent character, courteous, arbitrary and barbarous in turn. He is confident following the celebration on stage of a meeting of two Tatar armies. A skilled diplomat, this merits an aria complex, subtle and of rare appeal. He is prepared to permit an 'escape' if Igor agrees to a future alliance. The offer is proudly rejected.

Konchak must have instructed his daughter to win the affections of Igor's son, Vladimir. The plan works, so that he remains part voluntarily, hostage-like. Confused, he is rushed into marrying and effectively joins the enemy. As a sub-plot, the episode is a relaxing diversion, its sensuous music balancing the military spirit of much of the rest. How far is his supposed lover emotionally involved or just acting on orders? With a contralto voice, her song is ravishing. He is no medieval warrior but a 19th century Romantic, already calling her his wife during their love duet. She even offers to flee with him, and on offering to be his slave for life, sings in her father's diplomatic language. Vacillating, later he intends to leave without her; she calls the alarm and only Igor escapes.

There are oafish characters prominent in the second sub-plot. The fears for the home capital are not of much concern to Prince Galitzky who has been unwisely left in charge. A habitual rapist, he shows off by terrifying a girl, stripping her in public. This sinister episode sinks into obscenity with the connivance of the crowd, and two appalling deserters from Igor's army who are Galitzky's hirelings. They also fancy themselves as entertainers with the crudest rendering of fine old songs. The townswomen seek the help of Igor's wife who intercedes and frees the girl after threatening Galitzky, her brother, with disgrace when Igor returns. She has a humane, dignified role, and the women overall are very sympathetically treated. Not so the men.

In captivity, Igor sings tenderly of his wife, leading to sombre reflection on his situation to the noble theme-song of the opera:

The enemy holds the Rus within his claws, and for this the Rus blames me. Give me freedom that I may redeem my disgrace!

It is with the help of a defector, a Christian Tatar, that Igor does finally escape. His surprising return home will be celebrated by the townsfolk as if a victory. That is the final ironic note; the enemy are on the march and the town is part destroyed.

The overture had to be written from memory by Glazunov who heard the piano version only once. It takes nothing from this achievement that the overture has several exceptionally striking songs. That includes heroic themes of both embattled sides, an affecting one associated with Igor's marriage, and one with the lovers' duet. The contrasting music of two folk cultures is heard in the choruses at both capitals. The exciting Polovtsian choral and dance sequences are performed at court to delight the captive Prince. They have also impressed the world of ballet, unfamiliar rhythms and exotic melodies with a unique appeal within the repertoire.

Well known as ballet for the past century, *Polovtsian Dances* in their own right, they have added to the opera's international prestige. Along with the overture's popularity they have given it an ennobling image especially to those who have not experienced the drama. This is for the most part a grim, vivid chronicle, to be set alongside the two Mussorgsky works as landmarks in Russian culture.

■　■　■

Rimsky-Korsakov's fourteenth opera might have been his last but for the shattering events of 1905 and Russia's humiliation in the disastrous war against Japan. It was his expressed sympathy for the unsuccessful uprising against the Tsarist regime that caused his dismissal from the St Petersburg Conservatoire. This led to his composing *The Golden Cockerel*, his only direct political satire, and unlike any other opera in the existing international repertoire.

Dodon, King of an unspecified country, hopes at minimal effort to achieve military glory. This idea often seduces tyrants, but the resemblance of his behaviour to the realities of Tsarist Russia in 1905 was so clear that a ban was placed on the opera completed two years later. The composer had not seen it by his death in 1908.

Dodon's sons know even less about military strategy than his C.- in -C., General Polkan, and their argument is interrupted by the appearance of a mysterious Astronomer, a eunuch with a curious vocal range. He offers as tribute a Golden Cockerel who will crow whenever danger threatens the King. Could it in war become his secret weapon? He wants to try it out before paying the Astronomer who seems annoyed as he suddenly disappears. Dodon's taste for adventure has long since gone, but is briefly revived by a dream of meeting a beautiful princess, as he thinks from the neighbouring country, so he sends his unwilling sons off to occupy it.

Weeks pass before the Cockerel crows again; the war is going badly. Dodon is obliged to look for his sons, coming across them in a mountain pass but they are dead. He and the General sing a Slavonic lament. The enemy are hidden by the mists, but then the vision of a tent which proves to be indestructible. Out comes the beauty of his dream claiming to be the Queen of Shemakhan, a pagan of strange demeanour but radiant presence. Offering a *Hymn to the Sun*, she sings of her beauty and desire to find a real man, one who will dominate her. Dancing in seductive manner, she begs Dodon to join in, which he does; but in one of his age this is not short of grotesque. Still she professes to admire his kingship, and he is entranced. She is furious when General Polkan starts asking questions, and Dodon offers to execute him if she agrees to become his Queen. As when meeting the Astrologer, he can only accept events at their face value.

The people are told of his foreign 'victory' and how he rescued a Queen from a dragon. Assembled for his homecoming, the crowd are thrilled by the sight of two splendid corteges with the Queen and King in a golden chariot. It is halted by the Astrologer making a most untimely entry. This causes general alarm for their royal couple, which troubles him not; he is to be the spectre at the feast. Only the Queen seems undisturbed. He claims his reward, and Dodon is ungrateful, then shocked when the Astrologer will accept nothing less than the Queen. Dodon strikes him down with his sceptre, and for the moment she remains impassive. It is when he presumes to ask for a kiss that she tells him to clear off and take his court with him. A storm erupts, the Cockerel gives his final screech and springing onto the chariot, pecks the King who falls dead. In the darkness, the Queen laughs mockingly, then she and Cockerel are no more.

There is a short rising phrase suggesting a tale of mystery, a soothing rhythm merging often into the score. This is given dramatic impact by several recurring motifs: the Cockerel on muted trumpet, the Queen with a leisurely arabesque, the Astrologer accompanied by the magic of harps and glockenspiel. Act II builds up around the *Hymn to the Sun,* an exotic scenario with rich ballet sequences by the Queen and her slaves. Comparable in originality with *Shererazade* , this has since made for one of Rimsky-Korsakov's finest symphonic suites, with the outlandish themes for Astrologer and Cockerel preceding the Queen's music and the brilliant processional march. In that form, the suite is best known outside Russia; but the opera is of most significance, a satire of depth and foresight.

The reigning Tsar Nicholas II once said he welcomed war because it would draw him closer to his people. Having survived the 1905 debacle, his delusion reached its dramatic end in 1917 when he kept a million or two of those people company in death. Meanwhile, the Tsarina valued her Cockerel in the shape of the notorious Rasputin. Did the Astrologer represent the people and King Dodon the Tsar's inability to grasp realities? Any uncertainties should be answered in the epilogue when the Astrologer obligingly tells the audience that only he and the Queen were mortal, all the rest part of a fairy story.

22　*The Romantic Piano Concerto*

The term concerto suggests a contest between instruments, originally with what we would now call a very small orchestra at first grouped into two parts, the 18th century's concerto grosso. Except for organs, instruments at that time had not normally been heard solo unless a combination was not available. Even the harpsichord had just an accompanying role at first, though concertos were to be written for it. A plucked instrument, it was being replaced from about 1770 by the piano which had developed from it and had a more expressive range. This was operated by hammers and the name came from use of the terms *piano* and *forte* meaning soft and loud.

Mozart was the first to give the earlier pianoforte front-rank status well ahead of the harpsichord with sonatas and as many as 27 piano concertos, attaining perfect balance and establishing the Classical pattern. The solo instrument was poised against the orchestra, but there was a kind of partnership sharing themes, and following the symphonic plan, one slow movement between two, the first often brisk (*allegro*), the last quick (*presto*). The first movement was longest and in sonata form, the last a rondo (two themes 'coming round'). Beethoven's early ones were similar in structure and his 4th has in the slow movement an intriguing dialogue between piano and orchestra. This was a novel use of instrumental recitative which be important in the following generation of Romantic composers.

The early upright pianos had acoustics loud enough to make a big impact in a drawing room and to become an ideal solo instrument. The grand piano such as was developed in Britain giving much more variety of tone was a majestic instrument whose appearance brought in the age of virtuoso performers. In the early 1800s the pianoforte was to have a big effect upon art music and on the leisure of cultured society.

The piano was not superior to other instruments such as the violin for the concerto form, but its two major advantages have given it a unique appeal over 200 years. It was not part of the orchestra, so its tone was more distinct, making composing easier; and the sound contrast with the orchestra could be more dramatic. The early Romantics tended to follow the Mozart-Beethoven pattern though restricting themselves to not more than two piano concertos each: Mendelssohn, Chopin, Schumann and others, lyrical works not longer than 30 minutes with one solo passage (cadenza) to show off the pianist's virtuosity, often written by him/herself. The orchestra was generally relegated to a supporting role, and in Chopin's case quite ineffectual.

By 1856, Johannes Brahms conceived of the piano concerto on a grander scale: his first had an opening of greater emotional intensity than any concerto up to that time, and his second was regarded by many critics as a four movement symphony with a piano *obbligato* (accompanying). He did not argue the point, and dispensed with the cadenza, whilst for some minutes the cello takes over with a melody ideally suited to its tone in the luxuriant slow movement. The writing was so powerful that many pianists felt unable to tackle it for fear of damaging wrists.

Where Mendelssohn, Chopin and Schumann tended to the intimate, Franz Liszt's two concertos were extrovert, dramatic. The other instruments were used to far more individual effects than any previous concerto, creating a tonal show-piece. The E minor concerto opens with a commanding 7-note motto which retains its hold in variations through the whole work. This form was unprecedented, to be known as cyclical, the movements sharing certain themes. Liszt had broken the mould, with an exceptional range of contrasting sections in both concertos whilst reducing their length to just over 20 minutes each. Both have always had critics who called them vulgar and exhibitionist, and their popularity has declined as the demand for piano virtuosity fell.

Yet they stand as the prototype of the bravura concerto, and it would only need the right kind of box office film to put either of them once more in the front rank of popularity. Inimitable, they influenced Massenet, Grieg and Arthur Bliss among many others, each composing impressive single concertos. Bliss' was dedicated to the people of the U.S.A., confident and vigorous. In contrast, the five concertos of Camille

Saint-Saens are nearer in spirit to Bach than Liszt and have a classical elegance.

In Britain at least, the piano concerto was almost raised or lowered to the status of a 'popular' genre, and around the mid-20th century; this happened through the influence of the British film industry. It started with someone deciding that piano and orchestra could be used highly emotively as background music. Tchaikovsky was an obvious model, but the works could be specially composed, short but right for the limited purpose. For a war-time love story, the *Warsaw Concerto* was concocted and no-one was heard to comment publicly that it was based largely on salient themes from Sibelius' Second Symphony, with a Rakhmaninov veneer as required for the film.

There was a rush of films with stories about aspiring pianists – and death; but the summit was reached with one of Britain's greatest films, *Brief Encounter,* the emotional intensity of the story increased by the 'stiff upper lip' showed by two of the English breed to a doomed romance, with a railway station as the third 'character'. A most sensitive integration of parts of Rakhmaninov's Second Piano Concerto into the action was inspired like no other background music, the film's impact strong after the passing of half a century.

This concerto followed in a tradition looking back to Liszt and Chopin,: broad, lyrical melodies, but with a strong Russian appeal in its rhythms, commanding and nostalgic in turns. It was destined to achieve exceptional world popularity, and his next, the Third, was like a twin, though complex and more powerful. It has arguably the most thrilling cadenza of all concertos. His Fourth, relatively late on, was briefer and more reflective.

As near as any to Rakhmaninov is Selim Palmgren's Second Piano Concerto, *The River,* with an added Finnish strain, and he composed four others, probably his most durable works. Ravel composed two concertos in one year, not giving them numbers, as if representing the masculine and feminine sides of his musical personality. For a pianist who lost an arm in the war he prepared a part which in range and virtuosity concealed that it was for left-hand. The orchestral parts were lowered in pitch to give balance, with the sombre inclusion of a double bassoon, but building up to two fierce climaxes, with a storming march.

The other concerto is more like a *divertissement*: the three movements look in turn to his homeland and Basque melody, the 18th century and a heavy syncopation close to jazz.

In pre-revolutionary Russia, Prokofief's spiky technique offended his teachers as 'anti-Romantic', and his First Concerto was in one very assertive movement. Later some critics in the U.S.A. called him the Bolshevik pianist with steel fingers, though the popular Third was a seductive backward glance at Romanticism. His Fourth, obligingly written for the left hand like Ravel's, was not well received by the pianist. Others whose technique tended to the percussive included Stravinsky and much more surprisingly, Vaughan Williams. His was so complex that he prepared an alternative version for four hands.

In the 20th century there were several important Hungarian concertos, the three by Bela Bartok mixing the Romantic with what he called his barbaric style. The two by Erno Dohnanyi were on the largest scale and Brahmsian, but he is best known for his *Variations on a Nursery Tune,* the definitive tribute to the great concertos for piano. The styles of Mozart, Beethoven, Liszt, Chopin, Brahms and others are brilliantly parodied, the humour extending to the postures of virtuosi and the errors of juvenile aspirants. As a concert entertainment it is unique.

23 *G&S: Dynastic Problems*

William S. Gilbert has probably added as many phrases to English usage as any secular writer except Shakespeare, and he was master of the paradox. This was apparent in all his Sullivan collaborations where the plots were enlivened by characters with eccentric ways of thinking, but who are not altogether fools. The Gilbertian wit was directed at a parallel world of his own making. Specially familiar to the public of the time were his gentlemanly pirates, uninspired poets, flirtatious judges and an admiral who had never been to sea.

He sympathised with the idea of universities for women, which had been an innovation in the England of the 1880s and was promoted in Tennyson's poem, *The Princess.* So female emancipation escaped ridicule by Gilbert; but he was never short of an alternative. His sub-plot fits into place admirably on the absurdities of royal protocol, which had so often provoked crises and wars throughout Europe's troubled history. Gilbert's own comic 'per-version' appeared 14 years before he revised it for Sullivan to add music in 1884 with its title changed to *Princes Ida*, performed at the newly built Savoy theatre.

The arbitrary King Hildebrand intends that Ida fulfil her pledge, made 20 years previously at the age of one, to marry his son. His enforcement threats are celebrated by his courtiers in a thrusting *rataplan.* So when her father, King Gama, arrives with retinue but without her; so the royal visitors are courteously taken hostage.

King Gama is an irascible old buffer, a caricature of petty, arbitrary rule; as such, he is bored when things go right. He prides himself on his repartee, and on his home ground enjoys practising entrapment. He entices visitors to indiscretions before chastising them. This creates problems when tried out in a foreign court. His three sons, light of brain but heavily armoured, clatter around to a plodding military refrain. Equally insensitive to danger, they follow him cheerfully into the dungeon. In a display of royal logic, Hildebrand offers Princess Ida a choice: submit or be guilty of triple fratricide.

The most famous ballet internationally up to the 1880s had been *Giselle*, the suppliant and tragic hero being a Hilarion, hence Gilbert giving such a rare name to King Hildebrand's heir. But in contrast, this Hilarion is a man of action, promptly deciding to visit Ida at her college, Castle Adamant. He takes the ultimate risk with two friends, all disguised as women. In this bastion of feminism, most girls have no awarenesss of masculinity, and even playing with chessmen can lead to expulsion. Dancing a minuet is however considered a harmless diversion for ladies. That and certain choruses at Castle Ada-mant have an archaic flavour, such as the classroom anthem, *Merrily ring the luncheon bell.*

The intruders steal female clothing and employ the decep-tion long enough to find those girls most susceptible to male charms. Hilarion's friend has a sister, Lady Psyche, whom they most easily bring on side. Yet as Professor of Humanities, she has been pushing a strong feminist line, a per-version of the most fashionable evolutionary theories:

> *He bought white ties, and he bought dress suits, he crammed his feet into bright tight boots;. and to start in life on a brand-new plan, he christened himself Darwinian Man — But it would not do, the scheme fell through— For the maiden fair, whom the monkey craved, was a radiant being with a brain far-seeing — While Darwinian Man, though well-behaved, at best is only a monkey shaved.*

The idealistic heart of the story lights up the first half of Act II, with a dreamy female chorus which brings out the best in Sullivan, and Ida's invocation of the Goddess of Wisdom. Later, she leads a quartet, *The world is but a broken toy,* and in final disillusionment, *I built upon a rock.* Some admiring critics hoped that the G&S partnership would write complete operas in such lyrical vein, which they never did.

The intruders enjoy a reckless gallop of a quintet with those compliant girls, but the fun is stopped short; this is the moment for all to hold their breaths. In G&S plots, it is always the occasion to introduce a new face. It will never be a friendly one, but always formidable, a contralto powerful of voice and per-sonality. In this case, it is Lady Blanche, the manipulative Vice-Principal. She knows what a baritone sounds like, exposes the deception, then in complete command, closes it up again.

In order to subvert Ida's iron rule, she will even connive with men.

Ida is flattered by the report she is given of Hilarion's love for her, until one of his colleagues gets drunk and sings of the joys of kissing. In shock, she falls into the moat, emerging to protect her honour and chastity in armed conflict. The remainder of Act II and the start of Act III are a parody of 'heroic' opera.[29]

The women's fear of conflict is expressed in a poignant chorus, in turn defiant and imploring, a Gilbertian device. Tennyson resolves this issue in a concluding tournament, and here a combat between Hilarion's trio and Ida's brothers precedes the finale. In the florid manner of a G.F.Handel opera, they protest at the ineffectiveness of their heavy armour.

Of the 13 extant G&S operas, this was Gilbert's only one in blank verse, and the likely explanation that *Princess Ida* is only the tenth most performed. That is no reflection on its quality, and the lyrical music associated with the women's college was never excelled by Sullivan. He had welcomed this opportunity to move away from farce towards more serious opera.

Plots centred around a foundling were the most clichéd in all Victorian literature and Gilbert often reduced them to an absurdity. Beyond that, he rarely needed to repeat himself, though an infant betrothal would also feature humorously in a later work, *The Gondoliers*. There, the lecherous villain is Spain's Grand Inquisitor who had spirited away to Venice for reasons of state the child heir to the throne of Barataria. He has grown up incognito as a gondolier but no-one knows which of two he is. The Duke of Plaza Toro is the main figure of ridicule, famous for leading his regiment from behind except when retreating. He is the father of the yearling fiancée whose immediate sweetheart will have to be disposed of. Fortunately, as the audience should guess, he will be identified as the royal foundling. This will occur in a final recognition scene, another operatic cliché turned to fun. The two other 'candidates' are relieved to be discounted.

Gilbert had translated Offenbach operettas, one of whose less satirical works, *The Bridge of Sighs*, had been seen in London in 1872. With *The Gondoliers*, Gilbert also had a Venetian setting for a play superior to the one Offenbach used. It inspired some of Sullivan's most colourful and exuberant dance rhythms. Gilbert's wit was undiminished but notably less subversive than

in his early comic operas. That would not have displeased
Sullivan who was by nature an establishment man. He was at his
best concentrating on parody; *The Gondoliers* starts with burlesque on Italian opera, a lengthy *scena* in simple Italian without
spoken dialogue.

Sullivan's facility for composing a rollicking tune to match
the rhythmic demands of Gilbert's lyrics was exceptional:

In enterprise of martial kind, when there was any fighting,
He led his regiment from behind, he found it less exciting.
But when away his regiment ran, his place was at the fore-O,
That celebrated, cultivated, underrated nobleman,
The Duke of Plaza-Toro.

Take a pair of sparkling Eyes enjoyed exceptional popularity, an
English take on a Latin lover's serenade. Compliments were
also paid to Offenbach's style at times in the score, which
seemed to be blessed with Italy's sun. It was the last of their
most successful collaborations, though Sullivan's muse did not
fail him until ill health brought his death in 1900.

24 *Tchaikovsky as Melodist*

Tchaikovsky was a man of obsessions, of exaltation and despair, one who could bring full pathos to the story of *Romeo and Juliet* in his orchestral fantasy, More challenging was a description of the poet Dante's visit to the second circle of Hell where the Italian lovers, Paolo and Francesca, are suffering eternal punishment. Tchaikovsky had graphically described two of literature's greatest love affairs, placing him among masters of the symphonic poem.

Empathy with other characters of literature and history led to his composing large-scale operas, whilst his recurrent emotional complexities also found expression in symphonies, at least four of which deserve their place in the international concert repertoire. In the world of diversion and fantasy, his unique gifts enabled him to achieve the most loved of all ballet music.

Alongside *Romeo and Juliet,* his First Piano Concerto is a front-line popular classic, a virtuoso work in the bravura manner of Liszt. It opens with a tremendous sweep, yet so rich was Tchaikovsky's store of melodies that this introduction is not heard again. The rest of the work also succeeds within itself, but his remaining ones for piano and orchestra never repeated such success, partly because he was inclined to neglect the piano parts.

His melodic gifts extended to the more intimate world of art song and chamber music. From his *Album for Youth, Sweet Dreams* and *June* from *The Seasons* have special warmth and intimacy. What is popularly known as the *Andante cantabile* was probably the most famous movement to be from any string quartet, except one of Haydn's which became the German anthem. It was known to have reduced Leo Tolstoy to tears, in part because its melody came from a folk song.

Peter Tchaikovsky (1840–93) was an exceptionally fine melodist, and with a debt to Russian folk music. His fellow composers who were active in promoting Russian this resented his standing apart. In total contrast to them, he was extremely subjective, and his success with cosmopolitan (Western) forms was remarkable. Loving his country's music, he still saw himself as an eclectic, whilst we foreigners like the Russian strain within him. One cannot be certain how far a facility for absorbing the native idiom has influenced the shape of his own melodies.

The Russian style was important for his more extrovert works such as his first four symphonies and most spectacularly in the *1812 Overture,* where a Serbian tune is used also to promote Slav cultural solidarity. The First Symphony includes what sounds like the forthright, archetypal Russian folk song. The Second Symphony is even more linked with melodies, Ukrainian, hence its becoming known as the *Little Russian. The Silver Birch Tree,* the most famous of traditional Russian songs, takes command in the finale of the Fourth Symphony, causing alarm to some critics then about the intrusion of 'peasant life'. Far more listeners are now taken by the exciting crescendos of first and last movements.

Tchaikovsky put into words its programme for the benefit of his long-standing patron, Madame von Meck. The melodies' diversity, often compelling or frenetic, imply the appeal of escaping from oneself by merging into human society. Curiously explicit are two inclusions from Bizet's *Carmen,* a work which impressed Tchaikovsky greatly. One relates to the moment when Carmen reads in the cards her destiny. For him, fate is the unwanted pressures on humans. In his Fifth Symphony, it has a commanding motif reappearing to haunt the seemingly euphoric moments. Yet with so many fine melodies in one work, the overall effect is more likely to be elation. Its slow movement provided one of the earliest candidates for commercialisation when its international copyright came to an end in 1943.

It is only in the equally compelling Sixth, the *Pathetic Symphony,* that the pessimistic message hits head on. This was once called a musical suicide note, with a desolate bassoon theme which gives way to one which led to the work's unofficial title given later by Tchaikovsky's brother. The two middle movements are exceptionally uplifting: his finest march and one expressing the intoxication of love, in rare 5/4 time. As a symphony, the whole shape of the work is original, the emotional weight passing to the despairing finale of exceptional length. Mahler and some others of the younger generation would have been impressed by its innovative structure.

His earlier operas included *Mazeppa*, a Cossack rebel who fought against the Tsar's forces at Pultava in 1721 and with his Swedish allies was defeated. The plot centres around Mazeppa's putting into prison his lover's father, a presumed enemy, and killing him. The daughter becomes the central tragic figure, though losing some sympathy by siding twice with Mazeppa, much older than her, in his dispute with her condemned father. The plots's grim realism and violence is lightened by music in the folk style and relief comes with choral strains of traditional Church music. That applies also to the *Oprichniki*, a tale of Tsar Ivan IV's fearsome bodyguard.

Tchaikovsky was drawn to English writers, not for opera, but specially Shakespeare for orchestral works. His *Tempest* has a gentle love theme for the reclusive Miranda. Unlike that of several others', his incidental music for *Hamlet* is diverting and humorous in parts. Perhaps he thought the play gloomy enough.

It was to Russia's most respected writer, Pushkin, that he turned for more personal themes in operas and what we would term anti-heroes. *Eugene Onegin* had two lovers rejected in turn by each other over a period of years. The protagonist was also to suffer remorse for killing his best friend. This was in a duel provoked by jealousy after his flirting at a ball with the fiancée of the other. Two episodes have earned special praise for the cohesion of music and plot: Tatiana's letter song in which a girl confesses her ill-fated love, and the ball scene where the fatal quarrel erupts.

In *The Queen of Spades*, two die in an unfulfilled love affair, he for using a naïve girl to further gambling ambitions, she for infatuation with a dangerously unstable man. Such obsessions ensure the prominence of two powerful motifs, but the harsher tones are relieved in two directions. Tchaikovsky took the opportunity to compose a pastiche ballet in the spirit of Mozart and the music of the late 18th century when the action of the story occurs. The two operas also contain exquisite duets that sound like folk songs; refined young ladies enjoying forbidden fruit, though in one instance they are caught and rebuked for 'dancing like Russian peasants'. These girls would have been expected to speak French as their first language and dance with like decorum.

Among concert pieces deservedly favoured for their melodies are the euphoric *Serenade for Strings*, the *Italian Caprice* with its Neapolitan borrowings, the *Rococo Variations* inspired by the style of Mozart; and the Violin Concerto which is one of a handful in the virtuoso Romantic style most popular in the West.

For the world of fantasy Tchaikovsky could conjure up exquisite strains and instrumentation. Just as entrancing as much better known examples is the depicting of the Alpine fairy appearing in a waterfall in his *Manfred Symphony*, based on Byron's poem. Tchaikovsky felt an empathy with its hero wandering remorsefully in the mountains. The motto theme expressing his isolation from society is heard in each of the four movements of this largest of his symphonic works. It also contains his finest scherzo, of which there are none in his three final numbered symphonies. The work's conception was influenced by Berlioz' *Harold in Italy*, and is the most important of his orchestral works with a literary programme.

His three large ballets have set the highest standards and not been surpassed imaginatively. The *Sleeping Beauty* and *Swan Lake* were conceived on a symphonic scale, their symbolism representing permanent human values which called for grandiose music. Tchaikovsky had severe doubts about setting the third ballet, *Nutcracker*, because of its eccentric theme. In the event, its escapism offered him an atmosphere remote from his personal obsessions and he was inspired to write an idiosyncratic score. Act II is presented as a dream, starting with the child-like *Snowflakes* chorus. The colourful parade of foreign dances in Delibes' *Coppelia* was the model for the sequence which follows. A Georgian cradle song is transformed into an Arab dance, a Chinese effect comes from the combining of flute and bassoon, and fierce Russian rhythms cross with serene, authentically French melodies. A rare keyboard instrument, the celeste, was specially imported from France, so that he could be the first Russian to compose for it. The outcome was a world famous sound, creating an aura for the Act's mistress of ceremonies known as the Sugar Plum Fairy.

Tchaikovsky's tendency to use falling melodic lines is most prominent in the *pas de deux* where the theme is a scale descending from keynote to keynote, repeated several times; the gratifying effect comes from it being given a 'tail'. As for the concluding melodies, no more euphoric spirit ever justified such an absurd tale.

Stravinsky had the greatest respect for Tchaikovsky's achievements, particularly in such areas as melody where his own skills were very limited. It was in tribute to Tchaikovsky's *Sleeping Beauty* that Stravinsky composed a pastiche, *The Fairy's Kiss*. This did not inhibit him from finding ingenious ways of transforming the songs he selected to suit a ballet touched with a different kind of humour from what Tchaikovsky ever addressed. Its moral is that, like a kiss from the gods, humans should avoid one from a fairy.

25 *The Lesser-Known Sousa*

English football matches in the 21st century are often introduced by undistinguished music showered from P.A. systems onto largely indifferent crowds. We'd be right to envy the Americans with their endless supply of John P. Sousa marches and swaggering drum majorettes at big sporting occasions!

Yet as with the Waltz King, Johann Strauss II, there is one rare aspect of the March King's entertainment which is taken for granted. A typical Sousa march includes an introductory phrase and no fewer than four strains, rising to a climax on the final one, then finish. Strauss' concert waltzes tend to be even longer. Though both composers borrowed some material from others – by way of a compliment – the number of tunes each of them carried in his head could be counted in thousands.

In 1876, whilst touring the U.S.A., Jacques Offenbach told the young Sousa (1854–1932) his melodies were so good that he should write operettas. His commitment to a life as the most famous of bandmasters makes it the more remarkable that over the following 30 years, he wrote 15, thanks partly to his experience in staging those of others. This would add perhaps 200 melodies to the much larger number he wrote for other purposes.

Sousa's strength was the quick march, with exciting melodic leaps. Some material could be adapted to the varying rhythmic demands of operetta, but would require highly trained voices, which in the long run has restricted amateur performances. In contrast, Arthur Sullivan planned melodies that were 'easier' for the singers so that his comic operas have been attempted by countless English-speaking schools for well over a century, often with unfortunate results.

Sousa arranged music of many composers, from the popular and religious to Bach and Wagner, and especially for theatre, performances of Offenbach and Sullivan. His melodic style for those times was very different from both, but extremely catchy and with lively instrumental decoration, so apparent in his most familiar marches. Typical is the brilliant piccolo solo in *The Stars and Stripes forever.*

London's unofficial home of visiting operetta and dance has long been the Sadlers Wells Theatre. Some years ago, an entertainment of traditional musicals included Paris, Vienna and London; but the surprise and success of the evening was the singing for a fizzing Act I of Sousa's *El Capitan,* with jubilant choruses, and a conclusion which later had another existence as the popular march. This performance was the more welcome because its staging in a previous tour of England had been before anyone could remember.

In 1995, the BBC Radio 3's composers of the week once included Sousa and did not concentrate on the well-known marches, giving place for his overtures and songs, chosen for their panache and warm melodies. He was bracketed with Scot Joplin, whose music achieved immense popularity in Britain, thanks to piano transcriptions made six decades after his death. Sousa's choice comment on jazz, that it makes us want to bite our grandmothers, could surely not prevent him enjoying, say, *Marching Onwards* from Joplin's operetta, *Tremonisha.* One wonders what he would have said about the charming syncopation of the cakewalk, *Aunt Dinah has blowed de horn* from the same work.

With hindsight, the two composers stand not as far apart as once seemed. They enjoyed their youths in the same decades, as the U.S.A. was still looking to Europe for musical leadership, and when they learnt the technical skills of a great tradition. Yet each in his way would set out to progress musically in new directions, reflecting major features of America's life and personality.

For a century operetta was a cult which generated countless popular songs and dances. Though at least a hundred might be first class, barely one quarter feature in modern opera repertoires. This is because they are as demanding of quality and mostly of resources as operas. It is doubtful if any of Sousa's would make the 'top twenty', but even that cannot be proved. this year, except perhaps in some corner of the U.S.A. Even so, excerpts suggest he must have had many 'hits'. Not surprisingly, he could sweep audiences along, and knew much about stagecraft.

At least one of his operettas gained from remarkable innovations: a scene in a factory, with sand-paper added to the percussion. Then another at the 1898 Spanish-American war, the San Juan battle illustrated with the help of an actual cinema projector. In an admirably democratic spirit, the work was called after its heroes, *The Glass Blowers*. Enthusiastic reference is made to them by the ladies in an up-beat chorus, whilst the men add whistles, in unison of course. Unfortunately, that title kept the audiences away, so it was changed to *The American Maid*, and success followed.

Its patriotic fervour is matched by rhythmic invention, such as an early suggestion of a tango, and there is a cakewalk, *Cleopatra's a Strawberry Blonde*. Not, it had to be understood, that such a wayward pace was for bandmaster Sousa's professional soldiers, but it was relaxed and euphoric, taking him as near to Joplin and ragtime as his style permitted. One march recalls the Vienna of Franz von Suppé. This South German melodic affinity may be related to Sousa having a Bavarian mother; and like the best operetta composers, he was skilled in adapting the most attractive foreign rhythms, notably Latin American. His Portuguese name came from his father's family.

The hero of *The Freelance* advances from mercenary to king of a central European state, calling for an original kind of Balkan dance. This arrives in a novel variant of 3/4 time, a kind of polka-mazurka with extraordinary percussive effects. It might have intrigued Suppé, who used to offer a fine range of eccentric rhythms. In Sousa's *Irish Dragoon* there is a vigorous dance which sounds quite like the finale of Sullivan's *Ruddigore*. Yet considering how often both of them were given to parody, such similarities are rare.

Sousa had time to distinguish himself as a writer but was not apparently the best of librettists for what was musically one of his finest works, *The Bride Elect*.

He is well represented in the uplifting atmosphere of parlour songs, notably with *The Philosophic Maid* and *Lovely Mary Donnelly* whose enthusiasm for the dance is answered with a jig in the piano accompaniment. At the lighter end of his range, there is a neat patter song which settles for the warning:

You'll miss lots of fun when you're married.

If Sousa would like to be remembered for one song, other than *The Stars and Stripes forever*, perhaps it would be a ravishing violin piece which he was so often called upon to play as an encore, *Nympholyn*. His daughter thought it his finest melody.

26 *The German Strauss*

No composer since Richard Strauss has swept the world and walked through music with the stride of a Colossus, making dwarfs of his contemporaries. He was a sunset, an afterglow of Liszt and Wagner; only great men end époques ... Strauss sharpened the vocal style of opera; he quickened the vision and pulse of the orchestra. He tinctured Romanticism with worldliness; he made brutality and realism vibrant and sensuous and attractive.

These are the words written around 1940 by former *Guardian* critic, Neville Cardus, who had been a youth when Strauss made his major impact on the musical world.

Richard was born in Munich, a Bavarian citizen, and his South German musical culture was nearer to the Austrian than the North German or 'Prussian'. His father, a horn player who performed but detested Wagner's music, was delighted when the talented son seemed to lean towards Brahms, who was in the 1880s assumed to be the living antithesis to Wagner. Strauss wrote a witty *Burlesque* for piano and orchestra which parodied current styles. By 1888, aged 24, his four movement symphonic suite, *From Italy,* was a young man's tribute to another nation's musical style, the kind of gesture which was just becoming fashionable. The only convention it broke was by using, not a folk song but a vivacious popular one, *Funiculi, funicula.*

The turning point for Strauss was not the decision to compose a short symphonic poem; his first one, *Macbeth,* raised no dust, but what followed revealed his rare ability putting live events into music in what he called tone poems. *Don Juan* launched Strauss internationally, a story of unbridled passion, a man seeking the ideal woman, exhilarated but also experiencing its downside and a fatal duel. *Till Eulenspiegel* was on another legend of a popular rogue who thieves and jests his way with a boyish swagger to early death, including the gallows scene. The energy and picturesque detail astonished the musical world, exceptional orchestral virtuosity and tonal contrasts. He had gone far beyond evoking an atmosphere, creating in a few musical strokes a character, drama transferred to the concert hall.

Drawing on literature and exceptional moments in real life, these tone poems would increase in length and complexity, further than some critics approved, through to the year 1912. *Don Quixote* (1898) included an inspired use of instrumental recitative; the hero and the interplay between him and Sancho Panza are characterised on solo cello and viola. Charging the sheep, the windmills and other adventures were expressed more graphically than one had expected to hear. Some listeners even protested that such music was usurping its function.

Strauss' artistic struggles and battles with the critics from the time of his first opera, *Guntram,* were the subject of *Ein Heldenleben* (A Hero's Life), where he paraded some of his key melodies in retrospect. This self-promoting went further when he sketched his family's life in a vast orchestral work, *The Domestic Symphony;* some thought he had wandered along the path of realism to reach the cross-roads of bad taste. Not surprisingly, he failed to interpret the philosophy of *Zarathustra* in one 40-minute work, which however produced glorious passages and one adapted for film music, popularly called *2001, a Space Odyssey.*

No exhibitionist, he needed startling themes to inspire him. Munich had rejected his first opera, *Guntram,* written under the influence of Wagner. He had the chance to strike back at his home town with his second, *Feuersnot,* using a 'vulgar' Flemish legend. Even so, it had a genial message: that all warmth derives from Woman. In revenge for being rejected in love, a young man employs a magician to douse all the fires in the scornful one's home town. It was understood that no flame would reappear until the girl had stood naked in view of all, when fire would emerge from her backside. The citizens permit her to be so used.

Local satirist, Ernst Wollzogen, who would later become active in the Berlin cabaret scene, wrote the libretto. The wizard who took charge symbolised Wagner, and the script was decked out with allusions and witticisms at the expense of the supposedly unenlightened citizens of Munich, to which the action had been moved. No short opera could have been melodically more inspired and the orchestration was so rich that many acclaimed Strauss as Wagner's successor. The Bavarian idiom and local jokes in a complex one-Act opera are the only reasons it is rarely performed today, but its lengthy closing scene recalls many of the work's finest moments.

The Biblical account of Salome is sparse, but fleshed out, she has been given sympathetic treatment, as in Massenet's *Herodiade* of 1882. She had also become a titillating figure in fashionable art around the turn of the century. Another interpretation by Oscar Wilde was perverse, Salome having a Sado-Masochistic obsession for an asexual John the Baptist. The play was banned in England for years, but Wilde's tongue-in-cheek French melodrama offered Strauss rich possibilities. By 1906 the outcome was *Salome,* a work built around a few strong motifs, each representing a character. Salome's is based on a phrase familiar as the four notes of the 'quarter to' of clock chimes, developing into the most voluptuous sounds known until then in an opera house. Her step-father Herod's lust for her and superstitious fear of John reveal an irrational monster set against an anxious, manipulative wife. In this whirlpool of emotions, traditional opera's separate arias are replaced by the voices integrated closely into the score. Its opening notes suggest Salome's sensual appeal just before she takes centre stage for a prolonged symphonic rhapsody ending with her display of necrophilia and being murdered. The hypocrite Herod orders this, as if she were the only 'pervert' in the family.

The main plot is interrupted by three scenes: a political dispute between dignitaries, a row between Herod and his wife, and Salome's exhibitionist dance, properly performed nude, as it is today. The lurid episode when she kisses the lips of John's severed head would in lesser hands be farcical, and the theme was used in several staged burlesques before the actual play was permitted in Britain. The role of Salome required a dramatic soprano able to sing over an exceptional melodic range, with skills in acting and dance, though for that often a substitute is used.

The critical majority admired *Salome* as following on from Wagner's conception of music drama. Strauss' next opera, *Elektra* (1908), has close affinities in form and expression with it, demanding a very large orchestra, not to accompany but to compete with the singers. It is an adaptation of a classic Greek drama moving relentlessly from a revenge motive to ritual murder within a family as vilely obsessed as Salome's. It is a 'generation' feud, however, and there is much tender music between Elektra and her siblings. The theme suited the most radical harmonic and tonal experimenting, a direction which Strauss then decided he wished to pursue no further.

With *Elektra,* he had found a new collaborator, his most important one. Hugo von Hofmannsthal was a fine lyric poet, but an aristocrat, little in common with the unpretentious Strauss outside of their work, except that Strauss had a deep knowledge of German literature. They rarely socialised, but had a mutual respect, and a correspondence of great distinction touching on aesthetics and the music theatre. Strauss' South German culture underlay his melodic style, but with a sensual flavour often added.

Operetta was before 1914 at the height of its drawing powers. Though far removed from his music dramas, he joked he could write one to rival the great Johann. There was much to push him in that direction, a capacity for broad musical humour and parody. This is heard in his music for Molière's *Bourgeois gentilhomme* when he traces the gestures of three masters, of philosophy, dancing and fencing.

Hofmannstal did not see himself writing operetta scripts. A compromise was one of the greatest of all libretti, realistic enough to have been often performed as a straight play, *Der Rosenkavalier.* Strauss wrote:

> *A pompous, fat and elderly suitor favoured by the father has his nose put out of joint by a dashing young love. Could anything be more plain? Your characters are marvellous, drawn very sharply. Do not forget the public should laugh, not smile and grin.*

The young lover is Oktavian, the elderly suitor the uncouth Baron Ochs. The working out of his unsubtle schemes leading to humiliation occupy one third of the opera, knock-about comedy accompanied by music with the light allure of operetta. The remainder is its heart, a love triangle, intensely lyrical. It is sad for the older woman involved, the Marschallin, joyous for the other participants, Oktavian and his new infatuation, Sophie. The music is in turn radiant and bitter-sweet: young love and a lament for lost youth. This young man favoured by two women has always been one of the most distinguished trouser roles in the international repertoire. For at least three of the four main characters, the need for versatile acting is a formidable challenge, and its authentic performers have always been singers of the highest international repute.

The adulterous Marschallin has been the ultimate role for several of the world's greatest sopranos in their maturity, perhaps the finest-sketched and most loved female character in all opera. She is mistress of every social situation and as Strauss understood it, even of her heart. He once said she was of the kind who would soon recover from one man to continue her promiscuous life. This was by way of criticising an Italian soprano who had given a sentimental interpretation.

Strauss' operatic themes had been centred on personal conflicts but this time, on the lighter and deeper aspects of love. With the plot set in 18th century Vienna, his complex orchestration was to be heard alongside moments of elegant purity inspired by Mozart, especially in the closing pages. He borrowed a radiant waltz, *Dynamiden,* from the deceased Josef Strauss, suggesting a feigned glamour within the comical scenes, and adding several of his own in the Viennese style. There is an entrancing duet, within a lengthy recognition of first love, and the concluding trio must be the most impassioned for women's voices in all opera. It was a favourite through the years of a BBC radio programme, *Housewives' Choice.*

The lyricism of the work should have come as no surprise. By the age of 24, Strauss had composed songs of special tenderness, such as *Dedication* and *Serenade. Morgen* is equally tender, with a long introduction on piano, like a miniature tone poem, often heard to even greater effect on solo violin. The German Lied became a major occupation, over 200 in his lifetime. He next conceived *Ariadne on Naxos* (1912) as a sophisticated farce, a unique mixture of music styles calculated to confuse the protagonists, two troupes of entertainers. On stage, a *nouveau riche* patron insists that to save time, an opera and a farce should be performed simultaneously, impromptu, and regardless of the performers' feelings or adaptabilities. In it, classical singers struggle against a background of music hall clowns, Greek myth alongside German cabaret. The rich contrast of styles, especially clear-cut, singable melodies and almost non-stop humour have ensured its retaining a unique place in the international repertoire.

It was followed by the collaborators' most thorough-going epic, *The Woman without a Shadow* (1919). Here Hofmannsthal used characters representing human types. It was to be in scale and complexity, some would say in obscurity, quasi-Wagnerian. The vast musical resources of *Elektra* were to be used for the theme of pure love, not *Tristanesque* passion, the conflict over two lengthy Acts resolved in the exultant third. The demands on the finest of singers and the difficulties of staging such a symbolic work explain why it is less performed than the previous four operas.

Strauss' sympathy was turning away from grand opera, and he intended to relax, composing a farce in the spirit of Offenbach's version of the Helen of Troy legend. Hofmannsthal subverted the plan, giving him an eccentric libretto lacking humour, but demanding very passionate music. Some felt that *The Egyptian Helen* fell between two stools so that the powerful music score has not been fully appreciated. Yet it is some distance in feeling from *The Woman without a Shadow*, whereas the final Hofmannsthal collaboration, *Arabella*, is a love intrigue in the style of *Rosenkavalier*. *Arabella* has probably suffered by comparison and the text was incomplete at Hofmannsthal's untimely death in 1929. That greatly distressed Strauss, who had regarded their work together as developing a friendship.

Arabella is an entertainment about the petty aristocracy and their Yugoslav guests, with a splendid ball scene and a miniature Viennese carnival. Seizing the moment, by pretending to be Arabella, in the dark her sister gets a man into bed, and retains his affections afterwards; this leads to a comic finale of parental embarrassment. There are two duets based on beautiful Yugoslav folk songs, one for the sisters.

Strauss was always inspired to write superbly for the female voice, nor had he completed what he termed his gallery of women heroines. Social comedy was congenial to him, so he turned next to Austrian Stefan Zweig for an adaptation of Ben Johnson's *Silent Woman* (1934), its farce and wit giving scope for musical tricks in a modern Harlequinade.

From 1933, the Nazis were keen to profit from the support of Germany's leading composer, but within a year, Strauss had angered the regime because he refused to renounce his association with Zweig and other Jews. When he wrote to him in Austria criticising Nazi racial policies, the Gestapo intercepted the letter, but he was too famous internationally for them to do more than boycott his work. After that, he had to remain politically cautious for the sake of his half-Jewish grandchild. Known to be materialistic, he remained suspect for having collaborated with the Nazis, and genius apart, he was not among the most likeable of men. Nor was his wife Pauline widely loved. She had a reputation for exceptional rudeness, but he welcomed her music criticisms and their marriage was almost ideal, lasting until death. An operatic soprano, in the early years she sang his music and became his muse. The songs, opus 27, he dedicated to her symbolised aspects of their relations, and a brief marital crisis was given a fictionalised version in *Intermezzo* (1923). This experimented in the fusion of conversation and music, an opera for which he also wrote the text and which was regarded as modern for the 1920s. Four late operas were to come, Strauss placing traditional emphasis on melody, even *bel canto*, and more classical in style.

In the 1930s, Strauss composed two contrasting short operas for a possible double bill. *Daphne* was based on a Greek idyll, and *Day of Peace*, with a male chorus most prominent, an ironic choice of theme under a regime planning aggressive war. He never saw a full production of his later *Loves of Danae* because of wartime destruction, but Jupiter's metamorphosis in a shower of gold was perfect material for Strauss' inspiratrion. On the theme of gold and godlike seductions, the work was a return to his most passionate and lavish style, with Danae yet another of his fascinating female creations.

The final international stage success in his lifetime was *Cappriccio* (1941), an elitist discussion on the respective value of words and music. Its escape from the brutalities of war into a world of ideal beauty explains its lasting appeal. Strauss lived out in great anguish Germany's collapse through the war, finally implying publicly that the Nazis had destroyed European civilisation. This and the passing of an era he made the theme of his *Metamorphosen* (1946), an elegy for strings which included the funeral march from Beethoven's *Eroica*.

In his 80s, he had a late flowering of genial, small-scale works. A detached musical observer of the human comedy, Strauss' art was objective until the final stage when in his *Four last Songs,* the soprano voice exquisitely invokes nature's beauty and that of the world which Strauss was about to leave. There is a moment when is heard in the background the soaring theme from his *Death and Transfiguration*. This was a tone poem written as a young man when he had said that the mystic Swedenborg's vision of an afterlife had struck him. Into the new century, this poignant farewell is in Britain the most performed of all orchestral song cycles.

In the 1940s he was much taken on moving camera, and as a conductor he looks most casual, even bored. Those who played under his baton said this was an illusion, maximum effect for minimal effort. When younger, he had been a distinguished conductor and always drove his musicians hard. Total dedication, like Mahler's, but not so difficult to work with.

Strauss' funeral in 1949 was filmed for posterity, conducted then narrated by Hungarian conductor, Georg Solti. In the course of singing the trio from *Rosenkavalier,* all three sopranos in turn broke down.

27   Gustav Mahler, ultra-Romantic

For decades in Britain and North America Gustav Mahler (1860–1911) was widely known for just one movement, his Fifth Symphony's lyrical *adagietto*. Before then, when another of his finest melodies was used during World War II for a very popular song, the association was not publicly referred to.[30]

The obstacle to Mahler's wider fame was the exceptional size of his symphonic works, requiring nearly one hundred musicians, and sometimes far more. That problem was overcome by the invention of long-play recordings around 1950, enabling him to achieve posthumous cult status over decades. Beyond the exciting sound of these symphonies, they are appreciated on a spiritual level. Whilst he was still creative, much of the controversy about these works was summed up in his well-reported meeting in 1907 with Jan Sibelius. He had stated that his ideal of the symphony included severity of form and an inner connection between all the motifs. Mahler's view was in contradiction, that a symphony is like the world and therefore all-embracing.

Brahms was by then deceased, but as the recognised model of stylistic purity, he would have wholly rejected Mahler's view. In the 21st century, Brahms is long since held as the heir of Beethoven in the classic German line. At the time of his death in 1897, there had been lasting debates about the direction the symphony, the late Romantic version, should take in the wake of Wagner's revolutionary contribution, especially in melody and harmony. Wagner created no symphony as a model, but had developed a synthesis of that and opera, music drama.

Anton Bruckner, Brahms' contemporary, was a Wagner enthusiast. His compositions were developed leisurely on a very large canvas, some would say splendidly, works enthusiastic to the point of naivety. As a result, the plain-spoken Brahms had ridiculed him for writing symphonic 'boa-constrictors'. Bruckner's nine completed symphonies, each lasting about one hour, were half as long again as the supposed norm. There were accusations of rambling and formlessness; he had to face ridicule. Would his audiences fall asleep?

The young Mahler admired Bruckner's individuality, works typically Austrian in feeling, and with an emotional intensity reaching the ecstatic. Both men were visionaries, but in an Austro-German musical world where tolerance was in short supply. Fortunately, Mahler likewise felt free to follow his composing instincts, as if he were an amateur. This was because by the 1890s, he was secure in his profession as a distinguished orchestral and operatic conductor.

He had been born on the Bohemian-Moravian frontier, a Jew speaking both the local languages, German and Czech. Like so many fellow-citizens he was drawn by the cultural appeal of Austria, and as a boy was accepted into a Viennese music academy. Rapid advancement had followed.

Whilst conducting *Rienzi,* he once described it as Wagner's most beautiful opera. That sounded like a simplistic view, but no criticism was intended against a man whose later works he greatly respected. Compared with Wagner's mature compositions, *Rienzi* had the attraction of youth, surface appeal, popular melodrama. On a first hearing, its melodies make a strong impression, and were superior to most his competitors were writing. If *Rienzi* is neglected now, it is only because of Wagner's later achievements. The comment revealed Mahler's attachment to beautiful melody, for which today his own compositions are specially loved.

Mahler wrote the words for the four *Songs of a Wayfarer,* a tale of young love lost which he must have related to Schubert's *Winter Journey.* Yet where Schubert's rejected hero had thought of suicide by the side of the *Lindenbaum,* the lime tree, Mahler's had found consolation in nature. One of the *Wayfarer* themes, orchestrated, describing the morning pleasure of running across a meadow, opens his First Symphony (1888), and another is the uplifting second subject of the finale.

A second movement, relaxed and nearer to salon music, was later eliminated to start a new existence under the title, *Blumine.* Next is a scherzo, but with Mahler not in the traditional manner of Beethoven; instead, it is a rustic dance contrasted with a more polished slow waltz. The work's most intriguing movement is the slow one, a funeral march, but it raised some disapproval starting with gloomy variations on *Frère Jacques* in the minor key, followed by a startling theme of Jewish origin. Mahler intended no easy ride but felt obliged to explain:

> It is important only to grasp the mood being expressed and form which the fourth movement springs precipitately from, like the flash of lightening from a sombre cloud. It is simply the cry of a deeply wounded heart which is preceded by the uncannily oppressive atmosphere.

Programme notes refer to the life of the protagonist whose early death and spiritual life would be the subject of the Second Symphony, the *Resurrection*. The idea of a sequel was novel for a symphony; here it justified an opening funeral march. In future he would favour movements of similar pace and emotions, but without explanation.

From 1883 (when he was 23) to 1905 Mahler worked on well over 40 songs, some with depth, others unpretentious. Some would be expanded to fit into his symphonies with the human voice adding contrast and poignancy, an exceptional procedure for the 1890s, and one even Bruckner had not considered. Mahler was the first great composer since Berlioz to compose major orchestral song cycles. *Des Knaben Wunderhorn* (A Boy's Magic Horn) were folk-style verses which, like the Grimm stories, have elements of the macabre, and were perfect for Mahler's more naive melodies, often with a sense of irony or the grotesque. Themes included an angel's prayer, a march for phantom soldiers, a parody of early 18th century song and a lover's plaint.

He introduced into his three symphonies, numbers 2 to 4, songs from this cycle, given extra emotive power. Mahler claimed the model for his Second Symphony had been Beethoven's Ninth, with its choral finale where a version of Schiller's *Ode to Joy* is the resolution. This precedent helped public acceptance of the new work. As an example of human futility, Mahler uses a *Wunderhorn* song about St Anthony of Padua preaching to the fishes, converting it into a fierce orchestral scherzo. The song *Primal Light* is about salvation and it introduces the finale; Mahler intended a parallel here to a male soloist introducing the finale of the Beethoven work. The end of the world is tumultuous, instruments being used at the extremes of their range. The chorus brings divine intervention and forgiveness after the Day of Judgment; the opening notes of the *Dies Irae* are without any sense of gloom.

These first two symphonies' emotional range has exceptional thematic variety. The oratorio features of the Second's conclusion may have been acceptable to his audiences, but the Third Symphony, for the year 1896, was far more eccentric. Vaguely Pantheistic, Mahler was turning to things earthly and graphic in ways not imagined in the programme symphonies by Berlioz and Liszt. It had six (originally seven) movements, with all the drama and diversity one composition could sustain. In initial reactions, certain Berlin critics called him a megalomaniac, and that was before the work had been heard complete.

Its start has two strident themes, the first likened to the famous one in the finale of Beethoven's *Choral*. Mahler wrote that the first movement was a celebration of summer's approach. For its exceptional length of thirty minutes, he gave the second theme its own development section, an innovation. The solo trombone effects were unique. Richard Strauss felt the parallels in sound but not feeling with his own recent symphonic poems, such as the autobiographical *Heldenleben* (A Hero's Life) and *Zarathustra*. His support might make it easier for the grateful Mahler's work to be accepted.

At the conclusion of that opening in the first complete performance at Krefeld (1902), Strauss rushed forward to lead the applause. He said, for the raucous march which emerges late on, he imagined revolutionary socialists massed on May Day. The second movement is relaxing, balletic, with the feminine allure dominant for the first time. Then a turbulent movement describes what Mahler stated in programme notes as what he had *learnt from the animals*, whose play is interrupted by posthorns as they flee from the hunters. He uses the Spanish *Jota Aragonesa*, remote from any dance, as if far-off, pathetic, a 'street song' played on a 'vulgar' cornet solo. This third movement even today sounds the most idiosyncratic of all, a denial of stylistic purity, though that hardly offends modern audiences. In 1902, classical proprieties were still broadly observed, though bigger musical shocks than Mahler's were barely one decade away.

Two songs follow, the first a serene nocturne, the second for chorus and bells, angelic in youthful *Wunderhorn* style. The lengthy finale expresses the power of love, the first melody one of his most profound, held back in suspense but gradually emerging in its full beauty. It has an affinity with a second one, hymn-like, the music life-enhancing.

Only Tchaikovsky had written a comparably intense adagio finale for his *Pathetic*, but to entirely different effect. Both composers broke tradition by putting the emotional force on the end of the symphony. Another planned *Wunderhorn* song Mahler decided to withdraw and place as the spiritual climax of an entire symphony. So the genial Fourth emerged, in total contrast despite some thematic links, and written for a smaller orchestra, with more traditional proportions.

This opens euphorically in dance rhythms, and does not stray far. Describing the second movement as a scherzo, Mahler used slower or varying paces to Ländler-type, $^3/_4$ rhythms. The slow movement, in traditional variation form, is the weightiest, then the finale, the song which describes a child's view of Heaven. This symphony's unaffected warmth and directness have made it specially popular.

In the post-Wagner years, new music tended towards more chromatic sounds, with heavy orchestration often obscuring the rhythmic effect. The Fourth Symphony did not follow, his melodies clear-cut, influenced by the vibrant central European folk styles he had lived alongside, and Schubert's deep simplicity.

Many of his compositions were affected by memories of his youth. As a 6-year old, he had heard the gunfire from the historic battle of Sadowa, known poverty, racial prejudice, lasting insecurity, sudden terrors, and the relief of country music. He also had an affection for Viennese operetta, the intoxication of which many 'serious' composers envied. Funeral marches, military bands, waltzes and country dancing are prominent, elements of a 'lighter' kind, a kaleidoscopic effect not previously thought suitable for one symphony.

Mahler gave instruments, or groups of them, exceptional prominence, such as overwhelming brass, sometimes like symphonic chamber music. Where most symphonies tended to reconcile conflicts, Mahler emphasised fierce, sudden sound contrasts, as if reflecting the modern world. If some thought he often strayed from good taste into melodrama or weird fantasies, it was of no consequence. All of this was essential to his art, seemingly unrestrained, its pulse having a varied but strong sensuous appeal.

After this extrovert phase, he would experience under inner necessity two shorter creative periods. The *Wunderhorn* inspiration was working itself out, with further influence to be found in the score of the Fifth Symphony, notably in the first movement. Mahler is rarely concerned with introductions; instead there is the riveting thrust of the main theme, an extended funeral march of shattering power. Though so dramatic, it has a fine melodic flow, hardly less than the fourth movement, that famous *adagietto*. Between them are two dance-led sequences. The finale, brisk and optimistic, has an uplifting melody that finds an affinity with the *adagietto* theme.

The Seventh Symphony also in five movements has many similarities, starting with an impassioned march but ending very differently with an enigmatic rondo. There is no formal slow movement, but one of the two called 'night music' is to be played in 'amorous' fashion. It is like an experiment with fantasy; some listeners regarded it as spectral. In relation to his Fifth, it has suffered the fate of many companion pieces, not so well known and suspected by some of repetitiveness.

The Sixth Symphony's first movement is shared between two virile subjects, the second a rapturous melody which was an expressed tribute to his wife. It is the only note of solace, and the turbulence which dominates is mirrored in the following scherzo. Mahler was often of two minds about this, sometimes interposing the third movement, one of his most tranquil. The finale makes it the most uncompromisingly strife-ridden of all his works, now commonly called his 'tragic'. Its finale's concluding hammer-beats were interpreted as prescient of the disasters to follow in his life. At least one famous conductor admits that he can be disturbed for days whenever he performs it.

These three symphonies are more abstract, without voices, relating not to the past but to Mahler's inner struggle, spiritually ambivalent. There were no accompanying texts to clarify meaning, as earlier, but what followed was the Eighth, finding religious consolation, called the *Symphony of a Thousand,* but not by him. It consists of just two movements, first, opening on an organ chord, the declamation of a 13th century hymn, *Veni Creator Spiritus* (Come, Holy Spirit). For what was to follow, in a contrasting, near-operatic style he selected a text from the philosophical part II of *Faust;* in Goethe's epic, the character is redeemed as a seeker after truth:

Look upward to the gaze of salvation, all tender penitents, to be gratefully transformed into blissful fate.

By then Mahler was being inspired by the religious works of J.S. Bach, though it was more obviously an oratorio in the tradition of Beethoven and Berlioz, and despite the title it is not quite a symphony.

In that year, 1907, fateful events began to influence the course of his composing. His marriage in 1902 to a remarkable woman, Alma Schindler, inspired as well as reflecting the tensions in his music and she gave up composing to assist him. If there were anxieties about his *Songs on the Death of Children* (1905), superstitions grew soon afterwards when one of his two infant daughters died. Then he was informed he had a terminal illness.

Weighed down by the fear starting with Beethoven that composers could not live beyond their ninth symphonies, he began work on what he considered two simultaneously. *The Song of the Earth* is in total contrast to the 8th, just with two voices, male and female. The text was based on classic Chinese poetry, celebrating youthful enjoyments of life, but the sadness of leaving it. A mystical score, its finale, *Farewell,* is like a swansong.

The Ninth Symphony opens with a phrase which seems to despair of human life, expanding into a very long movement of unusual beauty; the finale is similarly elegiac. The broken phrases and chromatic melodies raised the question whether Mahler was moving into a new, post-Romantic musical phase, such as in the work of some younger composers by 1910. The two intervening movements are restless, fast-flowing, mocking the outer world. The one termed rondo-burlesque, of his middle-period symphonies, but mocking the world. He instructed the Ländler to be played in the rough manner of country dancing. The other termed a rondo-burlesque was intended to confound traditionalists with his skill in polyphony, the burlesque being a device he often used, here a musical joke about his Jewish background.

Of his Tenth Symphony (1911) left incomplete at his death only one movement of the five planned is accepted, and there was no falling off of inspiration. There was also a projected movement, *Purgatorio,* and the remaining sketches were of such compelling interest that a performing version was finally made.

It was by Deryck Cooke (1952) and it has gained much critical acclaim, though Mahler would probably not have welcomed the initiative.

In the years following his death in 1911, Mahler's weighty symphonies were not thought to be a performing option, especially in the sparse fashions of the musical world emerging after the Great War. Many admirers still regard him primarily for his orchestral songs. This can avoid the controversy still attached to his symphonies which his critics may always accuse of lacking unity. Yet the break-down of shared values in our own society may have created greater appreciation of Mahler's unique perspective in those many-sided works.

28 *The Historical Sibelius*

After the *Marseillaise,* among patriotic songs *Finlandia* is perhaps the world's best known, having become the national anthem for at least one foreign state; but it had arrived much too late to become Finland's. It has an enviable number of fine melodies for its length of eight minutes, but because it has no space for symphonic development, it is often called 'light music'. More importantly, it achieved its original purpose, reaching the mass of Sibelius' fellow citizens. To put so many fine themes into such a small space shows an excess of creative energy which several composers have enjoyed in their youth.

Patriotic music Sibelius was keen to use in the 1890s as an elusive act of defiance against the Russian government which was taking steps to increase control of what they called the 'Grand Duchy of Finland'. Finns resented Russian being imposed as the official language, and most young men did not want to be conscripted to fight for the Tsar in his wars, two of which would soon occur within a decade. Apart from this liberation phase, Sibelius would be too engrossed in his art to be politically active, as he moved away and into the more abstract world of his later symphonies.

Musical subversion might have brought imprisonment, so the political resistance had to use cautious titles. The Finns were educationally very advanced so historical and cultural allusions were appreciated. *Finlandia* first appeared in 1899 as if it were just one movement in seven 'historical scenes'. His *Song of the Athenians,* resistance to a foreign invader in the 3rd century BC, had an even more emotive effect when first performed.

Sibelius' first 'historical' work came in 1893 after he had initial successes with youthful compositions raising national awareness and related to legends, *Kullervo* and *En Saga.* It was called *Karelia,* probably the largest concentration of folk-inspired melody he composed. The overture is panoramic, suggesting the battle with nature, hunting horns, a defiant, pioneering spirit, as the Finns spread westward from Lake Ladoga. Then is heard the voice of their women, forthright, hardy, in a primitive style associated with ancient runes:

Be kind, forests, soften and bend, precious Tapio,[31] bring a man to the islet, lead him to that mound where a catch is to be made.

This solo song has a raw attraction with a full vocal power, riveting and strangely unlike operatic delivery.[32]

Karelia had been the Eastern Finns' homeland before they inhabited the interior and frozen lakelands; but its capital, Vyborg, had suffered Lithuanian, Swedish and Russian domination in turn. One movement relates to its castle' s founding in 1293, with music near to the Gregorian style touched with Sibelius' distinct harmonies; then an incident in 1446 with its ruler listening to a ballade. The city's tragic fate on being besieged by the Russians with the decline of Swedish power in 1710 starts genially in a scherzo with brass prominent, but political subjugation rapidly follows. The 1808–9 military campaign against the Russians eventually failed, but there was some consolation that Karelia was joined to Western Finland in 1810, even though there was to be a Russian overlord.[33] This leads to modern times, a celebration of union, ending with a rendering of the national anthem, *Our Land.* Composed by the German-born Frederick Pacius early in that century, its dignified beauty ensures it will not be replaced. Its inclusion in *Karelia* was a compliment to the elderly Pacius, but Sibelius later said the music had no Finnish link but Italian: which was true, uninhibited in a Verdian spirit.

These movements were subsequently broken up by Sibelius because he was dissatisfied with its form as a loose set of tableaux. The overture was later published separately and he reassembled three movements to form his now very popular opus 11, the *Karelia suite.* Of these the march had appeared complete in the original, and the ballade had been sung, the male voice later replaced by a cor anglais. The exceptionally fine intermezzo was arranged anew from earlier sections, onward-thrusting, the conquest of nature. The original work has recently been reassembled for recording with soloists and chorus.

Sibelius had the advantage of growing up bilingual in two cultures. The Swedes had colonized Finland's south-western coastlands and he had been born of that stock. During his youth, Scandinavia was enjoying much new drama, and a powerful subject affecting lands further West came his way. It was a violent historical episode about an uprising against the Scandinavian King in 1520.

King Christian II (1898) was a successful play climaxing with a bloody outcome at Stockholm, and it served for his first purely orchestral symphonic suite. It does show a slight melodic influence from Russian composers of the time, but a distinct lyricism is heard in the suite's two serenade-like movements. The first called *nocturne* is a rapturous expression of the central love affair prominent in the early stages of the action before the King's consort is assassinated in an act of revenge. It has two themes of great warmth, but late on suggesting the tragedy, sustained chords of the kind soon to be recognized as typically Sibelian. The suite was praised sufficiently to reach the London Proms in 1901, though one movement had been described as 'drivel' by a Leipzig critic. This was an unsophisticated, not to say repetitive dance for the Queen, a peasant ignorant of court etiquette. The elegy has a moving Scandinavian strain familiar to many listeners through Grieg's music. Laconic references to treachery follow in the *Fool's song*, with an intriguing slow waltz rhythm. This has some affinity with the wistful but alluring *Valse triste* which a few years later would become a favourite worldwide.

The slower, more reflective episodes in *King Christian II* show Sibelius' melodic gifts in the Romantic intensity of its late 19th century style. The final movements deal with the victory celebrations, skirting around the most unpleasant features of the story. Virile and precipitous, they show marked affinities with parts of Sibelius' First Symphony of one year later.

Sibelius often used the poems of Runeberg, likewise a Swedish-Finn, and he set an unusual work for male chorus and orchestra, a so-called improvisation about the heroic General Sandels' success against the Russians in a Finnish battle of 1809. It is a kind of melodrama, a declamatory form popular in those confident decades. It was for orchestra with male and female chorus, at first jovial, then leading up to a battle when Sandels led his troops in what sounds like a snow-storm. Apart from the strong Finnish flavour, it has a slight parallel in the English style, such as choral arrangements by Elgar and Grainger.

The political situation was becoming more tense with a new Russian governor restricting the freedom of newspapers. 'Pageants' were the safest way to avoid the censor, so the situation led to a 'Press Celebration', the main item being another set of tableaux glorifying Finnish history. Yet whereas the *King Christian II* music had been in extrovert manner, the opening tableau of the *Press Celebrations Music* (1899) has a mysterious, remote quality, an aspect that would become more evident in Sibelius' developing musical personality.

This is how he habitually evoked the spirit of the national epic, the *Kalevala*, subject of many of his greatest works. The symbolic baptism of the Finns is expressed archaically in modal keys. This is followed by revelries at Turku Castle and a sensuous bolero, justified by the ruler having had a Spanish wife. It is better known in the *Historical Scenes* as the *Festivo*.

For Finland, as for Germany, the 30-years War had been a prolonged disaster, the sudden change in fortunes suggested when a gentle minuet is disturbed by martial fanfares and a slow march. The 1710 Vyborg siege is in sombre language, impressionistic, with tone and atmosphere replacing flowing melody. Out of this, the challenging flourish of 'Finland awakening' introduces the famed note stated ten times[34], the call to arms and the themes known now as *Finlandia*.

Much of the material was later revised into the movements of the opus 25, *Historical Scenes*, but such initiatives and the Finnish folk idiom were just an early phase for Sibelius. Even so, it was a further 18 years before the Finns gained their independence, and not before a civil war. In 1905, a young Finnish patriot had assassinated the Russian governor, Bobrikov, and Sibelius considered writing a requiem, but the outcome, more discreetly, was the anonymous *In Memoriam* (1911). This ceremonial slow march might be the nearest he came to orchestration with a Mahlerian flavour, far more than Elgarian.

During the post-1917 civil war, Sibelius fell into the hands of the 'Reds'. Knowing that his historical and political views did not concur with theirs, they did not treat him as a national hero. Though he remained hostile to communism, he continued to interest himself in the music of the USSR, listening to Russian radio even when Finland was at war with them.

Mythology, not history, subsequently inspired his music, though the drama of humans was strong in his remaining seven diverse orchestral suites. Of these, only one is concerned with a figure of history, *Belshazzar's Feast,* for which he used delicately a small orchestra. Though Sibelius expert Robert Layton was less complimentary about its opening *Oriental March,* he admired the elusive poetry of the other three movements: *Solitude,* with its undulating, whispered string *ostinato*[35]: *Night Music, no less searching and inspired,* and the final dance, *an exquisite little piece of cool, fresh charm.*

Despite its quality, it was to be Sibelius' unique impersonation of a non-European culture. His skill in creating atmosphere in this and other drama-related works brought suggestions he should write film music in later years. Yet unlike some of his famous contemporaries such as Stravinsky, he can't be imagined treading the Hollywood way.

29 *1900: Turn of the Century*

The last social era which no-one is still alive to recall is that from around 1900 until 1914, taking in what we call the 'Edwardian' and a few more years to the outbreak of war. For this and certain other reasons, it may be remembered with nostalgia, such as a 'sunset glory of Empire'. There was no radio, but famous performers were recorded acoustically, the sounds in part distorted, our earliest aural link with history. There remain quaintly static, dignified ancestral photographs, and those of the privileged classes, then almost tax-free, enjoying the good life to apparent popular admiration: poorer people in large groups, at work, watching football or dressed in Sunday best. Opulence and poverty, separated by a gulf, but everyone wearing some kind of hat.

For them leisure was more valuable than for us because most had long working days, and we might even envy their innocent pleasures or some of the entertainments, which had to be cheap. In the creative arts, those 14 years were as eventful and exciting as any in Europe's history. Education and opportunities for participation had greatly increased the numbers of distinguished writers and composers; and they had reason to celebrate civilisation's spectacular progress through the 19th century. Collectively, there had never been sounds with so much confidence and splendour as the new music around the year 1900, with the largest orchestras ever used, and an attractive range of bands. Recorded music, existing in small quantities, was not yet a substitute.

To many people living in Western Europe, war had become a romantic notion, soldiers dressing in fine uniforms to impress, their officers to feature at balls and on operetta stages. In 1914, Europe's young men marched off hopefully, just an autumn war to prove themselves, to return home finally for Xmas. The unimagined death toll, suffering and squalor which followed was an obscenity which appeared to have no end, a testimony to human stupidity and the destructive urge, a denial of the civilization so recently boosted. Popular music might seek escapism, but the new art music would never sound the same again.

It is a historical curiosity that so many great composers died and so many young ones appeared or reached maturity around the year 1900, and with arresting new styles of expression. They were to become the last of the late Romantic generation, but did not escape the spirit of the age, and with hindsight we look for reflections of changing realities in their music. There were also less obvious affinities in their styles.

The first decade witnessed Richard Strauss' sensational development of German music drama, and Mahler's evolution as the most controversial symphonist of his time. In Italy, the cult of dramatic realism, *verismo,* was being followed by several successful operatic composers; of them Giacomo Puccini would achieve most lasting fame with such emotive works as *Madame Butterfly* (1904) and *Tosca.* The first great school of Russian nationalist composers had died by 1910, and Stravinsky was about to emerge to be during the 1920s internationally the most influential of the Russians. Meanwhile, Rakhmaninov had become Europe's leading composer-virtuoso, in one sense perhaps Tchaikovsky's successor, with a melodic inspiration and piano technique to win exceptional appeal.

By contrast, the most disturbing note within the Romantic idiom came from Arnold Schoenberg in a unique chamber work. *Transfigured Night* (1899) concerns a woman confessing to her lover that she is pregnant by another man. It has a sweetness, but underlying is a poignant dissonance, wistful. Schoenberg had expressed a saddened human relationship with a sharper conflict of harmonies than had been previously accepted. In later works, he rapidly progressed to the point where he abandoned familiar melodic patterns. This became the most revolutionary step in all Western music; he and his followers would establish the 'second Viennese school', to distinguish it from that of Haydn and Mozart.

French artistic Impressionism was influencing the music of Claude Debussy and Maurice Ravel, who both preferred to move away from classical rules of musical form. Debussy did not just find a new style but a new aesthetic. Listening to much of his music, such as the opera *Pelleas & Melisande* was a different kind of experience. The moment, the chord (vertical) had an increased importance in relation to the melodic (horizontal).

His works for orchestra, *Images* and *La Mer*, were models of a new kind of expressive harmony, strangely evocative. Ravel fascinated with his use of modal scales, often suggesting the other-worldly, and an original use of orchestral colour. He invoked Spanish life in the opera *Spanish Hour*, and Ancient Greek myth in a lengthy ballet, *Daphis and Chloe*. Vaughan Williams would study orchestration with him in Paris, returning home to create what had not been achieved in music before, a broad, vibrant impression of his city in a *London Symphony* (1908).

Debussy could have said it, but it was Sibelius who advised an aspirant to be cautious in the use of notes; every one should have its own life. Several composers would often be identified by just one chord or their use of instruments. These would often be played at unfamiliar parts or extremes of their pitch, even disconcertingly, a trend much associated with modernism.

In 1899, Frederick Delius advanced towards international recognition with the tone poem, *Paris, the Song of a great City*. Born in Bradford, he had welcomed an escape from the industrial world when his father paid for his stay in Florida. There he learnt to value Afro-American music, then studied in Germany Wagnerism and the other fruits of the Romantic tradition. Absorbing this, by the 1900s he had broken away from society and its conventions into a uniquely private world, composing in moments of frequent elation inspired by nature and a kind of Pantheism. His works have a leisurely flow, extended melodies, soothing harmonies and often the lushest of orchestration, notably *Sea Drift, Song of the High Hills* and *On hearing the first Cuckoo in Spring*.

Leos Janacek (1854–1928) had made conventional arrangements of music from his home province, Czech-speaking Moravia, before making a radical break in style, when he began to base his melodies on the native speech rhythms. Most famous of his operas is *Jenufa* (1904), a tragedy of peasant life suffering from village bigotry. His late works were startlingly original: a sequence of operas, passionate and on very realistic themes, but two with humour and strong elements of fantasy.

In Britain, composers Charles Stanford's and Hubert Parry's finer works are neglected now, partly because they are seen as 'Germanic', composed in the shadow of Brahms. It was unforeseen that one Edward Elgar (1857–1934) would displace them, achieving critical fame in 1899 with the *Enigma Varia-tions*. This revealed a strong individuality which initially made a big impression in Germany, 'English' but as he implied, far from folk music. Large-scale compositions of great depth fol-lowed, symphonies and oratorios, to supplement the popularity of his marches and other light music. Wilfred Mellors comments:

> *He accepted Edwardian society as zestfully as Delius rejected it. Both took over the idiom of German Romanticism, Delius to express an egocentric isolation, Elgar to express a social conviction no less purposeful than that of Richard Strauss. That Elgar could use this idiom with a technical expertise equal to Strauss' was a remarkable achievement; he was able to assume the existence of a great symphonic tradition which had never happened in Britain.*
>
> *He had the power to make us believe, momentarily, that the Edwardian world was as grand as his music; while at the same time he subtly suggests that in his heart he knows, and knows that we know, that the grandeur is in his imaginative vision.*

30 *Franz Lehar,* Paganini *and Tauber*

I t is difficult to find a clear-cut illustration of the difference between opera and operetta in the works of a single composer. An exception is Franz Lehar (1870–1948) who set out as an opera composer with *Kukuschka* (1896). It gave little suggestion that Lehar would become probably the greatest of 20th century operetta composers.

Kukuschka, later revised and now recorded under the title *Tatyana,* has the theme of exile to Siberia, with two lovers dying together. It is a tragedy which has a similar shape to that of *Manon Lescaut,* though the lovers are more admirable. Lehar strongly approved that recent opera by Puccini and they developed a mutual respect and lasting friendship. Their main themes were of love affairs tending to the tragic, music rising to similar levels of intensity. They moved in slightly different directions, but they are perhaps equally regarded among Europe's greatest composers, and certainly most popular.

Lehar's operatic model was Slavonic rather than Italian, and much of *Kukuschka's* appeal came through his feel for Russian melody. The opera was very well received initially, but its subsequent neglect was so disappointing that Lehar decided against a second one. Instead, he was impelled towards the most fashionable genre of that time, operetta, reaching to some 30 stage titles. Posterity does not regret this. At least one half are available now in complete recordings, mainly in German.

He was active when operetta stood at its final commercial peak over four decades. For some years after 1905, he would have been one of the few best known composers in the world because of the unprecedented popularity of one stage musical, *The Merry Widow.* Its world impact was immensely greater than any other one in the years before broadcasting. Today, for colour, melodic and rhythmic vitality it remains unsurpassed.

Lehar was born in the mixed Slavonic-Hungarian community of what is now Slovakia As a bandmaster's son then soldier-musician, he spent periods in numerous parts of the polyglot

Austro-Hungarian Empire, and became multi-lingual, a talent often associated with the Jews, of which he was not one. He acquired strong feeling for the music heard in the distinct parts of the Empire: German, Hungarian, Slavonic, Rumanian, Italian. Yet as an ethnic Hungarian, he wrote at least one operatic melody, *I hear a Cimbalom*, so popular with gipsy ensembles that it is widely assumed to be a folk song.

The ability to absorb so many idioms, and the excitement he brought to them, distinguish him as a composer. Unlike today when the performance of musicals in the world's leading capitals is hampered by near-monopolistic conditions[36], in Lehar's productive years there was the strongest competition. Hundreds of musicals were good enough to have a lavish production, and the best would come out on top. They might have well over twenty excellent songs each, rather more than expected in our modern stage works. His successes ensured rapid wealth, but he was modest about this because he had artistic integrity and priorities.

The creation of great classical operettas, the *Golden Age,* comic and satirical, had virtually ended by 1900 with the death of its most famous names. At first *The Merry Widow* was thought to continue in the mocking style of Johann Strauss' *Fledermaus.* The ruler of the actual Montenegro complained that he was being sent up in the plot about a certain *Pontevedro.* The world might assume from it that Montenegro was a corrupt, tin-pot state like Monte Carlo!

The Merry Widow was quickly followed by another prodigious success, *The Count of Luxemburg,* which ridiculed marriages arranged for aristocracies. Even so, Lehar asserted he was not in the long run interested in satire or writing 'funny music'. He intended to express great passions, ennobling ordinary people through the power of love, as his biographer Bernard Grun stated. *Gipsy Love* was a fine example, and it was a rare opportunity to present his native music idiom in its most sophisticated form. Decades later, he rewrote this full-blooded music as an opera, ill-fated to be premiered during the bombardment of Budapest in 1944.

After the 1914–18 war, he introduced the new dance rhythms into his scores, notably tangos and foxtrots, much reducing the waltz element. He also composed a complete act as a much extended love duet, judged by some as deliberate Wagnerism.

He refused suggestions it be altered to stop criticism. Yet there was a complete revision in 1930 as *How fair the World,* a work which avoided the sad endings of his four previous ones, though their tragi-comic vein was said by many critics to be his finest.

These had started in 1925 with *Paganini,* his twentieth stage work. Paganini had been a notorious exhibitionist, not too appealing when separated from his famed violins, and the kind of 'celebrity' no woman should become emotionally involved with. Napoleon's habit of placing his siblings to exercise power in his outlying Empire resulted in his younger sister Elisa being sent to an Italian puppet-state, Lucca. There she languished, married to the Prince who was having an affair with his opera's lead soprano, Bella. The historic accuracy of the events need not concern us; Lehar recognised a most suitable script, and arranged for the experienced Otto Jenbach to provide lyrics.

Lehar expressed powerful emotion without sentimentality, and he succeeded in avoiding romantically escapist plots so familiar in lesser works. In *Paganini* and the three following ones, each heroine is stoical as she renounces for honourable reasons her lover. This always occurs in the third Act, the first two being concerned with seduction, pleasure and intrigue. The operas were set in Italy, Russia, Germany and China, and to an extraordinary degree, Lehar's inspiration matched the need for local musical colour. There has since been no comparable sequence to rival them.

Lehar used none of Paganini's many compositions. As a violinist he wanted to assimilate something of the man's spirit before composing virtuoso passages for the first two Acts. Elisa had despaired of the freedom to find pure love, and she reveals her nature in a passionate aria, having concluded that Paganini is worth sinning for.

Her husband the Prince does not want him at Lucca, especially as he is alleged to have killed someone over a woman in a duel. When she threatens to expose the Prince's liaison with the soprano, he has to turn a blind eye, so for six months Paganini will be employed as music director. That is more than enough time for his affair with her to progress, seduction assisted by his composing a song for her. Yet it is not long before he desires Bella, so she in turn receives the dedication.

His carefree attitudes are reflected in one of the most male chauvinistic songs to have gained world-wide popularity:

Girls are made to love and kiss. And who am I to interfere with this?

Lehar did not drop the Harlequinade tradition that there should be at least one inadequate clown in a sub-plot. In return for money favours, Paganini tells the Mayor the secret of his skills in winning women's affections. When the Mayor tries it on with more than one lady, he gets a slapped face; but does have the consolation of a song in waltz rhythm.

Paganini has gambled away his Stradivarius, but the news of his scandalous behaviour has reached Paris and Napoleon sends a general to arrest him. He flees to the frontier, hoping that smugglers will get him out. Elisa is resolved to losing him, though she and Bella follow him until in a poignant finale for two women, he bids a cool farewell.

During the productive years, some 40, Lehar reduced the dance element in his stage works in favour of the dramatic. Yet with operetta committed to dance rhythms, he includes them effectively in his songs, such as in Bella's final aria, *Seductive Love.* It has a tango rhythm, but interspersed with a vigorous Italian strain from the chorus.

Lehar was specially proud of the 8-note motif, subtly varied, heard in the terse prelude, again when Paganini and Elisa first feel mutual attraction, dreamlike, 'ennobling', the musical climax held back until her explicit decision to be his lover. He responds with the motif, *In your eyes I read,* leading to an ecstatic duet. This is later complemented by another, *Love, you Heaven on Earth,* the equal of the even more popular, *No-one loves you as I do.* It was written at the last moment to replace a melody considered too difficult for the soloists; because of its easy vocal range (*tessitura*), any enthusiasts might try it. Elisa's possessiveness in Act II is answered with a radiant Italianate aria:

She: *You did not come to me last night. Were you with another?*
He: *Yes, I was with another. I was all evening with a love offering. I was composing it for you.*

The premiere in Vienna failed because of the production, but the work was saved in Berlin by the arrival of one of the greatest inter-war tenors, Richard Tauber. A heavily-built man, his appearance was the opposite of the skeletal Paganini and this upset London audiences years later when C.B. Cochrane brought the work to the Lyceum. Yet Tauber had a voice to conquer all, and as a high tenor he was equally at home with Mozart and Lehar, whose delicate serenade from *Frasquita* (1923) he had already graced. A distinguished musical partnership grew up between the two men.

By 1925, Berlin was starting its greatest if brief period of creative musical theatre, and Lehar decided to place it at the centre of his plans. He produced those next three works successfully at its Metropol Theatre, home of operetta, with Tauber and some of Germany's finest light sopranos. *Girls are made to love and kiss* came to be known as the Tauber song, one of seven so-called over the years. *Tsarevitch* begins in Russia but the story moves to Italy in the third Act, and his *Volga-Lied* was probably his most nostalgic song. *Fredericka* was the nearest of all to tragic opera, with *Maiden, my Maiden* as the Tauber song.

One song not superior to many others he composed achieved disproportionate fame world-wide. *You are my Heart's Delight* has suffered from over-popularity, which must have annoyed Lehar. It came from the fourth work, *Land of Smiles* (1929), with its exquisite Chinese flavours.

Bernard Grun writes of *Maiden, my Maiden:*

It is the great main theme of the work, slowly dawning, constantly growing ... first as a flute solo, then as a contrapuntal decoration on the love motif in the prelude; and the moment the curtain rises, in violin octaves to distant organ accompaniment. In the first act finale, it breaks through in its full glory.

But he cannot say as much for the other six Tauber songs:

They have in common the free, grand melody, vocal forcefulness, sonorous effect. Yet for all their brilliance and power, they fail from the viewpoint of musical drama through their dangerous transfer of weight in favour of the singing star. The action suddenly breaks off, the actor becomes a soloist, the interest of the audience turns away from the dramatic action to the song. This tendency did not stop at Tauber; it was reproduced by his imitators, who appeared everywhere, often an annoying part of a chiché. Lehar recognised this and tried to get rid of the habit; but in vain.

He would be appalled at the much increased cult of 'celebrities' into our times through the extensions and influence of the mass media. This trend has been to the disadvantage of most talented and dedicated musicians, and to the decline in the average quality of new musicals offered in the larger theatres.

Tauber performed for the final operetta, *Giuditta*, which Lehar intended as his *Carmen*, fiery, with Mediterranean colour, and a sell-out in 1934 for a long stay at the Vienna Opera. Their meetings were only interrupted by the 1939–45 war, Tauber having been persuaded to flee the Nazis on their occupation of Austria, his homeland. He died in England a few months before his friend, and the outcome of their collaboration is still to be heard extensively recorded again with modern techniques.

Lehar had initiated the 'Silver Age' of Viennese operetta. Musicologist Richard Traubner adds:

Had he striven to imitate Johann rather than Richard Strauss, the operetta picture in the 20th century might have been radically different. But Lehar was more interested in lyricism and beautiful love songs rather than comedy-through-music and character delineation.

31 *Kurt Weill and the Satirical Berlin Theatre*

No filmed documentary of Berlin in the late 1920s would
be complete without a sound track including snatches
of Kurt Weill's music evoking that period. It would
probably be from the spiky extracts for small band based on his
Threepenny Opera.

Still in his 20s, Weill became briefly the most influential
composer in Berlin's lighter music theatre. This phase was to
end tragically with the Nazis taking power in 1933, their racial
and artistic intolerance having appalling effect on the cultural
world.

The Tsar has his Photograph taken, by Georg Kaiser, was Weill's
first successful move into comedy. A group of anarchists take
over a studio long enough to shoot the Tsar, but the female
assassin takes a fancy to him, resulting in a kiss and dalliance
until the police arrive. The work is little known, the music
being too austere for musical comedy, but one innovation was
the playing of a seductive tango on a gramophone record.

By that time, 1927, Weill had joined the musical avant-garde.
Fortunately, rich melody had come to him through his Jewish
background and he could write strikingly original songs within
a popular idiom. He approved jazz whose rhythms he saw as
having a role in the 20th century comparable with that of the
waltz in the 19th.

*The negro music from which the jazz band had sprung is full of
rhythmic complexity, of deft harmonic traits, of timbral and modulatory niceties*[37] *... everything else the radio offers us as dance
music is surrogate.*

Yet he did make use of current dance measures, notably the
fox-trot and tango, most effectively and not in condescension
for several staged works. In traditional opera the audience
empathised with the characters, sharing their joys and suffering. He became one of those contributing to the post-war
reaction against these emotional demands. With a strong sense

of musical irony, he was able to comment in ways which viewed the stage action objectively. This matched the dramatic approach of Bertolt Brecht, who was promoting a theatre of ideas; a plot might be exaggerated or unrealistic provided it made the audience reflect, part of the 'alienisation effect'. The two men were able to have a distinguished collaboration from 1927 to 1933.

There had been for decades a style of musical farce, distinctive Berlin operetta, brought to perfection by composer and theatre director Paul Lincke and others. These included brilliant song-and-dance acts with a cheeky local flavour, often laughing at militaristic attitudes and other establishment symbols, such as the Kaiser. Alongside, there was a sophisticated cult of cabaret, attracting German-speaking composers from as far away as Vienna. Brecht, though musically untrained, had a flair for writing and singing his own pieces, even providing the melodic germ for Weill's later 'hit', *Pirate Jenny*. Brecht intended a theatre culture, drawn in by catchy songs; wider audiences should experience his political ideas acted out on stage. Weill could supply the music, offering a fresh alternative to Berlin's established music shows. By chance his young wife, Lotte Lenya, was very talented in cabaret songs. She was to succeed in certain of those works he was about to undertake and which did not demand singing of operatic strength.

Brecht had written a satire on the U.S.A., the Hollywood syndrome, and the quaint notions of it which many naïve Europeans had. He presents a society where money could buy anything and the sole punishable crime was poverty. From this the two men undertook their most ambitious opera project, *The Rise and Fall of the City of Mahagonny,* Its 'popular' songs were to be used in a short dance sequence, *The Mahagonny Songspiel,* set in a sordid night-club. It displays the vices of the 'paradise city' where there is a mindless search for pleasure. The casual dancing reflects a futile, desperate world of crime, lust and abandonment symbolised by the frantic *Alabama* song. The *Benares* song relates to an ideal city which the protagonists hope to reach. During the action its destruction is announced with its accompaniment denying the swooning, optimistic melody.

Public reaction to the *Songspiel* was inevitably mixed, the avant garde considered it a regression by Weill, and the Nazis, seeking publicity, frequently demonstrated violently against subsequent Brecht-Weill collaborations. Its 1980s TV version makes interesting comparison with the night-club sequences in the 1976 film, *Cabaret,* which the original version had inspired. The *Songspiel's* silent, sinister *Conferencier* (club host) is replaced in *Cabaret* by a gnome-like Joel Grey praising decadence in seductive wit, the phantom, expressionistic dancers giving way to grotesque high-kicking transvestites. In the film the pervasive menace was seen in the street behaviour of jack-booted Nazi thugs.

The Threepenny Opera was intended in similar disrespect as a stage diversion, to become the 20th century theatre's most famous satire on 'bourgeois' society. Romantic, heroic opera, is ridiculed with failed love and dirty deeds among London's criminal classes who feign respectability and are granted it by the Establishment. Instead of the lush violin tones of operetta, its glamour and escapism, there are vulgar emotions and simple ballads. These are played by a few musicians on street instruments with percussive effect, and with the cheapest décor to match. To suggestions of a run-down music hall, the songs have an earthy appeal, with ongoing trade in bombast and mock sentimentality. There is a masterly ascent or descent to the first half's nostalgic brothel scene with a searing tango which became most popular through the 1930s productions.

The Threepenny Opera like the original *Beggars' Opera* of 1742 ridicules the style of 18th century opera with a jealous slanging match between two girls. Musical parody is sharp in one other scene, the fast-paced finale hinting at the salvation of Margarita in Gounod's *Faust* but with an absurdly devotional chorus. In the 1930 Franco-German film versions, the farcical ending has the hero-villain Mack the Knife's admission to the privileged classes approved by Queen Victoria, an incident in celebrations of her 1897 Jubilee.

Happy End was in the style of *The Threepenny Opera,* an ironic love story of a Salvation Army girl and a gangster which had a plot likeness to Shaw's *Major Barbara* and the later musical, *Guys and Dolls.* Brecht's wife, Helen Weigel, performed at the premiere but angered at its lack of political content, she added a diatribe on-stage as an impromptu protest. This almost ruined the show critically, though Brecht agreed with her action. He then disowned the complete work, but it has lived to enjoy even commercial success in more recent times though falling short

Romanticism and Melody

of its predecessor. It is saved by excellent songs, such as the haunting *Surabaya Johnnie,* and that rarity, nostalgia for a disused ballroom, *Bilbao.*

Weill was not so concerned with ideological theatre, and the disagreements hastened the decline of the Brecht-Weill partnership. Brecht was to find in Hans Eisler a composer with a similar versatility to Weill's, but more acidic, and politically committed. The two would work together into their American exile.

Kaiser's contemporary left-wing play about financial exploitation, *Silver Lake,* became Weill's last opera to be premiered in Germany immediately before the Nazi take-over in February 1933. It included *The Ballad of Caesar's Death,* celebrating the passing of a dictator and aimed at Hitler. There is a charming duet of ingenuous girls trying to square the circle, eking out an honest commercial living. The most extraordinary scene has a banker swimming in paper money, his fortune made from simple and compound interest. These terms in German are *Zins und Zinseszin,* shouted out by him in triumph at the end of the refrain. This sibilant phrase has words taking over from music at the climax to startling effect. In *The Threepenny Opera.* a similar technique works starkly with the dramatic monologue, *Pirate Jenny,* when she orders her prisoners to be decapitated, *Hop, la*!!

The Silver Lake opened simultaneously in several cities, only to be closed down straightaway. Brecht fled into exile, Weill following to Paris within weeks, Kaiser more leisurely to Switzerland.

German was the original language of Weill's unique operetta, *Kühhandel,* hopefully to be performed in Berlin when the freakish Nazi regime collapsed; but Weill had to be reconciled to permanent exile. Without Brecht, he sought a style both more lyrical and farcical in the Parisian spirit of Offenbach. The music was less bitter and lightened with waltz and Latin rhythms. Its allusions to European and South American dictatorships were too much for 'non-political', Hitler-appeasing Britain of 1936, where the fashion in musicals was Ivor Novello's escapist Ruritanian romances. So for a production at London's famous Savoy Theatre, the satire had to be toned down, with 'music hall' additions. As a result the work's integrity was diminished. The Times correspondent commented that it was difficult *to tell when sentimental music was satirising itself, and when it is being itself . . . a kind of jazz with every beat of a bar of common time made into a strong beat.*

Once Weill had settled in the U.S.A, he assumed that, being in a classic European tradition, the work would not be revived and he used some of its best music in later works. What is now heard poignantly sung by Walter Huston as *September Song* opened originally with:

They say one cannot live by bread alone
But that's how I have lived since I came to the city.

A revised version for Britain's Opera North in 2006 bore the title, *Arms and the Cow,* a pointed allusion to G.B.Shaw's anti-war play, *Arms and the Man.* It is a satire on military 'strong men', arms dealers who sponsor wars and the sectarian exploiting of peasants also to be used as gun-fodder. It could fit the break-up of Yugoslavia as described by Lord Owen.

There is a full complement of operetta devices, patter songs, quasi-religious anthems, marches, political speech-songs, love duets, a drinking song (*fandango*). This lengthy stage work in the colourful genre of Bernstein's *Candide* received much more favourable critiques than 70 years earlier.

During his final 14 years in the U.S.A., Weill adapted his styles to a new language, tradition and environment, but his German works gained added favour after his death in 1950, largely through the stage personality of his widow, who had also recorded virtually all of his popular songs. *The Threepenny Opera* did not reach London until 1956 but with success in the U.S.A. even eclipsing many of the fashionable American musicals. Its new 'hit' was the *Morität,* (Mack the Knife), a deadpan catalogue of gruesome crimes, a memorable slice of black humour. Its song has an attractive banality, its popularity reflecting the increased appeal in recent times of monotonous rhythms.

32 *Bernstein and others on Gershwin*

From conversations around 1950, Leonard Bernstein quotes a music production manager stating that George Gershwin's *Rhapsody in Blue* throughout its variety and changes of mood and tempo breathes America — the people, the urban society, the pace, the nostalgia, the nervousness, the majesty. Bernstein wanted to qualify the praise because of defects in symphonic development, alleging Tchaikovsky-like sequences, Debussy meanderings and pianistic fireworks in the manner of Liszt. He suggests that certain sections could be removed without damaging the rest; there was no inevitability about it all. He called the equally enjoyable Piano Concerto the work of an apprentice learning fast.

In due course, Gershwin acquired the skills to orchestrate another concert work, *An American in Paris,* inspired tunes and rhythm, perfectly harmonised. Bernstein noted that it showed skills learnt from such as Richard Strauss and Ravel in linking and combining themes. An original symphonic thinker had not yet emerged.

It was a cultural reality that by the time of this conversation an abundance of great new melodies no longer flooded the stage as they had done in the times of Rossini and Verdi. That generalisation is related to the rise and fall of civilisations. Though a claim could be made for Kern and a few others, Gershwin was the rarest of exceptions. He was prolific in fine melodies which is why the production manager, unnamed, had cited him, worried that Bernstein's latest show had no 'hits'.

Years later, Bernstein would remedy this defect with such songs as *Maria.* One explanation was that he and Gershwin had come from opposite sides of the musical tracks. Bernstein had started off writing symphonies. This had involved becoming not just a song writer giving audiences what it was assumed they want, but an original one. Gershwin's way had been the more natural, an innate songster, to become as Bernstein believed the finest melodist since Tchaikovsky. He had grown into a serious composer, and with a rare sense of what works best in the theatre. That was where his destiny lay, and with one inspired opera before his progress was cut short by death.

Bernstein admired the entire opera *Porgy & Bess* as it had been written, but since Gershwin's death, productions had been turned into an 'operetta', such as by replacing the sung-speech with words. The manager suggested that was proof of a defect in the original version.

■ ■ ■

For 12 February 1924, in a pretentiously named 'experiment in modern music' at the Aeolian Hall, band leader Paul Whiteman would entertain New York's musical celebrities with 24 items under 11 headings. They might have been better advised to stay at home, except for the penultimate work which starting with its astonishing 17-note clarinet *glissando* was to be the outstanding work of the night. Gershwin always excelled in playing his own works at the piano, the leading instrument in his *Rhapsody in Blue* which had been orchestrated by composer Ferdy Grofé for Whiteman's large jazz band. Years later, a Second Rhapsody had a lesser impact, though Gershwin had good reason to believe it broke new ground starting as background for a film, then expanded. It revealed greater depth of feeling, and even by his standards, its forceful rhythms are intriguing.

Gershwin's future reputation for symphonic composition would rest on two works before he proved himself in an even greater challenge, opera writing. He orchestrated his successful *Concerto in F*; in a new American style, it has some affinities with Aaron Copland's.

If Gershwin had given it the title of fantasia or burlesque, he would have avoided much criticism about its form. The occasional glances towards Liszt and others could then have been seen as affectionate reminiscences. Modestly he described it as a sequence of musical paragraphs. The opening movement has a shock of contrasting themes, whilst a Charleston waits in the wings and eventually dominates. The slow movement is a leisurely, sophisticated comment on the blues, and the finale, suitably replacing the traditional rondo, is a sequence of themes delivered at an extremely fast pace. Whatever titles he chose, it was predictable that the combination of piano and orchestra would be a valuable option for the future. So he wrote a set of variations on *I've got Rhythm*.

An American in Paris followed two years later in 1928 and is most widely known from the film of the same title (1950), one of Hollywood's greatest musicals. There it is the accompaniment to an inspired ballet with a scenario on the Moulin Rouge and its famed artistes of the 1890s. For the concert hall it was a welcome innovation, a colourful symphonic poem describing a young man's exuberant romp around Paris with the confidence to capture the girl of his choice. It could have been heard as symbolising America's seduction of the Old World with the latest style of syncopated music. As a story told in episodes, it has a verve which can be likened to *Till Eulenspiegel.* Gershwin included four of his exuberant melodies; the fifth was a blues, nostalgic for the U.S.A.: the sixth, which had arrived decades previously from Spain via Paris, remains probably Western Europe's most compelling street song, the *Matchiche.*

As a youth, Gershwin had started composing for Tin Pan Alley, but its basic requirements were assembly-line production and he soon out-grew them. The popular formula was economical in music resources: one 8-bar phrase, repeated, then a different 8-bar phrase for contrast, then the first one again, but slightly modified to give a conclusion (cadence), This created a 32-bar tune, which could be repeated with different words, the object being to fit neatly onto the normal ten-inch gramophone (phonograph) record. *Lady be good* was a clear example. This song was also the title of his first unqualified success as a musical (1923) and introducing the Astaire siblings. Later the show was enhanced with the charismatic singer, Ethel Merman, whilst some of the most famous big band instrumentalists of the future accompanied. Unlike most composers, Gershwin might have to select from as many as 20 good songs for one show.

Ira Gershwin's lyrics apart, the stage plays used for 1920s Broadway musicals tended to the banal, and the Gershwins deserved better. It was in 1992 that a composite musical arrived to critical acclaim. It was *Crazy for you* partly based on *Girl Crazy* (1930), with some dozen other 'hits', escapist entertainment at its wittiest, versatile performers, a song-and dance spectacular. It was more than a worthy tribute to Gershwin; it pointed to his classic status over half a century after his death in 1937 aged 38.

He often worked alongside Jerome Kern, an older, classically trained composer of more sophisticated songs. His finest included *All the things you are*, in its original 'operatic' shape consisting of an arresting introductory phrase, then one full melody (refrain), leading to the climactic second one (chorus). The emotional effects there are enriched by fluctuations of major and minor scales, and other subtleties.

Both men had gained musically from their Jewish backgrounds, immigrants from Russia. Gershwin said he learnt from Kern how songs for musicals could be superior to 'popular' ones. This induced him to upgrade one of his best ideas which he had first withdrawn from the stage, probably because audiences had found it too intense, out of place. So he rewrote the song, *The Man I love*, giving it the introductory refrain it deserved.

Opera director Reuben Mamoulian described George's skills at improvisation:

He would draw a lovely melody out of the keyboard like a golden thread, then he would play with it, and juggle it, twist it and toss it around mischievously, weave into unexpected intricate patterns, tie it in knots and hurl it into a cascade of ever-changing rhythms and counterpoints.

The gift of being able to compose to a given text also set him apart from most, and a valued partnership developed from 1924 when his older brother Ira became his lyricist. To broaden his perspective, he visited Paris and Vienna, meeting many important composers, In 1928, Kalman's *Duchess of Chicago* gave the Charleston rhythms a leading part for the first time in operetta, and Kurt Weill's subversive *Threepenny Opera* appeared. That year in Vienna, Gershwin met both men and with his feel for stagecraft may have gleaned new ideas.

Popular stage hits slow down dramatic movement, reducing the drama's importance in musicals. One option was to seeking greater cohesion of words, music and action, using a manner more declamatory than traditional ballad. Gershwin would have known Weill's music, though there is no evidence he used it as a model. Some of his later works showed such interesting features, starting with *Strike up the Band.* They contained fewer lyrical songs and 'hits', which may explain why they have not been so much performed in recent decades. He was moving into 'serious' musicals, more satirical.

Gershwin was studying composition to face the ultimate dramatic challenge. At that time, operettas defined musicals requiring voices of operatic strength, but he would pass over this agreeably escapist option to compose a full-blooded opera. That had to be the powerful but depressing theme of his choice which came from a novel then adapted as a successful play. *Porgy and Bess* expressed sympathy for the down-trodden and its protagonist, a disturbed, crippled black beggar.

Many of his associates disapproved of this venture by Gershwin. Should not the first opera about blacks be more elevated? There was no shortage of black composers, especially in the world of jazz Surely 'popular' arias such as *Summertime* were more suited to musicals? Yet Romantic operas had always produced catchy, singable hits, and despite being 'modern', this one was also to be in the Romantic fold, notably in his inspired harmonies and rhythmic variety.

Gershwin wrote at least one impressive rag, *Rialto Ripples*, in the manner of Scott Joplin. He knew of that man's exceptional talents even for musicals. He may have known that only one European had composed an opera displaying the victimisation such people suffered: Delius' *Koanga*, and that as long back as 1897. Gershwin's long-standing interest in jazz encouraged him to go further, after visiting local communities and listening to speech inflections in the search for musical authenticity. His progress in composition was so rapid that by 1934, *Porgy and Bess* was ready, performed by an all-black cast and destined to be a long-playing success. It enabled him to prove himself in new areas such as characterisation and ensemble writing. This impressive score seemed to point to ways forward for his restless creativity; but fate decided otherwise.

Many have compared Gershwin's melodic gifts with those of Schubert who died at the age of 31. His last songs were among his greatest; *Love walked in* perfectly expresses swooning rapture, and his final comment (to his brother) described it as Brahmsian.

33 *The Music of the Ballets Russes*

By 1903, Isadora Duncan was famous in the West for her revolutionary if idiosyncratic approach to dance, and in locations remote from the ballet stage. The young Russian choreographer Michel Fokine could not follow her total disregard for tradition, but admired her naturalistic approach, such as refusing to dance on *pointe*. In the St Petersburg ballet, his creations were moving away from rigidities of classical style, but there was strong opposition to some of his changes in court circles. This was the capital where French fashions had dominated among the rich. Over six decades Russia's internationally famous 19th century choreographer had been the Frenchman Marius Petipa, through to Tchaikovsky's *Sleeping Beauty* (1890) and Glazunov's *Raymonda* (1898). Fokine was to be his successor and assembled the most famous-to-be dance team there, including Pavlova, Karsavina and Nijinsky; all four would eventually migrate to Paris.

He became interested in a circle which grew around two men who had met as undergraduates and were editing a forward-looking magazine *The World of Art*: Serge Diaghilev and Alexander Benois, painter and future scene designer. Diaghilev was multi-talented, but gave up his ambitions to be a composer when Rimsky-Korsakov told him he lacked talent. He was first taken on as an administrator by the Imperial Theatre; but would not compromise on a new approach to Delibes' ballet *Sylvia*, and was sacked. His destiny was to become a world-famous impresario, aristocratic in manner but able to pick the best collaborators.

Fokine was being obstructed, so his chance came when Diaghilev took a company in 1907, firstly for opera, on tour to Paris. He joined it to create by 1909 the ballet on Chopin's music now known as *Les Sylphides*, but Diaghilev sensed that the audience were ready for greater innovation. The *Polovtsian Dances* from the opera *Prince Igor* were given astounding choreography to music of a kind previously unknown, so vital and exotic. *Cleopatra* did not use the familiar personalised history, but was first in a plan to display the beauties of all great civi-lisations, an early kind of multi-culturalism. Its theme was based on an 'Asian' notion that a man would willingly suffer death for one night of voluptuous pleasure. Its ballet was a compilation from several Russian composers. Then came the aural and visual delights of *Sheherezade* based on tales from the *Arabian Nights*. In that time, before cinema had introduced sound, Rimsky-Korsakov's sensuous confection seemed to illustrate the unknown, the ultimate Oriental fantasy.

A Russian court painter, Leon Bakst's decor was able to evoke parallel responses, conceptions which are no less astonishing even in today's jaded post-modernist phase. He made original use of veils and harem pantaloons in place of the tutu, and his two works, *Sheherezade* and *Cleopatra*, had Parisians shopping for exotic home decorations. The original episodes of *Sheherezade* were not related to sex, but Fokine's version was carnal and violent. Rimsky-Korsakov, recently deceased, might have objected to this interpretation in a different medium, and his widow did so in vain. Two other new ballets on music from the earlier 19th century succeeded without controversy: *Carnaval* by Schumann and *The Spectre of the Rose* with a score which Weber had once used to make the waltz 'respectable'.

The visual and theatrical talent of the team Diaghilev had assembled brought ballet into a new century. Theme and music would be conceived together, incidentally avoiding such pro-blems as that over *Sheherezade*. Diaghilev then took a risk of historic importance, commissioning the unknown 28-year old Igor Stravinsky to compose music for a gorgeous, enchanting legend, *The Firebird*, (1910). This was once more ideal for Bakst's décor, sensationally matched by Stravinsky's use of instruments in a luscious score. It was inspired by the skills of his teacher, Rimsky-Korsakov, but his next step was in search of a new style, divergent, more austere and nearer to that of Mussorgsky.

Stravinsky improvised on the germ of a story, a *concertante* fragment between piano and trumpets. It would then be expanded and laced with several of Russia's popular and folk melodies. The piano part represented a puppet facing a hostile world, to be interpreted inimitably by the young Nijinsky. With Fokine collaborating, and Benois as designer, a pathetic story of jealousy emerged within a fairground scene, *Petrouchka*.

Startlingly original, like a Harlequinade gone wrong, it was a triumph of combined talents.

Diaghilev produced these two works by 1911 to great acclaim, and they initiated a move away from literary themes. Many ballets would in future have music composed to order; two years later, a third such work resulted in one of the most infamous riots ever by a supposedly civilized musical audience. It made Stravinsky the most notorious of young composers, one of the fastest promotions in musical history.

This was *The Rite of Spring*, depicting the selection, rape and killing of a virgin, an ancient Russian ritual to the earth god of fertility. The musical score affected the sensibility of many, and even the dancers found it very difficult to count the rhythm. The extremities of the choreography shocked probably no fewer; the dancers had to adopt animal-like postures, grotesque even moreso by comparison with the elegant upright stance of tradition. It was a lurch into primitivism, crashing harmonies, violently repetitive notes and rhythms. 1913 was a time when certain 'advanced' composers seemed to be taking leave of traditional melody, and some listeners were confused. In fact the melodies are broken but intense and thoroughly memorable. Visually and in emotive force, the work was reaching the ideal of an integrated work of art: music, scenario, choreography, decor.

An opera-ballet to *The Golden Cockerel* resolved a problem in the original work. The dance sequences the composer had insisted upon were too difficult for most lead singers, so the innovation was to have double casts, a practical device used later in Stravinsky's *Renard* and elsewhere. Diaghilev then found music with a restrained, perhaps more authentic Oriental touch. This was by the Russian Balakirev to become the ballet *Thamar*.

In between these works, Diaghilev turned to two contemporary French composers with a marked difference of approach to rhythm. Ravel's *Daphnis and Chloe* (1912) to a Classic Greek scenario was an orchestral *tour de force,* inspired flute passages contrasting pagan vigour with sensuous, elongated melodies. This was thought difficult, but Ravel's impression of a grand ballroom's mystique, *La Valse,* was more surprisingly rejected by Diaghilev. One likely explanation could follow from conductor Michael Thomas' experience:

*It requires such constant attention to balance, to nuance, to
articulation and to continual changes of tempi. Orchestras have
described the experience of doing* La Valse *with me as accelerating
around a racecourse without flinching in the turns.*

In total contrast, Debussy's *Jeux,* describing a search for a
tennis ball, has elusive and broken rhythms. His *Après-midi d'un
faune,* with its leisurely pace and chords suspended in mid-air,
was widely thought not to be danceable. Nijinsky found a
unique approach, dancing 'above' the music, finding a sensuality which helped to turn his performance into part of a
controversial legend. The Bolshevik revolution of 1917 brought
many Russian émigrés to France, and Leon Bakst decided to
stay. Sergei Prokofief, spending a lengthy 'holiday' from Russia,
would compose spiky, modernistic scores over more than a
decade. He started with the *Scythian* suite which was barbaric in
ways which suggested Stravinsky's influence. Diaghilev's late
choices included three more of his works: *The Buffoon, The Steel
Pace* (1927) on a modern factory theme, and finally *The Prodigal
Son,* more lyrical, and used as material for his Fourth Symphony
(1930).

Diaghilev had never intended his creation to become a
museum for 'White Russian' culture. Biblical themes were not
without spice, and Florent-Schmitt could provide some in his
Tragedy of Salomé. So Richard Strauss was given a divergent story,
Jacob's Ladder : he later confessed that its religious theme had
been beyond his sympathies.

Diaghilev reacted to changing conditions by linking with
contemporary artistic fashions, such as Surrealism which
encouraged incongruous relations between the music and the
theme. He requested from the idiosyncratic Eric Satie *Parade,*
with a light, jazzy score including a typewriter and later *Jack in
the Box,* both on amusingly commonplace themes. They were
admired by the young Poulenc because, as he said, they were
close to the spirit of Paris, as *Petrouchka* had been to old St
Petersburg. He and others wanted the new music to be clear,
healthy, robust and French. That could describe another success, *La Boutique fantasque,* (1918) except that it was Italian, an
even more exuberant romp which was a collage of Rossini
themes. An historic nationalist score by Manuel de Falla featured Spanish dancing and flamenco in *The Three-cornered Hat.*

The contemporaneous group of French composers, 'the Six',

responded favourably to the stimulus of the Ballets Russes. Darius Milhaud had put an extended stay in Brazil to best use, composing ballets such as *Salade* with its modern dance rhythms, and a French strain with his *Blue Train,* musically recalling the *naughty nineties* and popular theatre. A long-term success has been *Les Biches* (1924), flirtations with emancipated young ladies, teasing 'flappers' in short skirts, dancing to rhythms which range backwards two centuries from the 1920s. Its composer Francis Poulenc could span the ages even within a single movement, here creating one of the wittiest of all ballet scores.

In those excursions into magic, fairgrounds and pre-history, Stravinsky had astounded Western audiences exploiting the exceptional freedom in Russian rhythms; but some thought his *Soldier's Tale* (1918) was rhythm without feeling. His 'primitive' phase was unlikely to continue after 1914 when Europe's armies would practise barbarism on another stage. He settled for much lighter themes, such as *Renard,* a foxy tale, playing to his other strengths such as parody. Using small instrumental ensembles was a useful option, especially as Diaghilev had lost a fortune with London productions.

Stravinsky had greater success looking elsewhere for melodies and composing music for more traditional ballets such as in *The Fairy's Kiss.* This used at least eight of Tchaikovsky's lesser-known songs. Stravinsky exploited their potential to differing emotive effects, dreamlike or ironic as suited a disquieting story from Hans Andersen. He transformed them with some of his own bridge material into the genial central movements of his longest ballet about a man tricked into a false and disastrous betrothal. Its first section contains the disquieting *Lullaby in the Storm* and the enigmatic finale with its unsettling harmonies is built around Tchaikovsky's best-known song, *None but the weary Heart.*

Neo-classicism was rearranging music from earlier centuries, a fashion of the early 1920s when art music was uncertain which new direction to go. It was well adapted to the youthful style of Pergolesi's music in the comic ballet, *Pulcinella,* for which Stravinsky added piquant instrumentation. An entirely new direction was *Les Noces* (The Wedding), an ancient Russian ritual but influenced by African rhythms, with a new combination for ballet using chorus, four pianos and percussion. This music alongside those first three of his ballets show exceptional variations in style far beyond what could be expected in four works by any front-rank composer. He provided no more fireworks, but lastly a delicate essay in neo-classical style, *Apollo* (1928). These final contributions were relaxing and nearer to cool, abstract art.

As the shortest policy directive Diaghilev had said *Astonish me!* Yet the law of diminishing returns seems to govern human creativity. These new works of the 1920s could not generally match the originality and significance of the earlier ones.

Diaghilev remained the integrating force of the Company until his death in 1929. Stravinsky was distressed far beyond his concern that he might as a result lose his musical direction; he needed to go on his travels to find his creative purpose once more. Diaghilev's ballet troupe was terminated, though the name was taken up by others; one of his team, the choreographer Balanchine, successfully set up long-term in the U.S.A. Ninette de Valois started as one of his ballerinas, then became a leading force in Britain without whose work and persistence, it is said, the Royal Ballet would not have been born.

Constant Lambert had composed for the Ballets Russes a *Romeo and Juliet*, and in his distinguished book *Music Ho!* he wrote:

> *In his palmy days before the War, Diaghilev was a space-traveller, bringing to the Western world a picturesque oriental caravan laden with rich tapestries . . . appealing to a more intelligent audience than that sought by the ordinary commercial impresario, who would be forced into a policy of novelty and sensationalism that gathered speed as it went.*
>
> *In music his genuine taste was for the luscious, in décor for the opulent. In spite of all his convincing toying with post-war intellectuality, his favourite ballet was probably* Scheherazade.

34 *Cardus on English Song*

Of the generation after G.B.Shaw, Guardian music critic, Neville Cardus, was one of the most inspirational. His speciality was the Romantic period, including a masterly book on twelve of the greatest composers. Half a century later his writings are valued for their depth, warmth and imagery, dealing alike with the greatest works and significant minor ones. These would include a rarely performed opera by Delius, *Irmelin*. Writing in 1953, Cardus showed how significant and fresh its appearance would have been for the year 1892 when opera in English was at a very low ebb:

> *Already Delius had found the secret of his art, to express the fragility of young love and to feel the vanishing beauty of the world. Love in Delius is never erotic; voices and orchestra sing, rising and falling, high and low, of the passion of sensibility, not of sex. The harmonies mingle and dissolve, and the music achieves the sunset touch ... If anything, there is too much melody in* Irmelin, *every instrument is shaping a lovely curve, a lovely cadence behind everybody's back.*

Delius found his distinctive path, merging voices into the instrumental pattern in many fine orchestral works, though his subsequent operas lacked the dramatic immediacy to be placed among the great. Cardus elsewhere sums up the failure in opera of any British composers to enter the ranks of the most popular European ones, not necessarily from dramatic weakness. (Britten at that time was making his first impact). The main problem is a kind of national restraint, specifically the absence of sexual desire in their arias.

Among the great European song writers he includes Schubert, Schumann, Brahms, Wolf, Fauré, Ravel and Mussorgsky. In the inspiration of composing in that more intimate medium of art song with piano accompaniment, he says that the British have fallen short. Considering the status of English poetry, this is remarkable. Even Shakespeare has not been given ideal interpretations. Cardus admires Quilter's *Come away, Death*, though he places first Sibelius', one of his greatest interpretations. Cardus would have known that Beethoven and Haydn had made fine arrangements of songs from our islands.

He notices even a general reluctance to place British songs alongside Continental ones in recitals. Cardus thought Vaughan Williams' *Shropshire Lad* an exception, a song cycle strengthened with instrumental ccompaniment. There was a notion that our Victorian composers had spent too much time in organ lofts, as their achievements in choral music and oratorio were better. Even so, Elgar's arrival had been a surprise and had set the highest standards. He had been quoted as stating that Granville Bantock, his contemporary, had the most fertile musical brain of our time. This was generous tribute considering that both men had once been held in equal repute nationally.

Bantock did not call his *Omar Khayyam* an oratorio but it is a massive one, longer than most operas and allegedly his masterpiece. Based on a great philosophical poem, the *Rubaiyat,* it would have seemed very Wagnerian, expressed with the lavish resources which were available at that time by 1900 to Strauss, Mahler and others.

Cardus may have been first to assert Bantock was only of the second rank. Our generation has seemed to agree, having almost completely ignored his music. Bantock might well be prepared to be judged by *Omar*. Kodaly's *Psalmus Hungaricus*, a folk cantata, was an ideal model for Cardus who considered Walton's *Belshazzar's Feast* the finest English oratorio of its times.

Cardus had a nostalgia for the music halls of his youth, which had faded out in the 1920s, though much was taken over by the variety theatres. To true British popular songs, there had been 'international combustion' between the stage and audiences, and he specially recalled the songs of Albert Chevalier. He liked such as *I do like to be beside the Seaside* with its catchy rhythm, interesting enough to be turned into a tango by Walton for his *Façade* ballet.

The minor composers pre-1914 had contributed light music for once well-loved musical comedies, but those and successive ones would be forgotten. Cardus blames that partly onto passive acceptance of American dominance, and from the 1950s standpoint he wonders whether we have lost our collective desire to sing. It was a time when, unlike today, the symphonic repertoire was more prestigious than the operatic, which was largely unknown. Since his death in 1975, has anything happened to revive optimism in new British songs?

The first four decades of the 20th century were the second spectacular era of Continental operetta, seemingly losing impact in Britain as a result of the 1939–45 war when the stage world went quite dark. Over those years, the nation enjoyed our own successful efforts in topical songs. Cardus' judgment on his earlier years still holds good; the best British operetta consisted of Leslie Stuart's *Floradora*, certainly the famed sextet, and the Viennese imitation, *Bitter Sweet*. How Noel Coward, versatile in the creative theatre and for very witty cabaret songs, found time to compose in *Bitter Sweet* an excellent operetta remains a mystery. Yet it far outclasses the competition, including the sentimental, once-popular musicals of Ivor Novello.

Writers are rarely fully appreciated a generation or so after their deaths. Some of Cardus' views will shock many today, but that is good because we are living in an age of Hype, not least musical. In historical perspective his writings will stand very high.

35 *Bernstein's* Candide

A s a young man, Bernstein had already succeeded with light musicals in 1940s 'Broadway' style before he decided on two large-scale operatic projects. He started work on both at roughly the same time. One was a tragedy located in New York City, *West Side Story*, based on the theme of *Romeo and Juliet* to an inspired text by Stephen Sondheim. It was to have instant success in 1957, a modern opera with very broad appeal. The other was to have an uncertain start though no less innovative, an adaptation of the 18th century French novel, *Candide*.

Bernstein's intention was to follow as closely as possible the text and the narrative, so problematic that several collaborators fell by the wayside. The first version was too much directed at. political extremism in the U.S.A., the second was reduced in size and though it won a major award, Bernstein was not satisfied. The music was too good to be reduced and the play deserved the large-scale spectacular originally planned and finally produced by Scottish Opera in 1981. Like *The Threepenny Opera*, it stands as one of regrettably few great musical satires of the 20th century.

Voltaire had written a devastating comment on the human condition, drawing on real events in his own times:

The University of Coimbra had decreed that the spectacle of some being burnt alive on a slow fire was an infallible prescription for preventing earthquakes. So when the earthquake had destroyed three quarters of Lisbon, the authorities could find no more certain means of avoiding total ruin than by offering the people a splendid auto da fé ... *a Basque convicted of marrying his godmother and two Portuguese Jews who had refused to eat bacon were burnt, and Pangloss was hanged ... Candide was flogged in time with the anthem.*

Though the novel was short, this dramatic episode was just one item in a very long catalogue of disaster and misery, relieved only by Voltaire's wit. Tales of political corruption, extortion, mass slaughter and the sex slave trade were so common two centuries later that Bernstein felt no need to soften the effects.

As drama, in comparison *West Side Story* and even Verdi's *Force of Destiny* are uncomplicated. The story was two operas in one, a tragedy and a farce, an adventure to several parts of the known world, difficult to give coherent staging. There are very many characters, and most are observed to be infected with greed and lechery. The hero Candide with his blissful theme song is a model of innocence; influenced by his tutor's philosophy he will remain so until the end.

The reflections by him of tragic events have music near in feeling to the tragedy within *West Side Story,* especially in the epilogue where he is finally disillusioned about his great love. For the rest, Bernstein uses musical parody in thorough-going burlesque as outrageous as an 18th century lampoon, as sophisticated as classical operetta. It should be inspired by those of Offenbach and Sullivan for whom his admiration is apparent in the musical score.

The satire stems from the tutor, Dr Pangloss' fatuous assertion that we live in the best of all possible worlds. This is given a tune of suitable frivolity. He is tutor to Cunegonde, the daughter of a petty aristocratic family, who at the start display their collection of false, snobbish values. When their servant Candide wants to marry her and they are caught in dalliance, he is banished. Press-ganged into an invading army, he is expected to join in the rape and pillage. Since this is to happen on the family's estate, their pious chorale proves of no help, and they are scattered or killed. Candide escapes to Lisbon with Dr Pangloss, who has lost nothing more than his nose, and that through syphilis. Uncomfortable as Portugal proves to be for them, the *auto da fé* occurs at a most enjoyable carnival.

Cunegonde, having survived rape has become a saleable object and is shared on alternate nights by a rich Jew and the Bishop of Paris A willing slave living in luxury, she is reconciled to permanent degradation. As in *Faust* and some other operas there is a jewel song for a girl's corruption. *Glitter and be gay* is sung by her with panache and in coloratura style, speeding up to a samba and laughing song. It is the highlight of Act I and part of it in the much-performed overture.

Candide meets her, impulsively kills the villains and they escape, hoping for better in the New World. The sultry Latin rhythms heard in the entr'acte will be almost the only pleasure for him in those South America colonies. Music provides a sensuous background to the dialogue in this action-packed story. Once they reach Buenos Aires, Cunegonde opts for the appalling Governor despite his freakish behaviour and love-song; her chosen life-style will separate them until their final reunion many years later in Venice. Meanwhile, he ventures into the jungle, finding a land where the Jesuits rule and *Hallelujahs* are sung. Yet all is not bad. He reaches Eldorado, a social Utopia where there are countless golden-fleeced sheep and no lawyers. He now has hope of buying Cunegonde's freedom.

In Curaçao, he meets Martin, a pessimist who argues at length that we live *in the worst of all possible worlds* and warns him in vain against buying a ship from a Dutch merchant. A roll-icking chorus, *I'm a Boatman,* gives Candide a splendid farewell as he sets sail presumably for the bottom of the Atlantic. He is ship-wrecked, then astonished to find Pangloss who had not quite died in Lisbon has been one of his galley slaves. He also releases five deposed kings who have discarded vanity and desire *The simple Life.* They are among the very few people he has met who talk any sense. Finally, at Venice they can enjoy some relaxation, at least during the carnival

The most vital personality is the chaperone who accompanies Cunegonde from Paris through to Venice, encouraging her wayward lifestyle. Misleadingly called the Old Lady, she is in full vigour, also of voice. She never misses the chance to tell how, a pope's daughter, she has suffered extreme misfortunes though enjoying being despoiled ever since youth. Living on her wits and as an entertainer, to a tango she sings her *Adaptability* solo to a Cadiz audience before embarking with the lovers.

Voltaire gave much significance to the Old Lady's story and her survival to enjoy life, but in this opera, it is treated as a joke, mostly as if fictitious. Bernstein balances this by adding his own words to the original text in which she has a positive message for her feckless companions:

Life is life and all we know

Cunegonde now belongs to a Venetian casino owner and is seen inducing clients to gamble. How? Because *We are Women*, as she sings in the joyous manner of a Mahler *Wunderhorn* song, with the Old Lady providing a solid base. Since everyone is masked, Candide will once more be fooled, this time by a hard-luck story. This is an accelerating duet *I have Troubles* to the tune of Candide's optimistic motif and is capped with Offen-bach's best known barcarolle. Fixing the roulette wheel 'creates wealth' but 'protection money' takes it away. This vicious circle is the subject of a waltz, *What's the use?* for the casino owner and Cunegonde. *The Carnival of Venice* is tacked on, a tune tradi-tionally heard whenever it can give local colour to a musical.

Pangloss' opinions had always been expressed in absurd patter songs, so it is time for just one more. The fourth and final item in this exhilarating finale states his up-dated view of the optimistic life. In friendly counterpoint with the ladies, he rounds off the adventures in alliterative delight:

Lady frilly, lady silly, pretty lady, willy-nilly, :
Lady lightly, lady brightly, charming lady, fly by nightly
Lovely ladies, six or seven, this is my idea of heaven.

The farce is over but not the story. Every good opera deserves the drama of at least one recognition scene. The revelry ends abruptly with a less than joyous meeting when the two one-time lovers remove their masks. Finally disillusioned with this grasping woman, Candide asks:

Is this the meaning of my Life?

Voltaire who has given an ironic commentary throughout has the last words in the epilogue: avoid vain ambition, live in seclusion and cultivate one's garden.

36 Chicago, *the Film*

Roxie Hart is a nonentity with a pretty face and ambition to make a fortune on the stage. She has a large imagination, crude intelligence, a perverted moral sense with compulsion to kill any lover who cheats on her. She arrives in a prison also to be specially graced two other murderesses once driven by jealousy: a song-and-dance artiste, Velma, and a spoilt girl rich enough to be a 'celebrity'

Velma had hoped to monopolise the attention of journalists gathered to gratify public curiosity about a sexy-looking singer on murder row. Unfortunately, newshounds have no sense of absolute justice, and were diverted by the snob appeal of a socialite who had killed not one or two victims but three and at a stroke. What chance of fame would Roxie stand against this pair? She plays her master card, pretending to be pregnant, and the naïve victim of a cruel society.

Velma's lawyer, Billy Flynn, sees a 'human story' to be exploited; he thinks superlatively on his feet, a P.R. man who boasts he could have got Christ set free. He has Velma's trial delayed, so she finds herself in third place, bottom of the publicity pile. He alone can produce all the stunts to make Roxie's original one work. There is the slightest hint that the medical who confirms the pregnancy has been paid in kind. Thanks to a double bluff by Billy in the courtroom, Roxie is found not guilty, but at this unique moment of her public life, a fresh drama occurs and she is deserted by the yellow press. Another woman, a stranger, has had the cheek to kill a man just outside the court house. Local gossip needs no more than one good murder at a time.

The story based loosely upon real events had already been filmed in the 1940s and was ideal material for the partnership of Kander and Ebb as a musical, *Chicago*. The satire is sharp and pervasive, sweeping the audience along. John Kander composes tunes as distinctive and singable as any in our times, has a gift for characterisation and a flair for invoking the spirit of the jazz age. The former, perceived Hollywood image of gangsters

linked to the Chicago accent make for racy effect. Writer Fred
Ebb's wit offers an anthem for big-city show-biz, framing the
advice of the ultra-cynical lawyer:

Give'em the old razzle-dazzle, Razzle-dazzle 'em
Give'em an act with lots of flash in it
And the reaction will be passionate.
What if your hinges all are rusting?
What if, in fact, you're just disgusting?
Give'em a show that's so splendiferous
Row after row will crow vociferous.
Give'em the old double whammy, Daze and dizzy 'em
Back since the days of old Methuselah
Everyone loves the big bambooz-a-ler.

Bob Fosse would probably have directed a film version of
Chicago if he had lived, but his original conception and choreography were respected when in 2002 Rob Marshall directed
an imaginative and critically much regarded screening.

There is a fast-paced overture, introducing the stage Velma,
black-haired, with mid-'20s' flapper fringe, belting out the
motto-song, *All that Jazz*. The film version presents, in parallel
with Roxie's fantasies and stylised prison happenings, a vivacious cabaret with all five principal characters strutting their
stuff. As Velma's song ends, the police wait to carry her off to
prison, Roxie having watched her with admiration from the
stalls. About to murder her lover, she will soon follow Velma to
the jail where the most influential character is the wardress.
She charges the women exorbitantly for making 'helpful'
phone calls, a morality she dishes out in red-hot style:

If you're good to Mama, Mama will be good to you.

The inmates give lively account of themselves with a choral
litany of their pleasures in having killed men, to a seductive
tango. Not to be up-staged, Velma mimes and dances the story
of how she disposed of her own sister, but Roxie is only very
briefly brought back to reality. This is when a foreign prisoner
is hanged, sketched in a tightrope walker's *Hungarian Dis-
appearing Act*.

Mr Razzle-Dazzle, alias Billy Flynn, projects a saga of the
unborn child in a legal tap-dance. With the press in attendance,
this leads to one of the most stunning burlesques conceived on
film, a combined ventriloquist and marionette show. In an
inspired musical joke, there is an accelerating duet, *We both*

reached for the gun, for Billy and his doll, Roxie, with a compliant female journalist, feet flying as the puppet singing a Viennese-paced waltz, *Understandable.*

Inadequate and transparent, Roxie's husband has never been more than the poorest of meal tickets, a *Mister Cellophane.* This is his theme song, a Chaplinesque clown, in old-time music hall or vaudeville fashion. He is duped in the courtroom drama into appearing as the forgiving father-to-be. Billy invents a diary incriminating Roxie, then by 'proving' it is a fake, wins for her the sympathy of the jury to accept a plea of self-defence. As a reward for playing the major false witness, Velma through her triumphant lawyer in due course gains her freedom. So both girls emerge hardly more interesting to the public than if they were virtuous.

Roxie is duly rejected at numerous auditions, and finally trailed by the unemployed Velma. Since staged violence always has an appeal, she offers a truce and a proposition. Why don't they offer themselves as a song and dance team with a history? This is how we finally see them on stage, armed with plastic machine guns, in diverting variations of the Charleston.

37 *Opera into Film*

In its first half century, the familiar motion picture industry achieved remarkably little to advance the mass appreciation of the other arts. One exception in the 1940-50s was the Archers film company, led by director Michael Powell and his script-writer Emeric Pressburger. These men promoted Britain's creative prestige and increased cultural awareness in their films. Three with very high production values were most inventive in relation to dance, operetta and opera.

The Red Shoes was a ground-breaking dance fantasy and *Oh ! Rosalinda* a witty adaptation of Johann Strauss' *Fledermaus* (1874), given a contemporary plot set in Vienna post-1945 under four-power occupation. A new conception was to integrate ballet with innovative film techniques into a classic opera, Offenbach's *Tales of Hoffmann* (1880). Several of the finest talents in the performing arts available in Britain of 1950 were brought in. Musical director and conductor was Sir Thomas Beecham; the one-time Diaghilev protégé Leonide Massine mimed three roles. The film has been an inspiration to many who followed, as testified five decades later by Martin Scorsese, who has recently been directing films about musicians.

Early German Romantic E.T.A. Hoffmann's stories of fantasy had been adapted as a play by Barbier and Carré, the librettists of Gounod's *Faust,* including one which had inspired Delibes' ballet, *Coppelia.* The real Hoffmann was fictionalised as the protagonist, a foolhardy man doomed to failure. This was a difficult projection that few composers would have touched, demanding music in turn lyrical, farcical and ironic.

The hero cannot distinguish infatuation from love: one automaton and two women, relations in turn absurd, whimsical, and ill-fated. He is to become the victim, hardly more than reacting to the manipulations of his rival, the classic antagonist who pursues him in varying embodiments, frustrating his love affairs.

Hoffmann has become obsessed with Olympia, a mechanical doll, the latest Parisian fad. She is programmed to waltz and say *oui*, but has to be wound up like a clock whilst performing. Hoffmann has been presented with rose-tinted spectacles seemingly by an optical inventor, Doctor Coppelius. Olympia sings, coloratura no less, and sweeps Hoffmann into a frantic dance until he is exhausted. After quarrelling over copyright and a bounced cheque with her owner, Coppelius destroys her, the shattered remnants falling at Hoffmann's feet.

In Venice, Hoffmann visits a plush casino and fired with machismo, loses at the gambling table. He hopes for the ultimate consolation from the mysterious courtesan Giulietta, but this show is entirely set to the scheme of his antagonist, in another guise. Like Mephisto, his speciality is seizing men's souls, and he intends to add Hoffmann's to that of the freakish Schlemil who had been enslaved by Giulietta. She will do his bidding, acquiring Hoffmann's reflection, his moral self, so that he can be induced to commit a murder. The victim is to be the disposable Schlemil who has been watching insanely jealous as Giulietta vamps Hoffmann. So a deadly conflict is manipulated. Hoffmann snatches from his dying opponent the door key to Giulietta's room, rushing in only to find her gone.

In Munich, the Act where tender feelings uniquely surface, Hoffmann loves Antonia, who because of frail health is forbidden to sing. The sinister Doctor Miracle calls at her spacious home on the pretence of curing her. He conjures up the voice of her mother, once a famous singer whose portrait is on the wall, then hypnotises Antonia to join her in an intense duet. At the peak, she has a seizure and dies, with Hoffmann rushing in too late.

He has been telling students these stories in a *Bierkeller* opposite the theatre where Stella, his latest enthusiasm, is singing in *Don Giovanni*. Hoffmann tells the comic-grotesque tale of Kleinzach, the 'little fellow', puppet-like. When he refers to his funny face, *sa figure*, this could equally mean *her features*, so he starts to sing Stella's praise, though the rowdy audience prefer the Kleinzach story. By the time she comes to meet Hoffmann, he is dead drunk and she walks off with the rival, now the urbane Councillor Lindorf. He had previously boasted that there are easier ways to possess a woman than love. This is a perverse morality open to several ingenious interpretations. Hoffmann is finally consoled by the Muse of Poetry who assures him of her love. Suffering will make him a superior poet.

Offenbach was approaching this, his hundredth stage work and sixtieth year, but in failing health, with a race against time. His skill for parody would be brilliantly applied, moving from farce to tragedy, music to accompany a hero with the leisure to travel around Europe: Germanic drinking songs, a minuet and fleeting waltz for a Paris salon, Verdi-like fervour for the Venetian fantasy and an occasional Gounod-like pathos in the final scenes.

Though prolific in sensuous tunes, Offenbach was better known for humour than sentiment, but there are many passionate moments such as Hoffmann's love duets with Giulietta and Antonia. From his German opera, *The Rhine Fairies,* Offenbach converted one piece destined to become the most famous of all barcarolles; it was first heard as a dream-like soprano duet at the start of the Venetian scene.

The lack of a definitive opera version gave extra interest to this filming, a sophisticated treatment of the macabre[38]. The music was performed first then the ballet added. There was no spoken dialogue and nearly all the cast were singers or dancers who mimed the action. Stella's role was altered and enhanced visually into a famous dancer. Vistas are interspersed of her performing in a short ballet, with the opera's melodies adapted. It is choreographed to recall the style of *Giselle* (1842) but she wears tights fashionable for the 1880s in place of the tutu, with a *pas de deux* to a restrained variant of Hoffmann's Venetian romance, *What rapture enflames my soul ?* Moira Shearer dances Stella and Olympia whose appearance is set within a marionette show. She is wilful, not programmed for flirtation, spinning with Hoffmann on an unending staircase until he collapses. This Act ends with horror, a bare leg twitching in mid air and the eyes of the severed head blinking at the spectators.

Here and in what follows, the singer Robert Rounseville's face reveals how far Hoffmann lives in his head, and arriving in Venice, he is scarcely aware of a discreet orgy going on around him. Then more intimately, magic takes over, to the symbolism of burning candles, as in the *Diamond* bass aria[39] the rival bribes Giulietta into subverting Hoffmann:

Oh! Gleam with desire, in diamond the sun lies reflecting. So gleam with desire, with splendour steal her heart. As the moth flies round the candle, woman ...

In a scene attractively stylised, with moments of intense eye contact, Giulietta is briefly seen wearing a diamond necklace. Or is it just another illusion? Her role is played by Ludmilla Tcherina in an exquisite burlesque of a *femme fatale,* at first with apparent abandonment to Hoffmann's ecstatic romance, their duet reaching a peak for the time it takes until his reflection has disappeared. Then springing away from his embrace, coldly, she struts in triumph around him. For a moment, he regains his senses, alarmed at losing his reflection. Massine enters as Schlemil, an obsessive, humanity already drained from him. He and other sinister creatures press in upon Hoffmann, a threatening tableau which climaxes in an explosive septet. The doomed Schlemil duly makes a melodramatic challenge, the tension resolved as he and Hoffmann are rowed away along a canal to their duel. For the first time in the film, the rival is hooded as the Grim Reaper but as such, visible only to the audience. Now as if to be transported into a lagoon, Giulietta preens herself in a hugely ornate gondola with her decadent retinue, in picturesque silence indifferent to the fate of her lovers: a scenario that has surely been imitated in some later musicals.

The Munich scene is changed to a villa alongside a sun-lit Grecian amphitheatre, the lovers playing duets in Antonia's spacious home until disaster calls. By then Hoffmann has left on the arrival of her father who distrusts him. Doctor Miracle with fearsome incantations impels Antonia to sing with her mother whose statue he has brought to life. They are heard on a celestial stage, where magic violins accompany, but it is from a cliff that she is seen to fall to her death.

Of those who had danced two years earlier in *The Red Shoes,* Robert Helpman has the commanding acting roles throughout as the villain. He makes the film's first entry, surreptitiously, and is the last to leave, his plans achieved. Just before that, he peals off his three facial disguises to the barcarolle music introducing a second *pas de deux.*

The film is memorable for its sustained irony, rich imagery, rapidly changing backdrops, close-ups and exciting visual detail: the ornate medieval setting for the Nuremburg *Bierkeller*: a cameo danced by choreographer Frederick Ashton for the midget Kleinzach among giant beer mugs: the transformations seen through those rose-coloured spectacles: light and shade, idealised beauty alongside the grotesque.

38   *Albert Hall Highlights*

The 'Last Night of the Proms', world famous as a distinct event seen by increasing numbers over one hundred million on TV, now has much of the spirit of those 'pre-historic' promenade concerts of light music back in the mid-19th century. This was never more completely demonstrated than on Saturday, 8 September 2007, perhaps even beyond the expectations of the organisers. The choice of most accessible music, with attractive young soprano and violinist of potential world appeal was the reason. The evening became the finest live advertisement for an exciting variety of styles enjoyed within the Romantic era: a Shakespeare overture (Dvorak), a dreamy interlude (Rakhmaninof), Imperial pomp (Elgar), gipsy-inspired virtuoso fireworks (Ravel), an intimate German song (R. Strauss), a *bel canto scena* (Bellini), a popular Mexican song (Ponce), and operetta with an overt sexual flavour (Lehar). This last song, with flowers thrown from the stage by the beautiful lead soprano, fired the audience as rarely, even by Last Night standards.

London's promenade concerts in their modern guise, well documented, have been organised every summer for 113 years, long since the largest and most famous music festival in the world, and lasting for two months. The sense of continuity is symbolised by the fountain in the arena, which around 1900 was treated to unscheduled 'water sports', unthinkable in today's decorum, as recollected years later by Thomas Beecham.

By then conductor Henry Wood had done much to end London's status as a musical backwater, such as introducing orchestral works by Mahler, Skryabin and Sibelius to international fame, and even Strauss' first operatic 'failure', *Guntram.* No-one in 1895, not even young Wood, could have expected the long-term success and scope of an institution which he played a major role in starting and continuing as director. He lived to conduct impressively in its 50th season, sadly to die within the month. His musicianship, integrity and organising skill were a major factor all those years, and his memory is still celebrated.

Because of chaotic conditions in the music industry, arranging to have a regular orchestra playing for the whole of an evening and over the season was one of the largest problems Wood had to overcome in the earliest seasons. This achieved, the aim was gradually to introduce more substantial works by the great composers, and to give some opportunities for younger British ones, whilst dropping off some musical items past their day without upsetting too many listeners. Yet until the English music's revival from the turn of the century, it was less than prominent at those early Proms. At a British evening in 1898, the most memorable items had been Hamish Mac-Cunn's fine Scottish overture, *the Land of the Mountain and the Flood* and Elgar's *Bavarian Dances.* Beethoven and Wagner evenings became the norm, with other composers sharing certain concerts regularly, two at a time.

Financial problems threatened for 20 years until the BBC took the Proms over in 1927, so that apart from an uncertain period during the 1939-45 war, the institution's stability was guaranteed. The Proms' home, the Queens Hall, was destroyed by German bombs in 1941, and since 1942, the regular venue has been the Royal Albert Hall, with a capacity four times the size. This is Kensington's Victorian red-brick spectacular, modelled on Rome's Coliseum and splendid for ceremonial and sporting occasions, but far from ideal acoustically. So in 1969, fibreglass baffles were installed on the ceiling, the so-called flying saucers.

For decades, programmes often included an overture, then a concerto before a symphony, with Romantic composers in a big majority. After the interval, lighter music featured, so making a very full evening, and that practice lasted for at least 60 years, sadly being discarded in a slick public relations exercise. There have been exceptions when very long works such as oratorios and operas are performed.

Visiting musicians became more frequent, but a foreign orchestra was not invited until 1966. Sir William Glock as director from 1968-73, intended to broaden the repertoire, especially with 'modern' works, not to everyone's taste. No such objection could be applied to the pre-classical music which was becoming more fashionable, such as the medieval with its serenity and other-worldliness; and many welcomed the over-due recognition of England's Purcell. Of over 70 programmes, a few such as chamber concerts are now performed away from the Hall, and there have been exceptional nights, such as Indian, jazz or in 2005 Scottish and gipsy mixed.

The concerts have generally drawn audiences younger on average, that tradition often being passed on through families. The 'regulars' became an unofficial pressure group, but dec-orum was observed except on the last night when a display of Union Jacks and funny hats became the norm after the world war until now. The final stage begins with the time-honoured playing of Henry Wood's arrangement of sea songs ending with a furious acceleration which, some thought, created excessive excitement among the audience. Patriotic feeling was also stirred by two works when the audience joined in: Elgar's *Land of Hope and Glory* and Parry's *Jerusalem.*

For this final evening, many queue for a day or two, but TV viewers abroad may get a false impression from that occasion of apparent frenzy whereas all but one or two evenings are treated with utter seriousness. For the last night, only British compo-sitions used to be played, but that rule has been relaxed for years, with specially tuneful foreign ones being selected. In 2005, Walton's racy *Portsmouth Point* overture set the pace, fol-lowed by another highly syncopated work, for piano, chorus and orchestra, *The Rio Grande,* by Constant Lambert, who did so much for English ballet before 1950. In between was the pop-ular Guitar Concert by the blind composer Juaquin Rodrigo. Korngold's suite taken from his music for the film *The Sea Hawk* and a traditional song *Down by the Sally Gardens* were the final novelties. After that, the celebrations began with some audi-ence participation in the three time-honoured pieces com-posed by Wood, Elgar and Parry.

Outside of the Proms, the Albert Hall has at least one evening which in musical terms is massive and requiring astonishing degrees of synchronisation. No one-off, it is given by an equal array of musical resources most years. Such school events are rarely pleasing to few beyond the participants and their parents, but among those organisations good and large enough to reach the Albert Hall, that by the Harrow Borough schools is excep-tional. They always give it minimum publicity out of deference to those families who form ninety percent of the audience.

Planning and co-ordination are far beyond what would be expected from an amateur event. The senior symphony orchestra of nearly 80 are on the platform, two more large ones below them, with a string orchestra, five wind bands and one steel band, the groups filling the arena. Several school choirs occupy the thousand or so seats behind the orchestra. The only professional assistance comes from the conductors and opera singers brought in as principals. Most pieces are played by from three to six co-ordinated bands together, and at least four items involve dance troupes.

In 2007, music from eleven popular films included the composers John Williams, Maurice Jarre, Shostakovich, Goldsmith and Herrman, opened the event, followed by six *Nutcracker* dances. Each side of the interval, the steel band performed *St Thomas* then *El Nino*, respectively in jazz and Latin style. There were excerpts from *Tosca* and *Porgy and Bess,* and the five bands played a suite, *Natural Wonder,* music by Stevie Wonder.

Every year, spectacular episodes for the complete ensemble are played out on platforms in the arena: this time, part of the text of *Henry V* with Walton's music as composed for the 1944 film, the sixth and final movement being the *Agincourt Song;* and a very dramatic waltz scene from Act III of the *Rosenkavalier,* the farcical episode when the villainous Baron Ochs is publicly humiliated, requiring acting as well as singing of the highest quality.

For the 2008 performance, the integration of groups was most ambitious. Latin American song and dance featured memorably, and the large ensemble for the finale of Verdi's *Falstaff.* Narrative accompanied excerpts from the film *Scott of the Antarctic* with Vaughan Williams' orchestral score, and the Hall's massive organ heard at the climax of the tragedy.

39   *Tango*

During the decades when ballroom dancing was dominant, in Britain the tango was widely regarded with awe, the superior dance, the 'difficult one'. Following the waltz, fox-trot and quick-step, it would be introduced to classes alongside the rumba, flamboyant but less formidable. The first tango routine is unusual, partly because one does not face the partner full on but diagonally whilst the hips are generally the closest area of contact, with freer movement elsewhere. The basic rhythm is very deliberate, and though the steps are slow, quick, quick, slow, quick, quick, slow, the rhythm is very different from the waltz's. The one feature they had in common is that they were almost the first to be recognised as permitting the male to place his arm round the partner's waist.

For the British, the most familiar tangos have been heard in *Jealousy* and *La Cumparsita* with their assertive rhythms and theatrical in a Latin way, very elaborate. Less able dancers tended to withdraw from it, leaving the field for the most skilled. The tango became elitist, very prominent in British dance hall competitions. A less daunting option, also very artistic and of a similar speed was the slow foxtrot, because it gave similar options subtly to vary the pace. A main attraction is its unique glide, though curiously it had developed from the original, jerky foxtrot which has long since disappeared, with its unnecessary arm movements. An intriguing feature of the foxtrot is that one does not step on the beat.

The tango we knew had features in common with other ballroom dances. Its 'head click' was an invention which may have started in imitation of a Spanish style, but was not used in Latin America. Not everyone realised at first that the ballroom tango was so far from the 'authentic' Latin dance. It held sway for a long time, though it is less danced in one evening than other items in British ballrooms. In recent years, learners have increasingly opted for the original Argentinian dance, and we are most likely to see it on T.V. in its native setting.

The *habanera* originated in Cuba and is best known as the

one from *Carmen*. Its rhythm influenced the original tango which was being danced by the poor in the dives of Buenos Aires and Montevideo by 1900. In South America, these events took place in crowded rooms, the upper parts of the bodies remaining close, so suggesting the possessiveness of the male. Experts however state that it is sensual but not sexual in spirit. The basic step is not slow-quick but suggests the creep, seeming slow, leisurely by European standards. The partners may describe differing patterns, the female very mobile, moving elegantly around the male, their legs briefly intertwined. Casual dancing partners are not the way forward; there is every suggestion that intense preparation is desirable.

The tango was among the early 20th century dances which began to edge out the traditional waltz and it rapidly became fashionable especially at parties for the rich in Europe. By the 1920s it entered operetta and musicals, and to our times enjoys its high musical reputation internationally. There are many institutions to maintain its status and encourage innovation. In the Argentine, it is often played by 'classical' musicians, normally a minimal combination of piano, bandoleon and double bass, and as such a form of chamber music. The bandoleon, an instrument not unlike the concertina in appearance, gives a distinctive flavour to the music. Some of the melodies, like those of other Latin dances, are becoming popular in Europe; they had not been so commercialised as many for the ballroom tango, but the dance's intricate appeal is drawing increasing numbers to attend classes.

In the Argentine there has been a succession of influential participants. Carlos Gardel was probably his country's most admired personality at his untimely death in a plane crash, 1935. The classic period lasted for three more decades, but because it was very nationalist in sentiment, it was suppressed during the political dictatorships, which instead encouraged pop music inspired from abroad. After democracy was restored in 1983, the tango regained great favour at home and increasingly abroad. Into our time, it has inspired creativity with such exponents as Astor Piazzolla (1921–1992) who started as a bandoneon player and progressed, also with related compositions for the concert halls.

Notes

1. A trio is a chamber work for three instruments. This second definition can be misleading; it is the second theme, to balance the scherzo. In this sense it was also used by Elgar for the familiar tune in his first *Pomp and Circumstance* march.
2. A manuscript for Schubert's unpublished 7th is held in a London museum, having once been held by Mendelssohn.
3. Key changing is termed modulation. There is some analysis of the emotive effects of these changes in Chapter 2 and the Appendix to Volume I of this book.
4. Smooth transition between notes. *Staccato*, the opposite, notes shortened ('dotted'), gives more space between them.
5. Ballade. Romantic single movement.
   Barcarolle, a boat song. Gently swaying.
   Berceuse, a cradle song, lullaby.
   Cappriccio. Light, carefree.
   Etude, a study. Often displays technical aspects of piano playing.
   Fantasia. Free style, imaginative.
   Intermezzo, entr'acte. Any style, but originally performed between scenes of a play.
   Nocturne, *notturno*, a night song, restful.
   Prelude. Often the opening movement. Any style, but many composers have completed sets of 24, one for each diatonic key.
   Rhapsody. Free style, expansive, exciting.
   Serenade, *serenata*, an evening song. Often had four or more contrasting movements.
6. Central Europe's gipsy bands are specially admired for their lilting use of rubato. Pablo Sarasate's *Zigeunerweisen* (Gipsy Melodies) are the most famous concert piece.
7. *Castrati* were much used in Church music. The operation was banned in civil laws following the French Revolution.
8. *Robert the Devil* was debated in detail in Balzac's novella, *Galbarra*. Charges of bribery were often made against Meyerbeer. Corrupt practices over opera were commonplace.
9. A call to arms, sung to drum accompaniment, a cliché of Italian opera.
10. G.B.Shaw's comments are quoted on page 22 of volume I.
11. Vasco's enemy who is killed during the shipwreck was in reality

Don Pedro Cabral who 'accidentally' discovered Brazil; but Scribe was not concerned with historical truth.

12.   A 1980s Covent Garden production with Domingo as Vasco compressed the playing time to 3 hours, but remained cohesive.

13.   Sitwell argued that the most famous *Rhapsody no.2* has had a bad, long-term effect on popular music, which is by nature derivative.

Four rhapsodies were composed at a much later date and do not fit the original pattern. Liszt wrote a *Hungarian Fantasy* based on *Rhapsody no.14* dominated by one of the greatest of folk tunes, *Mohac's Field.* It consists of six consecutive notes of a major scale rising then falling from and to the key note, powerfully assertive.

Better to appreciate the rhapsodies, contrast a typically fine 1960s Hungariton recording of certain gipsy songs on authentic instruments with a curious alleged collaboration of Liszt and Tchaikovsky, with several of the same melodies, but which lacks spontaneity.

14.   One phrase from the final version of *Petrarch Sonnet no. 104* was used with the words, *Things that have happened once before,* as part of one of his most sensitive melodies, *Where or when ?* by Richard Rodgers. This was not plagiarism but a compliment. Its companion piece, *Petrarch Sonnet no. 123,* has a similar intensity and may have inspired Strauss' Italianate aria in *Rosenkavalier,*

15.   This classic melody was used by Glinka, Saint-Saens and many others, but none probably as idiosyncratically as Mahler.

16.   The diminished 7th has a tonal ambiguity, and composers often used it for moving into another key.

17.   The chromatic phrase G, G♯, A, A♯ appears briefly on the piano in Liszt's passionate song, *Ich möchte hingehen* (I may enter). Its tonal instability creates exceptional tension, the concept of death in love also transferred in Wagner to the tragic fate of the two lovers in the opera, *Tristan and Isolde.* This is an historic example of what inspired the extension of chromaticism by other composers in the late- and post-Wagner phases.

18.   Notes of a chord spread out as on a harp.

19.   For this reason, the *Prelude* and *Liebestod* are often performed in sequence at concerts, with or without the vocal parts. The overall *Tristan* effect specially on young listeners could be shattering, like a drug, Mark Elder had recalled.

20.   Two English musicals became war-time spectaculars, with memorable songs: *Chu Chin Chow* and *The Maid of the Mountains,* seen in London by countless thousands of soldiers before returning to the front line in France.

21.   The Habsburg Empire had at least ten major races within it but had become an anachronism, a society based on privilege. But it

had positive features: a central European 'common market': the cultural influence of Vienna and Budapest, both of which were its designated capital cities.

22. Using one theme in more than one movement was unthinkable before Beethoven. Refer to Liszt's use of cyclical forms, and his concertos, page 109.

23. Saint-Saens could not understand why his operas were not as popular as Massenet's. G.B. Shaw wrote very disparagingly, see pages 11-12, Volume I.

24. The key of C major is centred on the note C. When those same notes are centred on another note, they sound 'unusual' and are called modes. Most common in England was the Dorian mode centred on D, others were on A, E, F or G.

25. See G.B. Shaw's account, volume I, page 22.

26. There were queens in Sheba but whether one really visited Solomon is uncertain, despite her famous entry with its operatic potential that had also attracted Handel's interest.

27. The *Habanera* was based on *El Arreglito* by Sebastian Yradier who composed the classic popular song, *La Paloma.* Contrast *Carmen's* style with Falla's adaptation of wild gipsy themes in his ballet, *El Amor Brujo,* (Love the Magician).

28. Diatonic scales sound 'normal' to us. Modal scales may intrigue, suggesting other times or places. See Appendix.

29. Musical parody ideally should be as 'interesting' as the original and only a few composers such as Benjamin Britten achieved it brilliantly. Sullivan was one of the finest of parodists, along with Offenbach. Classical operetta tended to the satirical, often very funny. The mixture of styles is prominent in G&S and if the many parodies are not always easy to identify, they certainly have melodies enjoyable for their own sake.

30. Singer Vera Lynn greatly popularised *I'll be seeing you.*

31. Tapio was the god of the forests, hence the title *Tapiola,* his final symphonic poem.

32. Sibelius also pays tribute to the folk instrument, the *kantele,* here and in a fine symphonic poem, *The Bard.*

33. Vyborg was ceded to Russia in 1940, becoming the capital of the Karelian Soviet Republic, later disbanded.

34. There is a repeated nine-note phrase ideally matched to the oboe in the scherzo of his Second Symphony.

35. Phrase repetition can raise tension powerfully and the *ostinato* is a common device. Sibelius uses it often to unique effects, notably in the brass, groups of chords repeated many times as background against a changing melodic pattern.

36. The author once wrote to a leading impresario suggesting a

range of classic musicals any one of which would enhance West End staged entertainment. His courteous reply stated that although he would very much enjoy them, the expense of lavish productions which they deserved would be too much of a financial risk.

The subsidised opera companies occasionally oblige, but the Sadlers Wells Operetta with two works each season, one G&S, the other Continental, lost its grant in the 1980s, despite excellent productions.

37.   Timbre is the sound and quality which distinguishes instruments and voices. Modulatory relates to key changes.

38.   Offenbach had a musical taste for the macabre, to which Parisians had not warmed in his earlier operetta, *Three Kisses from the Devil*. He should have tried it in London!

39.   This aria was the inspiration of Ernest Guiraud's revision, the exquisite melody taken from Offenbach's *Voyage to the Moon*, and used since 1904. It is therefore sometimes omitted in productions, including an 'authentic' one at E.N.O.

Song and Dance

The following are among shorter pieces that have given the author much pleasure over time. They exclude operatic arias or any items referred to in the chapters and are not placed in any order of preference:

Kalinka (Russian folk)
Barco negro (Portuguese fado)
Parlez-moi d'amour (French) composer Lenoir
Bacchanale (French) Saint-Saens
Amapola (Spanish) La Calle
Havanaise (French) Ravel
Kapri Fischer (German) Winkler
Guapango (Mexican) Moncayo
Orchids in the Moonlight (U.S.) Yeomans
Chiquititta (Swedish) Andersson
Csardas no. 4 (Hungarian folk) arr. Hubai
Creole Love Call (U.S.) Ellington
The Northern Lights of old Aberdeen (U.K.) Evans
Skyliner (U.S.) Barnett
GreenEyes (Cuban bolero) orig. Soares
Ciribin (Italian folk)
Plaisir d'amour (German) Martini

The most exciting rhythms seem unexpected and complex, the most beautiful melodies simple and inevitable.

(W.H. Auden)

Appendix A

Classical Personae in Romantic Music

The earliest operas favoured gods and heroes but the Romantics seemed more interested in ill-fated heroines, the rebels, outsiders or losers.

Aeneas (*Iliad*). Trojan adventurer, lover of Dido, credited in Virgil's *Aeneid* with founding Rome. Berlioz' *Trojans*.

Ajax (*Iliad*), anti-hero who preceded Quixote in attacking a flock of sheep. Two clownish Ajaxes appear in Offenbach's *Belle Hélène*.

Apollo, sun god and music lover.

Ariadne. A Greek lady often seduced. Massenet's *Ariane*. Strauss' *Ariadne on Naxos*.

Bacchus, god of wine and dance, often invoked in poetry.

Briseis (*Iliad*), slave taken by Agamemnon, causing Achilles to sulk in his tent. Chabrier's opera *Briseis* was unfinished at his death.

Cassandra (*Iliad*). Trojan princess whose warnings about the Greeks were ignored. Berlioz' *Trojans*.

Catullus. Latin poet and lover of Sappho. Orff's cantata, *Catulli Carmina*.

Cleopatra. Egyptian Queen. Massenet's opera.

Clytemnestra, wife of Agamemnon murdered by her son. Strauss' *Elektra*.

Danae, seduced by Jupiter. Strauss' *Loves of Danae*.

Daphne. Tragic heroine. Strauss' opera.

Dido, ill-fated lover of Aeneas. Berlioz' *Trojans*.

Elektra, Agamemnon's daughter who avenges his murder. Strauss' opera.

Galatea. Feminine creation of the sculptor, Pygmalion. Suppé's operetta.

Helen (*Iliad*). Greek wife of Menelaus, Greek King and famous cuckold. Her willing abduction by Paris was offered as main cause of Trojan war. Operas by Strauss and Offenbach.

Hermione (*Iliad*). Helen's daughter whose jealousy of Trojan Queen, Andromache, leads to tragedy. Rossini's *Ermione*.

Jupiter (Greek, Zeus), the supreme god, notorious for planning seductions in disguise (his 'metamorphoses', celebrated in poetry).

Leonidas. Spartan leader at Thermopilae. Mock-hero of Lincke's operetta, *Lysistrata.*

Orpheus (musician) and Euridice. Classic lovers sent up in Offenbach's operetta, *Orpheus in the Underworld.*

Penelope (*Odyssey*), wife of *Odysseus.* Fauré's opera.

Phaedra, sister of Ariadne. Massenet's overture.

Prometheus, punished by the gods for bestowing the gift of fire on humans. Liszt's symphonic poem.

Sappho of Lesbia, Greek poetess. Gounod's opera. Stage name of Parisian actress in Massenet's *Sapho.*

Thespis, Greek actor of 6th century BC, credited with inventing tragedy. Sullivan's comic opera.

Tiresias. Punished by the gods, being turned into a woman. Poulenc's farce, *The Breasts of Tiresias.*

Troilus and Cressida (*Iliad*). Trojan lovers separated by war. Walton's opera.

Venus (Greek, Aphrodite), goddess of love, often invoked in opera.

Vestal Virgins. Pagan priestesses sworn to chastity. Spontini's *Vestale* and Bellini's *Norma.*

Appendix B

Harmony & Polyphony

Harmony, melody and rhythm are the elements of our music. Harmony was at first unique to European civilisation, but through its special appeal it has become familiar known in most parts of the world . It had evolved in the sophisticated development of chord systems.

A chord is a simultaneous playing of two or more notes, said to be harmonious if it sounds well, discordant if not. The common chord in the key of C major consists of the triad C, E and G, the dominating notes of the seven in the key on which a melody may rest. It has a soothing effect (because those notes have the closest mathematical relation), but if one note is changed to another in the same key, the sound creates a tension which is resolved only by a return to the common chord. This 'resolution' is a cadence , how nearly all songs end, with a sense of satisfaction or finality.

These chords are all diatonic, but any which use notes outside the prevailing key are termed chromatic. Wagner made revolutionary use of these and 'discovered' the so-called *Tristan* chord, thought of by his enthusiasts as miraculous, and a landmark in music's history. It is heard in the prelude to his opera, but is not resolved for another four hours until the finale, the *Liebestod* or *Love-death*, symbolising the anxiety of love unfulfilled. Many listeners think this is too long to wait, which helps to explain why some dread Wagner.

This lengthening of suspense began to influence younger composers, hence music tending to sound more 'difficult', with increasingly complex harmonies as the later 19th century progressed, and moreso into our own times.

As written down, harmonic relations are called vertical, melodic ones horizontal. The simplest tunes stay close to the notes of the common chord, such as nursery rhymes, and much that is popular, including the opening of the *Blue Danube*. The late 18th century style ('Classical' in the strict sense) had been simplified from the previous age, with clear-cut diatonic melodies; the diatonic ones are most familiar to us, using the major and minor scales taught at schools. Moving to other notes (accidentals) creates special tensions (a chromatic feel).

Other key systems (modal), taken from the Greek modes, are sometimes used, sounding unfamiliar, remote or 'old-fashioned', but perhaps having a special appeal, along with their harmonies. English folk music was often in the Dorian mode (centred on the note D), with Vaughan Williams and some others imitating it , looking back to Renaissance models; whereas modes were virtually banned in the Classical period (approx. 1750-1815).

Early Romantic music sounded freer, also influenced by the *bel canto* style from Italy (beautiful, clear melodic lines). Yet by the 1860s, it was moving away from that to more complex melodies, increasingly chromatic, requiring more concentration by the listener. As a result, many music lovers, especially of opera, believe that by the mid-19th century, the melodic heights had been achieved. It is a fair argument.

Through the whole of the Romantic century, harmonic and melodic practices were gradually relaxed, but in more recent compositions, such rulings are often ignored or considered irrelevant : hence the term modern music – though this does not apply to the popular kind which generally plays safe by staying with the traditional key (tonal) systems.

The notion of what may be termed a concord has broadened with time, though there are different views of the boundary as to what might be called 'a noise'. Many composers from Liszt and Debussy were often ahead of their time in an adventurous approach to harmony.

J.S. Bach was a master of polyphony (or counterpoint), playing two or more phrases or themes (melodies) simultaneously. The Romantics favoured it but not all were masters; those who were such as Richard Strauss used it in new ways to raise the emotional impact.

Polyphony is an aspect of harmony but not all harmony is polyphonic.

Index of Names in Chapters

From the Italian Girl to Cabaret

From the Italian Girl to Cabaret fills a gap in modern bibliography about burlesque and musical humour, describing theatre performances and the diverting evolution of the cult since the *commedia dell'arte*, specially of the great era of comic operas, from Rossini, forward to innovative 20th century musicals. Paris, Vienna, London and Berlin are highlighted as theatre entertainment centres. This is supported by the author's experiences, having attended capital venues across Europe.

'A headlong dash down the by-ways of musical fun'. Anyone following *'has a good chance of stumbling on something surprising, intriguing or previously unknown'.* (BBC Music Magazine, Oct.1998). By **G Colerick** ISBN 09524964 37. 181 pages.

This book has been bought for Music and Drama Departments in upwards of 500 U.K. institutions.

New Chekhovs

3 PLAYS, 2 FIRST TRANSLATIONS by **E Gamberoni**. Includes one amusing play for 3 male and 3 female parts, and a farce about primitive dental surgery in 19th century Russia. Ms Gamberoni who has produced both plays in London has written and included a penetrative 3,500-word introduction on Chekhov's life. ISBN 09524964 45. 94 pages.

Romanticism and Melody

As the BBC Music Magazine stated (November 1995), *few books about classical music speak directly to the non-specialist music-lover.* The first volume's *cumulative effect is refreshing in its directness and enthusiasm*: and successfully *idiosyncratic.* ISBN 09524964 29. 246 pages.

Significant terms are defined or clarified in both volumes to assist the layman in becoming more articulate about music. The approach in volume two differs however in one intention; it is less personal but quotes several distinguished critics. The author draws together some of the strands in mainstream music, notably in the development of the symphony, opera and programme music.

The Author on Music and Humour

The first four extracts are from his book, *From the Italian Girl to Cabaret*, the later ones from his first *Romanticism & Melody*

COMMEDIA DELL'ARTE

Italy had the best-known tradition of stage humour in Europe back to the Renaissance, especially the *Commedia dell'arte* based upon well-loved stereotyped characters. These became part of a popular culture enlivened by the constant improvisations of the actors. Early plots often involved a young man played by a *soubrette* (light soprano) and a gullible old woman, a comic *(buffo)* role for male voice. More elaborate forms evolved: the more familiar comic trio might include the skittish Harlequin, the charming Columbine and elderly Pantaloon. These three would fit respectively into a musical pattern of tenor, *prima buffa* (soprano) *and primo buffo,* deep-voiced and the object of ridicule, hence the English term *buffoon.* What we still call the Clown was a later addition.

SHOSTAKOVICH'S MUSICAL COMEDY

The Priest is an exploiter of human labour and takes on Balda wage-free, hoping to discredit him before the expiry of one year when he would have to pay him a lump sum. Devils abound in the community but behave more reasonably than the Priest who is superstitious. They dance boisterously in the market place without harming the citizens, and their assault on the church bells cheers up the music. The loyal servant wins the affection of the Priest's family but is deliberately set an impossible task. He is to visit the underworld and extract from the devils payment for debt.

The burlesque calls for a curious range of sound effects.

There are fleeting reminiscences of Mussorgsky and others back to Mozart, imitation of a balalaika band, well-known songs receiving eccentric orchestration: saxophones, wind instruments at the extremes of their range and the xylophone which is known to favour diabolical rhythms. The pantomime effects are increased with a child's song, a race between a devil and a hare and the dance of a Russian bear.

TRADITIONAL BURLESQUE

Young William Gilbert gave the Gaiety Theatre a good start with a new burlesque of Meyerbeer's *Robert the Devil*, a man prone to wicked deeds unless the fair sex could bring him under control. All English burlesques were given comic subtitles and *The Nun, the Dun and the Son of a Gun* set the scene. For Robert's famous ordeal with naughty nuns, the audience thought Tussaud's Chamber of Horrors had been brought to life. Even so, waxen ladies were a safe option compared with a trendy 1990s production of the genuine *Robert* in which defrocked nuns would be unfrocked nymphomaniacs.

Gilbert might laugh at sex but once he produced his own works, he'd never place it on stage.

EXTRAVAGANZA: LEICESTER SQUARE

During the 1880s, a variety of extraordinary reports emerged concerning the goings-on at the Empire Theatre, Leicester Square, one of which was of considerable social concern, others relating to pure frivolity. In April 1884, the magazine Era described the stage performance of the brothers Tacchi. While the one sang with guitar, the other appeared to have swallowed a bassoon which continued to play internally. A novelty, but was it not incongruous in a quasi-operatic presentation of courtly events in pre-medieval France with an enchanted forest, Gothic camp and 'electric ballet' of 40 Amazons? This 'integrated' stage work conceived and composed by Florimonde Hervé was *King Chilperic*, a famed parody of grand opera already 14 years old, but according to the Era, a spectacle still unequalled *on the modern stage.* So it had been the clear choice for the opening of the vast 3,500-seater Empire.

Hervé's chorus girls scandalously revealed their calves. His experiments with revolving props, trapdoor techniques, real and pantomime animals and cardboard armies caused him to be known as the master of stage illusion. He could be regarded as the inventor of classical operetta, c.1848.

WAGNER ENJOYS A MUSICAL JOKE

One evening in Paris when Wagner was addressing a distinguished audience on his 'integrated' musical theories, explaining why he preferred to compose to his own lyrics, a stranger asserted that he did likewise. It was Monsieur Hervé who proceeded to play his own compositions on the piano. According to a witness, the astonished Wagner observed him as a lion would a monkey leaping between trees, before relaxing to laugh at the musical improvisations late into the night.

KISMET, *A FILMED BURLESQUE*

Lalume is an inventive musical comedy role, such as in the scene where she turns her charms onto Hajj whilst giving her husband cursory stabs of jaded flattery. Her skill in parody and her vocal range are challenged in two contrasting songs. There is a satirical travelogue, *Not since Nineveh,* with preposterous references to the trumpet at Jericho, 'hot' Gomorrah and that wall writing at Babylon. *Bored* has long sustained passages, sensuous swoops into the lower register. Lalume has a duet with Hajj, an oriental send-up on the nature of virtue, with much reference to *Rahadlakum* (Turkish Delight) and jazz trumpet backing.

G&S: THEIR MOST SATIRICAL WORK?

Utopia Limited climaxes with a mini-cantata in praise of the English Lady and an heroic Verdian finale. This is to celebrate the triumph of capitalism in the conversion of the state of Utopia into a limited company – did lawyer William Gilbert foresee Britain after the Thatcher revolution?

One song gives advice, equally relevant today, on how to make easy money: set up a limited company and if it loses, file a petition and start another one, whilst:

The liquidators say, never mind, you needn't pay

and the King of Utopia declaims:

Well, at first sight it strikes us as dishonest, but if it's good enough for virtuous England, it's good enough for us.